Until The Lights Went Out

BRIAN F SIMMONS

Copyright © 2018 Brian F Simmons

All rights reserved.

ISBN-10: 1983705810
ISBN-13: 978-1983705816

DEDICATION

This book is dedicated to my dear son and daughter Robert and Maria and to my loving and ever-patient wife Marilyn for her support, encouragement and advice. She must be very relieved it is finally done.

ACKNOWLEDGMENTS

No tale can exist without its players and in my story there have been many. They all played their parts, consciously or not, in bringing me from the immature twenty year old who started this journey to the wiser, and fulfilled if somewhat battle scarred fifty year old who emerges at the end.

These include my dear and sadly now departed parents, my sister Angela, two wives and my children Robert and Maria.

Many friends and work colleagues have been named and their contribution acknowledged along the way whilst others have played their parts anonymously and a few have been assigned pseudonyms where I thought appropriate to afford privacy, spare their blushes or avoid them pursuing me with a big stick.

Whilst the majority of photos included are from my own archive or other non-attributable sources others relating the garage days have been kindly provided by Jill Butcher.

Thank you all..

In those days of light
I believed I was invincible.

When the darkness fell
I knew I wasn't.

TABLE OF CONTENTS

1 A NEW BEGINNING 1
2 EWELL DOWNS MOTOR SERVICES 6
3 CAR SALES 1960s STYLE 23
4 LOVE ARRIVES 36
5 A STEP UP THE LADDER 41
6 MOVING ON 46
7 WEDDING BELLS 51
8 LIFE GOES ON 58
9 A CONSTABLE ONCE AGAIN 63
10 SANDGATE 66
11 REIGATE DIVISION 72
12 DORKING DIVISION 86
13 I'M A DETECTIVE 104
14 GUILDFORD 112
15 PROMOTION 122
16 I BECOME A TRAINER 128
17 ASHFORD 135
18 LETHAL FORCE 142
19 A COUNTRY COPPER 152
20 THE HORSLEY HOME FRONT 164
21 MORE HORSLEY 168
22 EMMA 176

23 PUBLIC RELATIONS	193
24 A SAD TIME	206
25 A SORT OF FREEDOM	211
26 RECRUITMENT	223
27 PROMOTION	236
28 COMPUTER TRAINING	244
29 MORE COMPUTER TRAINING	254
30 SELF BUILDERS	259
31 A NEW JOB	265
32 DREAMS DASHED	268
33 MY DARK NIGHT	273
THE FUTURE	279
ABOUT THE AUTHOR	281

INTRODUCTION

At this point in my story I am just twenty years and three months of age and already somewhat surprised at many of the things I've seen and done and the places my short life has taken me.

Following on from my secure and happy early childhood the last five years make a less than impressive CV, unless that is, you value variety over persistence.

1960	- mediocre school performance results in my leaving at sixteen to start work.
60-62	- a couple of years or so spent in an electro-chemical research laboratory.
62-63	- six months as a steward with P&O including a five month round-the-world voyage; a very steep learning curve.
63-64	- a brief dalliance with a supermarket management training scheme.
1964	- just ten months as a copper in one of London's less salubrious areas.

However this is a new start and the following pages recount the next thirty years of my life. These also saw a lot of fun plus some real joy and happiness, but predictably I guess, much more adult drama. Such events have included bereavement (two), marriage (two), children (two), and divorce (one). Also, significant career change, a demanding but interesting working life, inheritance, house building and house selling and not altogether surprisingly a major breakdown.

Dear reader please note that this memoir describes aspects of life as it was in the 1960's and '70's so please excuse language or expressions that today we might regard as politically incorrect or inappropriate. It has been included because the words or something like that was said at the time.

1 A NEW BEGINNING

i

It's still dark and raining steadily and a rusting drainpipe on the wall we're parked by gushes water across the pavement. The street outside is an alien landscape compared to my village in rural Surrey and the windows are misted with our anxious breath and the fug of cigarette smoke. It's 1974, a couple of weeks after the Guildford pub bombings.

At half-four in the morning I'm sitting in a police mini-bus in a Brixton back street with a Smith and Wesson .38 Special revolver strapped to my waist wondering what the hell I've got myself into. The butterflies in my stomach are doing aerobatics and I'm stiff with inactivity having sat around for several hours since being called from home about half ten the previous evening.

Over the last three years I have blasted to shreds any number of cardboard man-sized targets but this is my first live call-out. I know the same is true of almost all the other police marksmen sitting in vans at four or five other locations around London and the Home Counties.

Kevlar body armour has yet to be invented. My uniform feels very thin, my body vulnerable. I'm nervous. No I'm not. I think of my wife and kids. Actually I'm very frightened.

According to the intel; of all the addresses to be raided, this is the one where the terrorist ringleaders are thought to be. *"That'd be right. Just my bloody luck."* especially as they had apparently vowed never to be taken without blowing themselves and all around them to kingdom come.

I'm sharing the van with Surrey's Detective Superintendent Ron Underwood, a D/I from the Met's anti-terrorist branch; and a major from the Army Bomb Squad who is apparently able to spot trip wires, booby traps and so on. There are also two or three other detectives, me and one other marksman from Guildford.

Ron checks his watch and says *"OK. Let's get this done."* We pile out and walk quickly around the corner and into a stair well of a tenement block and up to the first floor landing. Ron makes questioning eye contact all round and we nod.

In true Jack Reagan style the D/I takes a pace or two back and aims a hefty kick at the door which unlike those in the films remains obstinately closed. The D/I bounces back arms flailing and smacks Ron Underwood in the mouth splitting his lip so we have blood drawn even before we're inside.

A second kick. The door goes in and now it's our turn. The bomb squad guy takes the lead with his powerful torch and with me and the other shooter either side, guns drawn and eyes straining down the tunnel of light. We are in a long narrow hallway. Suddenly the click of a turning door handle on our right and we drop into the crouch, guns held out in the double handed combat grip. *"Stand Still. Armed Police"* we shout in unison as our eyes strain into the darkness.

Fortunately he doesn't stand still or we could be here all night. The door continues to open to reveal three points of light in the darkness that gradually resolve into the whites of two widely staring eyes and the white teeth of a large naked black man who drops to his knees with the word *"Jeesus!"*

Seeing that we have apparently not breached a terrorist hideout the D/I steps forward. *"Don't worry mate. It's only the police. Looks like we got the wrong place. No worries OK? Oh, and sorry about the door. Just send the bill to the Commissioner. He'll sort it,"* and with that we march out of his life with the split door frame being the only proof we were ever there.

But all this is jumping forward ten years from where this part of my story actually begins. What follows is the account of how I got there and came out at the end of it all.

ii

In order to provide some context and continuity to the following pages, it is probably worth explaining briefly what has brought me to this point in my life.

After a few unsettled teenage years that saw among other things a five month voyage around the world working as a steward for P&O; I eventually joined the Metropolitan Police at the beginning of 1964. My first, and as it turned out, only posting was to Kennington Road Police Station in Lambeth where I was shown the ropes by a very experienced Irish bobby – well 'his' ropes to be more precise. This unofficial information included such gems as where we could find a hot drink and sandwich or hot-dog on the streets around Waterloo at any time day or night and probably for free. There were also places where it was possible to comfortably sleep away two or three hours of a winter night duty without falling foul of the sergeant or inspector and of course the local pubs where a pint would find its way out to a thirsty policeman at the back door

Both of these jobs, whilst hugely interesting, and fairly steep learning curves, were if I'm honest, a bit of a culture shock to a young Catholic lad from a somewhat sheltered background in leafy Surrey.

I enjoyed the police job but at nineteen, I was probably a bit young and immature for the rough and tumble of life on the seamier side of Lambeth. This, coupled with the distance from my Surrey mates, lack of my own transport (I'd written off the little Austin I bought on my return from sea), and then Mum's cancer, led me to casting around for an alternative career closer to home.

During the previous few years, and especially since learning to drive, I had become a bit of a car and motor sport enthusiast and although unable to afford another one myself, I made every effort to get as involved as I could with cars in general.

This meant developing friendships with people who had a car – the more sporty (as in fast) the better. Together with these friends and all the other 'wannabee' boy-racers of the time we would read the Motor Sport magazine avidly, talk 'confidently' about things we didn't understand and take every opportunity to get to race meetings at Goodwood or Brands Hatch. Here we could drool wistfully over exotic machinery whilst revelling in our (mostly) unfulfillable daydreams. I say 'mostly' because a couple of my friends actually did get really quick cars and at quite a young age too.

Funny isn't it how we use understatement for emphasis, as in, we say quick when we actually mean bloody fast.

The two guys in question were my friends Reg James and Charles Page. Reg's father was a self-made engineer who had worked hard to build up a business from which he was able to live on Givons Grove, a very nice private estate in Leatherhead and indulge his son by giving him a Ford Lotus Cortina. We were all green with envy, as this was the car raced so successfully by the late Jim Clark and other well- regarded drivers of the day and was pictured almost constantly in our Motor Sport magazines.

The other enviable car was the one used by Charles Page whose father owned Page Motors in Epsom. They were Jaguar dealers so unsurprisingly Charlie managed to secure not just any old Jag but an E-type which was pretty much the most enviable set of wheels within our knowledge apart from the Italian exotica which in those days were rarely seen in our neck of the woods. Unlike nowadays when the Ferrari, Porsche, Mercedes, and other seriously fast and expensive marques seem to be almost ten a penny.

Friends with less exotic cars included my long-standing friend Ken Thorn who had his own Triumph Herald plus access to his mum's posh (leather and walnut) Wolseley. Then there was Bob Cloutte whose car while not particularly fast or comfortable was both interesting and beautiful. It was a bright red Triumph Roadster, circa 1949, with the huge dinner-plate headlights and dickie seat that popped up out of the boot. They are worth a mint now having been made the more desirable after appearing in the hands of actor John Nettles in the popular 1980's TV series Bergerac. Bob was actually still on L plates when he first got the car and I remember being his accompanying 'qualified' driver on occasions. Talk about 'blind leading the blind'!

So what all this background is getting round to is explaining a little why, when it came to seeking to leave the Met, I focused on the motor trade and, quite amazingly really, managed to get myself a job as a junior salesman at a garage on the Ewell by-pass near Epsom.

It was a bit surreal coming back home to the same little room after my various adventures and travels in London and at sea – almost as though the clock there had stopped. The same candlewick bed cover that was the subject of such drama the day I managed to put a big black stain on it whilst trying to make Post Office ink with my home chemistry set. The same carpet, curtains and wallpaper and little desk built by Dad that had seen so much of me over the years. This was where I had pored over homework, stamp collections, Meccano, chemistry sets, furtive cigarettes with the windows wide open and even the occasional 'naughty' magazine in the later years.

However the odd feelings rapidly evaporated as I settled back into domestic normality 'Bramley Way style', and dropped into the familiar routines that are just ordinary life although my relationship with Mum and Dad had certainly changed.

A bit like when I came back from my time with P&O, they seemed to acknowledge my maturity up to a point but this time there seemed a real acceptance that I was very much grown-up and my own person. Possibly because I now had seen and experienced a great deal more than they ever had or would.

Mum said *"It's lovely to have you home again and together like a normal family."*

Whatever Mum's thoughts were, domestic normality was certainly not what I wanted from life. For me, the new, and to my mind somewhat glamourous job in the car showroom was the first move towards what I imagined would be the step-up the life-ladder that Mum had always hoped I would achieve.

2 EWELL DOWNS MOTOR SERVICES

i

Ewell Downs Motor Services was a Rootes main dealership. For any readers who don't know, of which I imagine by now there are quite a few; Rootes produced the Humber, Hillman, Singer and Sunbeam ranges of cars which you may not know either. God, this is making me feel old!

I guess not a lot changes really because the above mentioned had at one time all been independent British car makers that were brought together under the Rootes umbrella. And you only have to look around today to see how many supposedly different marques are Volkswagen, BMW or Ford under the skin or at least by ownership. I mean who could possibly have imagined a few years back that the iconic British marques of Rolls Royce and Jaguar would now be owned by BMW and Tata, the Indian steel company.

Dating from about 1935, the garage where I went to work was a single storey white walled building with large sliding showroom windows and the curved corner room typical of the 'modernist' period. This was the office occupied by Geoffrey Welton the managing director. By the time I arrived he was certainly past normal retiring age although showing no signs of giving up the reins.

To the right of the main office and showroom building was a petrol forecourt selling, if I remember correctly, National Benzole fuel in two grades – Regular and Super. I think National eventually became BP. At the time I was there, and incredibly compared to today's prices, you could buy four gallons (about 4.5 litres to the gallon) for just under a pound. That was roughly eighteen litres for one pound. How amazing is that!

A small separate forecourt dispensed diesel fuel which back then was only used by a neighbouring taxi firm and passing commercial vehicles. Diesel family cars were still many years off. There was also a paraffin pump, because at the time this was still used in many homes for auxiliary room heating and even cooking in some. Central heating was not then for the majority. We always had some paraffin around at home but in our case it was mostly used in Dad's greenhouse to keep the frost at bay and on occasions to encourage a recalcitrant Ideal boiler or garden bonfire that refused to get going. Remember the TV advert – "Boom Boom Boom – Esso Blue" ?

This view of the new workshop was taken at the grand opening exhibition in the late fifties.

Between the main building and the forecourt a ramp led down to the workshop which was a vast double height structure with a corrugated sheet roof and no insulation.

The only heating when I arrived was via several tall coke stoves although hot air heating and fairly inadequate roof insulation came along a bit later. In all honesty, environmental considerations and worker comfort were not major considerations at the time. People were just expected to put on another layer and get on with it which amazingly through today's eyes we generally did. I can certainly recall fitters working in woolly gloves.

Two lubrication ramps and several fitter's bays occupied one side of the space while the remainder was taken up with the parts store and offices; a reception office; staff canteen; a car-wash bay at the foot of the entry ramp, and parking space for the vehicles in for service.

Ewell Downs was something of an anachronism with three of the four directors stuck fairly firmly it seemed back in the early 50's and doggedly determined to ensure the company remained the same.

Geoff Welton the MD was quite a kindly and somewhat bumbling old gent who, as I said, was pretty certainly beyond normal retiring age. He did however have the running of the place pretty much at his fingertips despite it being a few years behind the times.

The Company Secretary, Ethel Murfitt was a spinster and probably also in her late sixties. She too had her hand securely on the financial pulse of the firm but was equally determined that things should stay the way they'd been since Adam was a boy, or at least that was how she came over. Persuading her to spend a few pounds on something a bit new, modern or different was very much a 'blood and stone' situation.

Frank Lee was the oldest director and it has to be said was starting to lose it a bit. In his white working coat and pipe billowing some sort of rough cut tobacco smoke, he was responsible for the Stores side of the business and always professed to know what was in stock and what should or shouldn't be ordered in. I had so many circular conversations with Frank about whether this or that part had been ordered and why parts couldn't be fixed rather than replaced and the relative benefits of not allowing fitters to spend hours trying to mend a part instead of bolting on a new one. You'd have thought it was his own money being spent and in the end I'd walk out wondering if it wasn't me that had 'lost it'. I suppose it was not that surprising really. They were all born when Victoria was on the throne, survived two wars, years of no welfare state and somehow or other between them built and maintained a working, if not exactly booming business. I guess in the circumstances change was not a natural option to them whereas for my over-confident twenty years and 'vast' experience change was everything. *"Sweep it all away and get this show on the road."* Oh the simplicity of youth.

The fourth member of the boardroom quartet was a good bit younger – fifties I would guess. Works Director Bill Burton was an experienced motor engineer and was the perfect man for the job and more often than not able to diagnose a fault purely based on a verbal description and without setting eye or ear on the car. He was however a pretty rough diamond whose vocabulary was rich to say the least and was sexist in the extreme (certainly by today's standards) when it came to expressing his views on the relative merits of any female who chanced within his field of view. I am tempted just by way of illustration to quote a few of Bill's choicest and funniest expressions but even with the defence of 'reported speech' I would surely cause offence to some.

Yet another character of note was the workshop manager Doug Turnbull of who my main recollection is the permanent headless chicken. Doug was the principal customer interface (note the nice modern term) and his prime responsibility was accepting telephone requests for service, allocating slots and checking vehicles in on arrival. He also had to deal tactfully and respectfully (the difficult bit) with owners who invariably thought that the company existed solely for their benefit and wanted their cars back the day before yesterday if not sooner.

Whilst these were all working directors and were around the place all the time, my main contact was with Jack Moxley the sales manager. Jack and I seemed to hit it off from the beginning and I felt sure it was his influence after he was called into my interview with the MD that had clinched it for me and got me the job.

It was Jack too who offered me a lift back home after the interview as it was on his way and it was during the course of the journey that I realised why his name seemed familiar. His daughter had on more than one occasion been the object of my thus far unsuccessful attempts at losing my virginity. Fortunately she kept mum, so no harm done, at least as far as my new job was concerned. We never did go out together again. Bit close to home for both of us I guess.

So my new working life involved comfortable nine to five hours including Saturdays and a day off mid-week to compensate. I had also been told that I would be able to use a company car; in fact it was the main incentive for my interest in the motor trade. What was not specified however was precisely what car that would be so I was less than excited when I was told my own runabout was a somewhat weary 1958 Hillman Minx. It had been taken in part-exchange and having done a lot of miles it was relegated to use as a company hack.

My self-image took a bit of a knock but at least I was mobile and once more in the running in the girlfriend stakes. Also, I did feel somewhat less aggrieved on discovering that apart from the MD who had the Sunbeam Rapier demonstrator, all the other bosses were managing with similarly mundane modes of transport.

Showroom in the 1950's about ten years before I arrived

The showroom at the garage was wide across the frontage but only one and a half car lengths from front to back. So while there was plenty of space from side to side it was really only possible to display five or six cars with enough space to move around them. Just as an indication of how times have changed it is interesting to recall that the cheapest new car we sold was the Hillman Imp basic version at £489 while for £503 you could have the De Luxe model. What you actually got for the extra £14 I can't remember. Floor mats perhaps - Doors even!!

At the other end of the range stocked on site was the Humber Sceptre, a luxury and sporty family saloon at the princely sum of £998. Doesn't seem much now but given that £1000 a year was a good salary at the time it was only the fairly well-off who could consider it.

So the usual showroom stock would have been an Imp or the Singer version of the same which just had a superior level of trim. A Hillman Minx and the larger Super Minx or again the slightly better finished Singer versions. (Called the Gazelle and Vogue for anyone who like me is enough of a nostalgic car freak to even care) The last of the four marques sold was the Sunbeam Rapier, also in convertible form that was quite a nice sporty and fairly quick (for the time) set of wheels.

There were other cars in the range that we did not sell enough of to justify holding in stock. These included the large Humbers that were almost limousines and the Sunbeam Alpine sports tourer which is now regarded as something of a classic of its time.

We had several demonstration cars available but from time to time we had enquiries to try other models so I had to go to Rootes in west London and collect one of theirs. This was great because after completing the demo I usually arranged to pick up the latest girlfriend and impress her with a ride to London in a seriously posh car but then to be driven home in my rather sad old Hillman Minx. However it did have a bench seat if you get my inference.

It was around this time that the minis were having some success in motor racing so Rootes got in on the act by producing a rally version of the Imp. But they were rather caught on the back foot when one of them actually won the Tulip Rally in 1965 in the hands of Rosemary Smith. Luckily for the Rootes publicity machine she provided not only driver skill but a bit of glamour too.

There was a huge panic at Rootes HQ to put on a press reception to publicise the result and staff from all main dealers were invited as rent-a-crowd to which I was very pleased to go. Got to drink free champagne and then drive home. Terrible I know but that's the way it was in those pre-breathalyser days.

It may have occurred to you to wonder what qualifications I had to justify my appointment as a car salesman. The answer is absolutely none. Apart perhaps from the fact I turned up on time for the interview, looking smart and confident and was able to give a sufficiently satisfactory explanation for my short time in The Met. Perhaps the very fact of having been in the police may have counted for something – who knows?

Cast somewhat in the Arthur Daly stereotype, car salesmen in general were not well-regarded and coming from the police some of my more cynical friends saw me as a bit "gamekeeper turned poacher". However, as I was to discover, compared to some of the more "back street" car dealers of the time, Ewell Downs was a genuine, honest and well-regarded operation.

Sales in those days was nothing like the competitive and quite sophisticated profession it apparently is today. Mostly we just waited for customers to come to us at the showroom. Jack had his own established clients and our dealer network to worry about, so anyone else who phoned or walked through the door was down to me. There was certainly no theory, psychology, or particular technique to be followed or certainly none I was told about.

To be honest, back then, if a person came into the showroom to look at a car the job was usually at least half done. One only had to supply all the information, be suitably charming and knowledgeable and as soon as possible get the person behind the wheel of a demo car which usually clinched the sale. There was often the part-exchange issue but one way or another we usually managed to allow as little as we could get away with as well as selling a whole bunch of profit earning extras. It may be hard to believe but in those days, equipment like radios, spot lamps, wing mirrors, rear window de-misters, and in some cases, even screen washers were offered as chargeable extras.

In one back corner of the showroom there was a small enclosed office with a couple of desks that Jack and I occupied for the fairly limited amount of paperwork involved and which we filled with a dense fog of cigarette smoke and whisky fumes when not dealing with clients. But it soon became apparent that when, as sometimes happened, we both needed space to deal with customers at the same time there was a problem. A desk out in the showroom was out of the question because it was like an icebox in winter and although there were some radiators, there were times when the showroom windows were totally iced up.

Until then Jack and my predecessor had just muddled by but at my instigation we somehow managed to get the board to cough up for the creation of a second small office that gave Jack his own Manager's office and space for me to deal with my own clients.

I am not going to kid myself that I was the best salesman in the world but one way or another Jack and I established a good working relationship. Perhaps in some way my very youthful enthusiasm helped to rekindle his own. Anyway we did some good deals, earned a few pounds and in a short time had become quite close.

Jack with his lovely wife Monica

I never actually got to know much of his personal history apart from the fact that he had been in the RAF, but I think Jack by name had at times been quite a 'Jack the Lad' by nature according to a few of the stories he did tell. Prior to coming to Ewell Downs he had been an independent motor trader buying a vehicle here and selling there and eventually he took on an open air site somewhere in Epsom. I think that like me he just had a passion for cars and bought ones that interested him rather than those that would necessarily be good earners. He revelled in the memories of exotic vehicles he'd bought and sold especially a classic D-type racing Jaguar that was apparently set up for road use and which he used to drive around the district, sometimes with his mother on board and scaring people witless with its ear-splitting exhausts. I guess that inside most men there's a little boy who refuses to grow up, and why not indeed?

I hadn't been working alongside Jack for very long before I realised that he liked a drink, which is actually a bit of an understatement. Initially, during perhaps the first few months or so that I was there it wasn't too bad.

He usually went off at lunch time a mile or so away to the Glyn Arms at Ewell where he had got in with a group of people several of who were motor trade cronies.

Whilst not necessarily an everyday occurrence it was often obvious on his return that he'd had a few, both from his breath, eyes and over-affable and garrulous demeanour but at the time it didn't seem to affect his grip on the work situation. Perhaps the underlying knowledge that he was the entire sales department had prevented him from letting go completely, a situation that changed quite quickly during the first few weeks after my arrival.

Now I can't deny that at the time I was quite keen on a drink or two myself, so when Jack started to ask me along to The Glyn I was quite happy to do so. And that was really the start of a rather slippery slope for me. I'd thought that some of my erstwhile colleagues on the ship could drink a bit but they were left pretty well standing by the Glyn Arms lunchtime club. I certainly couldn't match their alcohol capacity nor keep up money-wise but they were all well off and more than willing to take me along for the ride so to speak and I'm embarrassed to say I let it happen.

In my case, I always seemed to remember that this was only lunchtime and that there was still a job to be done so one way or the other I managed to extricate myself while I still could and return to the garage (driving again I'm ashamed to admit). Not so Jack. And as time went on his lunchtime sessions often stretched from around midday to three in the afternoon when he would arrive back on the forecourt, stumble into his office and more or less pass out.

I'm not sure whether Geoff Welton knew quite what a state his sales manager was in on occasions but it was quite a challenge keeping the two apart. I also had to take calls from our sub-dealers on his behalf and somehow manage to put them off until Jack became sufficiently coherent to talk to them. Another problem was that if I was talking to a customer in the showroom I was on tenterhooks wondering whether Jack would give a mighty snore or worse still emerge from the office all red-eyed with a big inebriated grin and attempt to get involved. Fortunately that never happened.

There was also a slightly funny side to all of this. After Jack had dozed for a while he would come round looking like death and needing the loo. However, in order to do so he had to make his way down from the showroom to the workshop level. Now, regardless of what the MD did or didn't know, Jack's lunchtime excesses were common knowledge to everyone else and the fitters in the workshop had become so used to watching his attempts to negotiate his route to the toilets that it became a diversion they looked forward to.

It went something like this. Jack emerges dishevelled from office, stands for a moment to get his balance, treats me to a sort of twisted grin and says *"Desperate for a pee Brian."*

He then totters through the door at the back of the showroom that opens immediately to a flight of seven or eight wooden steps down into the workshop. I wait for the crash. Fortunately that never happened either although there were a couple of close calls.

Hanging on with white knuckles to the handrails he gingerly and slowly descends, breathes a very obvious sigh of relief and treats anyone nearby to the same whisky grin and then stops.

Stage one complete, he now has to cross the workshop to the toilets. He sort of braces up as he takes a bearing on the toilet door and then attempts to stride confidently in the right direction. This doesn't happen. Instead he wanders, mostly sideways, diagonally across the workshop to finally disappear from view. Once he even had a round of applause from the workshop staff.

One evening as we were leaving the showroom together Jack said *"Do you fancy a quick half at The Locomotive?"* This was a pub halfway along East Street on the way into Epsom. I knew I probably shouldn't as Mum usually had a meal planned for around six o'clock. The truth was though that I did fancy one so I said *"OK. So long as it is just a quickie."*

When we went in it was immediately obvious from the manner of the greeting, not just from the landlord but also the group already there that this visit was clearly not a one-off quick half on the way home. At one level I felt I'd been had over but bizarrely I also felt somewhat flattered that he wanted to introduce me to more of his friends, associates, brother alcoholics or whatever you want to call them. I only remember four of them and only one by name. This was a guy called Roy, who together with his father had a scrap metal business somewhere in south London. I guess I was quite easy to impress at the time but Roy sticks in my memory for two reasons. One was a stunning white 3.8 Mk2 Jaguar parked outside. It was a Coombes conversion with a seriously modified engine, sporty louvered bonnet and sparkling chrome wire wheels. A dream car as far as I was concerned. The other thing was the enormous gold Omega watch that he so casually wore to work in his scrap metal yard. A self-made man and no mistake. As Dad had often said, *"There's money in muck."*

Another guy was the son of the landlord who I thought was a bit of a prat but was interested in because was he was talking about buying a Sunbeam Tiger and could we set up a demo for him.

Being the car freak that I was I had wanted for some time to get my hands on a Tiger. This was a high performance version of the Sunbeam Alpine sports into which Rootes had shoe-horned a monster Ford V8 engine and according to the figures it went like a proverbial rocket. Sadly it was discontinued a couple of years later after Chrysler took over the Rootes Group. They discovered that unfortunately their V8 engine couldn't be squeezed into the Tiger and obviously there was no way they would use the Ford engine.

Having set the scene of my first few months at the garage here is probably the point to cut a long story short.

Sufficient to say that I did only have a quick half on that occasion because I really didn't want to upset Mum. But thereafter, this stop at the Locomotive became a regular, indeed an almost unconscious action which led to Mum laying down the ultimatum.

"Brian we can't afford to waste good food you just don't turn up for. If you'd rather stop in the pub that's your choice but you can sort out your own dinner if and when you do decide to show up."

They weren't happy but I guess for them it was just another step in the process of letting go. But the question we should all have asked was *"Letting go to what?"*

Well health-wise to start with, it was not a good scenario. I'd been smoking at some level since my early teens. Not, I think, because I especially enjoyed it but it was what you did; due I imagine to the fact that in those days pretty well everyone around did and of course the younger generation always follows on. So, without realising, I'd got the habit although now we'd probably say addiction. I suppose if I inherited a single negative thing from Dad it was smoking.

It had become far worse when I was at sea with cigarettes being so cheap too. We were paying eleven pence (pre-decimal) for twenty so it was not an expensive habit to feed. In the police there was no special incentive to stop and the health risks, even if sufficiently known were not at all publicised, so around the time I'm describing I was getting through thirty or more a day.

Alcohol too was also taking a hold; a taste I'd also developed in my teens and in the same way as the smoking. Unchecked or even thought about, it was now well established so that the lunch time and evening sessions with Jack were simply added on to the skinful I usually managed at the weekends with my mates. So overall not a good situation but let me change tack slightly and talk a bit about what was going on for me away from Ewell Downs Motor Services.

ii

Prior to joining the Met Police; my social activity, in addition it must be acknowledged, to a fair amount of drinking; largely revolved around heading off to the various dance halls around the district. This was with the primary object of meeting some pretty girl for a few dances and who knew what else. As I no longer had a car I was usually with Ken but not having independent transport didn't help at all with the 'what else' possibilities.

Favourite stamping grounds for us Surrey lads were The Orchid Ballroom at Purley, Wimbledon Palais, Streatham Locarno and if feeling adventurous and could afford the fuel – even at four gallons a pound – The Hammersmith Palais or one of the venues at Brighton.

You'll note that all these locations involved a good bit of driving and as I said before this was all pre-breathalyser time so we didn't give the matter much thought. To be honest I turn to jelly now when I think how stupid and irresponsible we were and how easily we or worse still, some other innocent person could have been killed or maimed. Actually I suppose I was more blameworthy than most; having been in the police I did know the law on the subject and even before breath-testing appeared, 'driving under the influence' was a serious offence.

It was at The Orchid that I'd met Theresa a year or two previously. She was a stunningly attractive and petite girl with real 'film star' features not unlike Audrey Hepburn. We became regular dancing partners and after a while evolved into what might have been considered 'an item' in today's parlance although to us it was 'going steady' and to my Dad thirty years before, 'courting' or 'walking out' would have been the expression. It's funny how these expressions develop over time although I guess they reflect the reality. In the 30's and 40's young people's lives were pretty much controlled and buttoned up so that 'walking out' was about the strength of it until marriage or at least engagement came along to allow a bit of unbuttoning to happen. I'm probably being naïve though as love and certainly lust can usually find a way around most barriers.

How different to today when a one-night-stand seems quite acceptable, particularly with the younger generation but was certainly a bit strong even in the supposedly permissive 60's or at least what I saw of them. I guess that then and now it depends where you look for your fun but all I can say is that where I was looking didn't seem very permissive. As I remember, Ken's girls did and mine didn't. Short straw again!

When I first joined the police I saw a good deal less of Terri as the training was pretty full-on and I still had no car. However a short time after my posting to Lambeth she decided to move to London and got a flat in Bayswater. Well, I say flat: it was actually a room in the first floor apartment of a Georgian terraced house that she sub-let from two gay guys.

They all had to share the kitchen and bathroom and the other two who were probably in their 30's seemed to have taken Terri rather under their wing like a couple of big brothers. It was rather touching really the way they seemed to care for her. So, with her actually living in town we were able to get together more often and the ballrooms and bars of the West End became our regular haunts. It was great and I was completely in love.

Terri did some kind of secretarial or administrative work at the International Wool Secretariat (IWS) which if I remember correctly was somewhere around the Holborn area. Strange, because although I knew who she worked for I didn't have a clue what the organisation was about and it has only been in the process of recalling those times that I took the trouble to find out via the ever-amazing Google and Wikipedia. Apparently the organisation came into being in London in the 1930's in order to unify wool producers (many of whom were in the Commonwealth countries) and present a more united front to compete with the newly emerging man-made fibres from Germany and elsewhere. These included rayon which later, when produced in the UK, made the fortunes of the Courtauld family. One legacy of their wealth is the beautiful and imaginative modernist restoration of medieval Eltham Palace in south London which is well worth a visit.

The IWS was mainly about marketing and promoting wool against other fabrics and among other promotional activities; prizes were offered to fashion designers who used wool in their creations. In 1954 awards were made to the young Karl Lagerfeld and Yves St Laurent who went on to become major players in the fashion world.

If ignorant of the IWS itself most people will be very familiar with their Woolmark. This was the swirly black and white logo introduced in 1964 along with the phrase 'Pure New Wool' and after which IWS became the Woolmark Company.

Theresa and I were still very much together when I left the police and started at the garage and although our meetings were a little less frequent we saw each other as often as possible and if I had to return a demo car to Rootes in London, Terri's flat was just round the corner. – Result!

As all the silly stuff around drinking with Jack continued, our sessions at The Locomotive got later and later and there were often occasions when I'd phone home to say I wouldn't be in. Then at eight or nine o'clock and with a skinful of alcohol , I'd get in the car and drive up to Bayswater. I always phoned first though as even in that state I was in gear enough to make sure she would be there.

Just recalling all this makes me realise how much we take our ever-present mobile phones for granted these days. Back then I either had to use a public phone in the bar against all the background clatter and general hubbub or go out in the street to use the box a hundred yards away.

I must have sounded dreadful over the phone but to give credit where its due Terri never turned me away and always made a real fuss of me when I arrived. Although in retrospect it would have been safer if she'd told me to go home and sober up.

So, by the mercy of God and my guardian angel, time and again I'd arrive in one peace, slump on her bed, drink the proffered coffee and go to sleep. Great company! – heaven knows why she put up with it.

I'd usually rouse about half six when she got up and drive back home for a wash, shave and a clean shirt and then quite miraculously turn in for work at nine o'clock. Jack did too and to the rest of the world we were fine, although we weren't at all really.

iii

Meanwhile, real sexual experience was still proving elusive. Notwithstanding the availability of time, place and privacy, and despite both being enthusiastic to move things on, Terri never seemed able to take that step and consequently we never got to make love properly and my virginity remained stubbornly present. It seemed such a big thing to me at the time that despite our protestations of love and surging libido there was this block and I became convinced that I was doing something wrong or that she didn't feel the same as I did about her.

Then one day it all came tumbling out.

Tears welled in her eyes as she started to explain. *"Brian, you are lovely and none of this is about you. It's me and only me and somehow I have to work a way through it."*

She paused and seemed to be finding it hard to find words. I said nothing because I didn't want to interrupt what she had started. *"I really want things to be right with us and I so want to be able to make love to you properly but keep coming up against this barrier that I need to explain to you."*

I said *"You don't have to explain anything. I'm sure things will be OK eventually and I don't want us to do anything you don't feel ready for."*

"That's the problem." She said. *"I am ready but don't know if I'm ever going to get there with you or anyone else and believe me I've tried in the last couple of years. I've never told anyone this before but I'm hoping that if I do it will help to make things easier between us."*

To be honest, this was all sounding seriously heavy duty and I wasn't entirely sure I was ready for whatever she was about to reveal so I said *"Look, only say what you are comfortable with because I wouldn't want you to regret anything."*
"You know I used to live in Australia don't you?"
"Yes but what has that got to do with us now?"
"Just let me explain. OK."
"Right go on then." I said.
"When I was about fourteen my father started touching me whenever Mum wasn't around and then one day he started again but wouldn't stop and in the end, well, basically he raped me in our sitting room."

"I didn't want anyone to know because I felt so embarrassed, hurt, confused, all of

these emotions that I just didn't feel able to explain coherently or in a way I thought anyone would believe. My father knew he'd gone too far and I think he was terrified I'd say something so whenever he could he'd try to cuddle me and say sorry but every time he touched me I just felt the hate build up inside me even more."

By this time I was probably open-mouthed with shock. Obviously I knew what rape was, at least in terms of the legal definition from my previous time in the police but to hear it described first hand was a very different thing. Anyway there was worse to come as she went on.

"I somehow managed to keep up appearances for the next year or so but as I said, in my head it was always there and I just kept re-living it until I thought I'd go mad.

One day when I was about fifteen and a half we all went on a hunting trip and he came and found me behind a truck and started on about it again and trying to cuddle me. Something snapped in my head. There was a shot gun on the back of the truck so I grabbed it and shot him. How I actually missed I'll never know but it was just as well I did or God knows what might have happened. Anyway, then it all came out but instead of him being kicked out by my mother it was me. They sent me back to England to live with friends in Mitcham which is where I was living when we met."

Somehow Terri had managed to keep control of her tears through all of this but when I said *"Oh my God. You poor thing. Come here."* She just collapsed into my arms and sobbed until I thought she'd never stop. Eventually she did and said that despite being so upset, she really did feel better now she was no longer carrying the secret alone.

To say I was shaken by her revelations would be a huge understatement. At one level I was very flattered that she clearly felt enough for me and trusted me enough to share her secret but on another level if I'm truthful, I was a bit overwhelmed by it all.

Although I spoke to her almost daily for the next week I didn't go up to town again until the following week and when I did I made a point of not arriving in a drunken state. I'd got to town reasonably early so we went out for a drink and meal in the West End and then made our way back to her place,

She'd seemed a bit distracted all evening which was hardly surprising given what had passed. In spite of that she was warm and affectionate enough but when we went to bed she just wanted to be hugged which is how we went to sleep. Terri kissed me awake in the early hours and very gently and slowly she loved me and it was the most beautiful, intense and loving experience of my young life.

I smiled as I lay there afterwards and the thought flitted through my mind that at last my manhood was complete although to be honest it somehow seemed much less important now. A rather trifling, pathetic detail compared to what Terri had endured.

Sadly, it was all rather downhill from there. Not in any dramatic or unpleasant way but rather a very gradual and gentle drifting apart. We made love several more times but for all the beauty and intensity of that first experience she never again seemed able to commit as fully and something of the barrier she had described still remained and it was never quite the same.

My visits to Bayswater gradually became less frequent until imperceptibly they stopped and I guess that we both just moved on. I only hope that sharing her secret with me helped in the long term although I suspect that there was still a fair bit of baggage to unpack. I did try a few months later to make contact again to see how she was doing but she had changed both job and home and in pre-mobile phone days there was no longer a number I could call.

3 CAR SALES 1960s STYLE

i

By about six months in, although still having plenty to learn, I was beginning to feel pretty much the smooth car salesman and life at the showroom took on a certain amount of routine around following leads, tying up sales, organising pre-delivery servicing and vehicle handovers. As I said, Jack and I had developed a friendship as well as a very good working relationship even if a fair amount of that revolved around me covering for him on bad days.

Fortunately, and despite the relatively poor economic conditions at the time the situation for Ewell Downs and our subsidiary dealers was quite positive, and aided by the enthusiastic take-up of hire purchase and credit-sale possibilities we were doing quite well thank you. So much so that Jack and I felt we could do with a hand on the sales front so we advertised for another salesman.

This was when I first met Michael Fahey although I already knew his father in a sense as he was the band leader at the Orchid Ballroom in Purley where we used to go dancing. Brian Fahey was a well-regarded conductor, composer and musical arranger through the 50's and 70's. He became principal conductor of the BBC Scottish radio Orchestra in 1972, and continued to work for the BBC after the orchestra was disbanded in 1981. He was also Shirley Bassey's musical director for a time.

Tall, slim and sharp-witted, Michael proved a great addition to the team and together we had a good few laughs whilst still pushing up the sales. As you might imagine there are any number of stories about life on the Ewell by-pass where we worked and one in particular had to do with the second hand car stock. These were displayed on the grass verge in front of the showroom but because of the somewhat exposed location they had to be taken in at night and brought out again in the morning.

What no one had realised was that due to the continual starting from cold a certain amount of unburnt petrol was mixing with the engine oil each time.

One of the cars was a very nice little grey Volkswagen Beetle which took the eye of a certain Mrs. Howarth who asked for a test drive. *"No problem madam"* says I and within a few minutes I had the trade plates on and we set off with me driving up the Reigate Road which was our usual demo route.

We had probably gone about a quarter of a mile with me busy chatting away and extolling the virtues of the car when there was the most almighty bang from the rear engine compartment. As we came to an ignominious halt I looked in the mirror to see a huge cloud of blue smoke drifting away to reveal the steel sump off the engine and a large patch of oil on the road behind us.

Well how embarrassing was that? I was full of apologies of course but at that point actually had no idea what had happened apart from the fact that it seemed the engine had blown up. As I said we were fortunately not far from the garage but being pre-mobile phone days I had to walk my customer back to the garage and I can tell you it was not easy to maintain relaxed conversation in the circumstances.

Mrs. Howarth went off with my promises to get in touch shortly ringing in her ears whilst we had the car recovered to find that the engine itself was fine apart from the fact that the sump had blown clean off. As soon as Bill Burton heard the story he realised immediately what had happened, namely, that the afore-mentioned petrol that had gathered in the sump had vaporised as the engine warmed up, hit its flash point and exploded. In the event all that it needed was a new sump and an oil change for the little car to be running again as sweet as a nut.

"Well". I thought *"In for a penny in for a pound."* So I had the car polished till it sparkled and then drove it round to Mrs. Howarth's home where I explained the reason for what had happened and then after another test

drive managed to sell it to her after all.

I was so pleased with myself. *"Fridges to Eskimos?* I thought. "No *problem – bring it on"* Cocky little sod that I was.

It wasn't altogether surprising that this trouble arose with the used cars because we had some real 'stickers'. One was a 1962 Humber Hawk estate that we had taken in part exchange for a new Sceptre. It was a tidy motor but had done a bit more than the average annual mileage which is probably the reason it didn't sell. I think we sang Happy Birthday to it once if not twice until after it had been there all that time it was no longer a high mileage car but pretty low for its three or four years which is what actually clinched the sale when it eventually did go.

Looking back on those times, life there was nothing if not eventful and hardly a week passed without some drama to fret over or incident to laugh at.

We sold an automatic Hillman Minx to a customer with only one leg. He'd lost the right one and in order to drive needed an automatic car with the accelerator on the left instead of the right. We had the adaptation done in the workshop and put huge notices both on and in the car "**Caution – Left hand throttle**"

Shouldn't be a problem then. Not so!

We had a car cleaner at the garage called Eric. A willing lad, probably about 35 years of age who we might have described as "a sandwich short of a picnic." So, not the brightest body but very good at what he did, which was car cleaning and delivery driving.

After its pre-delivery test run I'd left the car on the front for Eric to collect and clean which meant it had to be taken down the ramp and into the cleaning bay, and I imagine that by this time you are ahead of me. Right?

I passed him on my way back into the showroom saying *"Don't forget the different pedals Eric."* *"No. That's OK Brian"*. He said jumping into the car.

Down the ramp he goes, applies the brakes, except he doesn't but hits the throttle instead. This launches the car towards the back of the wash bay where it demolishes the stud partition wall of the toilet block and comes to rest against one of the stalls where Les the painter is sitting studying

Playboy and doing whatever he was doing if you get my drift.

In the event the damage to the car was not that catastrophic so we had the necessary repairs done, changed the pedals back and eventually sold it as a used car.

There was another and almost much more serious event a few months later. We had a Hillman Super Minx demonstrator that we'd decided to sell so technically it was a second-hand car but was actually only a few months old and with almost no mileage.

One afternoon a guy came in, had a quick look over the car and started asking what our best price would be whilst producing several bundles of folding money; a ploy which is pretty much guaranteed to catch a salesman's attention. It certainly did mine, so when he asked for a test drive I had him in the car like a shot and away up the Reigate Road towards Epsom Downs which as I mentioned previously was our usual demo route.

Normal practice was for me to drive initially in order to demonstrate a car's features, equipment, performance and so on and then hand over to the customer for them to continue. This particular guy seemed extremely hesitant and not at all sure of what he was doing – more so than just unfamiliarity with the car. Anyway we got started and I directed him back towards the garage feeling distinctly insecure but unwilling to interfere too much for fear of putting him off me and the sale.

Arriving back at the roundabout outside the garage I said *"Turn left here please and then take the second right into the garage."* which he did but unfortunately right into the path of an oncoming coal lorry.

I of course was in the passenger seat when the lorry hit us broadside on shoving us some distance down the road. Back then seat belts were not mandatory and I had not put mine on which turned out to be fortuitous. In the split second before the lorry hit us I instinctively leaned forward and away from the point of impact which I could not have done had I been wearing a seat belt and in doing so avoided very serious injury because the door pillar came in about eighteen inches.

We were actually very lucky because the lorry had managed to brake a bit or the damage would have been far worse or possibly even rolled us over. As it was we were both very shaken and when Jack came running out he dragged me out of the car first with me shouting *" Jack, the bloody idiot nearly killed me."*

The driver was less shaken than me so despite my protestations I was the one that finished up on a blue light run to hospital feeling a bit of a fraud sitting up in the back of the ambulance smoking a cigarette with the attendant.

Whilst I was away the police turned up and it transpired that our customer didn't have a driving licence. So he was reported for driving without a licence or insurance and the officers came back a couple of days later and reported me for permitting him to do so. In the end I wasn't prosecuted because Geoff Welton the MD had a word with someone about it seeming a bit unfair especially as the police had been very much less than effective in solving a burglary we'd had at the garage a couple of months previously.

However, despite the damage our wonderful body repair people did an excellent job and I sold the car a couple of months later. It was perfect although I didn't actually volunteer the information about the accident damage.

Apart from the accident and another nasty moment when the throttle jammed open on a Mk10 Jaguar we did have a lot of fun including occasionally getting to drive some quite exciting machinery.

The garage was visited from time to time by other motor traders who used to buy our part exchange vehicles that for any reason we decided not to sell ourselves either because they were a bit scruffy or the mileages were a bit on the high side. I imagine that our high mileage cars were probably sold on in the trade, had the speedo's clocked and eventually wound up on a site somewhere as 'low mileage gems'.

One of these traders came in one day with an E-type Jaguar which he was more than happy to let me take for a test drive and on another day the same guy turned up with a bright yellow Iso Grifo. Never heard of it? Not surprising as it was quite a rare bit of Italian motoring exotica produced by the Iso Company who were better known for their little Isetta bubble cars.

The Iso however was something else. "Sex on wheels" really. It had the most beautiful lines and under the bonnet lurked a monstrous American V8 engine. I got to drive that too – although he did come with me on that little run. With up to 500 horsepower on tap they were apparently good for up to 170 mph so you can imagine how exiting that was for us to even be near it.

So life at the garage went on apace but there was much more to my life than just cars that mostly revolved around girls, parties, dancing and drinking.

ii

On the home front I was still knocking about with Ken although I was no longer dependent on him for transport which was good. By the end of 1965 Theresa and I had run our course so naturally quite a lot of energy was expended in getting about in the right places and meeting girls with the principal ambition of getting laid although that expression was not in use back then or at least not in my experience.

On which subject, it has to be admitted I was still markedly unsuccessful compared to my mates if their boasts were to be believed although I suspect that quite a bit of it was wishful thinking. I still seemed to find the good girls who would only go 'so far' and who were really looking for a nice boy to take home to their Mums and hopefully get married which was certainly not my plan at that time.

I did meet a very attractive girl one night at the Orchid in Purley. Her name was Carol and she lived with her parents in Wimbledon. We'd been seeing each other for a few weeks and getting on so well that I actually was taken home to meet the parents. During the course of conversation with them a bit about my background came out as it does and they somehow concluded correctly that I was a Catholic.

Although they didn't say anything directly at the time Carol told me later that her parents didn't want her to see me anymore as they imagined that if we married I'd do the catholic thing and she'd end up with loads of kids. I couldn't believe it and was really hurt as I was very fond of her and could actually have seen us together but it wasn't to be.

One day while we were still going out together I went to meet her from where she worked at a travel agents in Putney. Being the poser that I was back then I stopped to comb my hair in a shop window, straightened the tie and then marched confidently up to the door of the agents, stuck my arm out to push the door open with a flourish only to discover that it opened outwards. My forward movement brought me rapidly into contact with the door where my nose hit the glass and I was left on the outside looking in at Carol and all her colleagues with my nose bleeding down my shirt and feeling a complete idiot.

This must have been a good day because it was when I discovered the border between being laughed at and looked after. I guess I must have looked quite shaken and there was certainly a lot of blood so rather than laughing at me, Carol and several of her friends came out and brought me inside the shop. They sat me down and fussed around like little mother hens or nurses, tidying me up, bringing me tea and generally being so very kind that the experience was almost worth the discomfort and embarrassment. I bet they did laugh about it afterwards though. I did in retrospect as I am now in the telling.

Apart from frequenting The Orchid, Locarno and Wimbledon Palais dance halls one of our other regular activities was party crashing. This was no way as bad as some of the horror stories one reads from time to time these days about parents coming home to find homes completely trashed to the tune of thousands of pounds. True to say, it was the same in principle but we were far better behaved and even after a few drinks were always much more respectful of property.

I think a major part of the reason it has had the occasional disastrous consequence in more recent years is the availability of mobile communication and social media which allows news of a party or rave to be distributed incredibly fast and also indiscriminately. As a result, what my Dad would have described as *"any old Tom, Dick or Harry"* can get the information and turn up in droves to wreak mayhem.

In our case the distribution process was by word of mouth at The Marquis of Granby pub in Epsom. We'd usually fetch up there about seven o'clock on a Saturday to pick up the information about where the house parties were that night. Our grapevine was pretty good so often one of our crowd would know the person hosting the party and so could usually arrange for us to be invited. If not we would just turn up and hope to talk our way in which we usually managed to do. I never knew of anyone back then that forcibly crashed a party. We just didn't do that.

The parties didn't usually go on too late and invited guests tended to drift off around midnight which we all thought was a bit early for a Saturday night. Quite often we would phone the King Alfred Bowling Centre in Brighton and book a couple of lanes for one or two in the morning and then the race would begin.

I acknowledge once again that this was extremely irresponsible and am ashamed of myself now but this was back then, not now. I usually managed to borrow something a bit interesting from the used car stock which for quite a few weeks was a lovely powder blue 3.4 Jaguar S-type or failing that I used our Sunbeam Rapier demonstrator. So with mates Reg and Charlie in their Lotus-Cortina and E-type and any other mates who fancied a fast run we would set off for Brighton with the express intention of seeing who could get there first. How we survived I'll never know. Apart from the drink element which was so wrong the only saving grace was that in those days, by after midnight on a Saturday the roads were almost completely empty which at least minimised to some extent the danger to other people.

iii

Around this time I also met a guy called Richard Whittingham who became a life-long friend. Dick, as I always knew him, lived at Burgh Heath not far from Epsom Downs. His parents were really nice people and always made me welcome as did his stunningly beautiful sister Josephine who had done a bit of modelling although she didn't pursue it as a career which was a pity as she could probably have done well. Dick also had an older brother John who was already married. I think they got on well enough at that time but they fell out in a big way later over some property and were sadly estranged forever thereafter.

Just a month older than me, Dick was quite tall, dark and good-looking with a confidence ahead of his years that I always envied and I hardly ever remember him being ill-tempered. He was always up for a laugh and more often than not the ring leader of some of the silly daft things we got up to.

However, shortly before I met him he'd had the terrible experience of seeing his girl-friend Ann die from cancer. I can't remember all the details now but it had certainly knocked him back and it was a long time before he was able to tell me about it in any detail. Actually, losing Ann was just the first traumatic event of his life and although we couldn't have known it then, his life was going to be anything but boring. He has over the years had so many set-backs and still he seems to come through. I should spend a bit more time on him later.

Dick's company car was far from exotic; a little grey mini-van in which he carried around all of his samples including zips, buttons, pins, elastic, lining materials and threads etc. He worked as a sales rep. for a company called William Gee based in the East End that I was delighted to see when I checked on line are not only still in business but in exactly the same place. Nice that some things are constant.

One type of thread that Gee's supplied was a very fine nylon that was virtually invisible and it was this that we employed for a fairly silly but highly amusing prank one evening at The Locarno. Given the low level of lighting the situation was ideal for our plan. Whilst Dick kept hold of the reel of thread I took an end and went wandering off through the crowd, round and round, back and forth as we watched the antics of people totally perplexed at this invisible (in the dark) but incredibly strong thread that was getting caught around their legs, and bodies as though some 'super spider' had them ensnared. On another occasion we draped swathes of the same stuff from the balcony onto the heads of the dancers beneath and watching them trying to disentangle it from their hair and bodies was like witnessing the birth of some new and outlandish dance moves. Stupid I know but very funny.

Quite often after an evening at The Locarno we'd go for a curry at a restaurant nearby and in addition to our main order we used to get a dish of hot curry sauce to spice it up a bit if necessary although it did have to be used sparingly. One evening we were in there when a group of four chaps came in and sat at the next table to us. One of them was a real show-off. You know the sort – all mouth, and what he didn't know about curry wasn't worth knowing.

Dick said "*Watch this.*" Then he passed our dish of hot sauce over to the guy saying *"Want some gravy mate?"* *"Oh Yea. Cheers"* he says and starts sloshing the stuff all over his food.

Well you'd have the give the guy credit for sticking it out. It was soon obvious as he started to tuck into the meal that he was in trouble, at least judging by the reddening of his face and the amount of water he kept drinking and the fact that he was having a lot less to say than previously. Poor guy, but he clearly didn't want to lose face. It was so hard not to laugh out loud but I should think he learnt a lesson.

Not long after we met, Dick decided to move to London as most of his clients were in that area and travelling up and down from Burgh Heath added a couple of hours to his day. He found a nice little bed-sit in quite a handsome Georgian town house in Frognal Lane, Hampstead where I used to visit time from time to time. We liked the Hampstead atmosphere with the trendy bars and pavement cafes which were starting to appear back then. So much more sophisticated than Epsom or so we thought. Dick also used to let me use the flat sometimes if I needed somewhere to take the current girlfriend for a little private time.

iv

So life around the back end of 1965 was good for me. I was having a great (if sometimes irresponsible) time socially, scoring occasionally in the girlfriend stakes and really enjoying my work at the garage.

The only negative issue was that Jack and I were still drinking too much during the week and the after work sessions at The Locomotive had become far too firmly established. The worst of this for me personally was that I then had to go home instead of heading off up to town to visit Terri and as a result Mum and Dad became more aware that I had a bit of a problem. Well, I say this was bad but on reflection it was probably the start of my recovery because both parents spoke to me about my drinking and in Mum's case her greatest concern was that I would ruin my life as she had seen at least two of her own brothers do.

For Jack and I this scenario rather became the norm – photo kindly provided by Jack's daughter Jill.

On top of all this, Jack had got into a relationship with a woman we'd met in the pub and started to disappear with her some afternoons often not coming back to the office at all that day.

Well at least it stopped me calling in at the pub on the way home but it was terribly difficult having to fob off Jack's wife Monica if she called to speak to him and even worse if she called in at the garage to see him which was not unknown. I was fond of Monica and he treated her very badly and me too now that I look back on it by putting me in that position.

Despite all of the above we still stopped off at The Locomotive most nights where we had become very much part of the 'fathers and sons' club. As I later discovered Jack knew that our drinking partners thought I was his son and he never chose to inform them otherwise. *"Brian my boy."* he'd say *"You're the son I would love to have had."* Whisky talking, but touching none the less.

Well, the fathers and sons thing came to a head for me when I discovered that there was to be a "fathers and sons" night out and we'd been included in a booking made at The Red Coach restaurant at Banstead.

What I hadn't realised was that The Locomotive 'fathers and sons' were just a small part of a much larger network of business men comprising fathers and sons that worked together. I wasn't very keen to go but when I discovered Jack had paid for me I felt I had little choice.

The Red Coach was a very good restaurant where we were served pre-dinner drinks that seemed to work very rapidly to get everyone in the mood. An excellent dinner followed with loads more to drink but there was more to come. A floor show had been arranged. *"Oh how posh"* I thought. Well, how naïve can you be?

Tables and chairs were pushed back to clear the 'floor'. Copious jugs and bottles of beer came around and it dawned on me that basically I was at a stag party which I had heard about but never experienced.

Of course it was a strip show with first one girl then two and eventually three strutting their stuff and casting off their costumes like it was going out of fashion. *"Well, that wasn't too bad"* I thought. *"Pretty sexy too."*

Then the action began to ramp up a bit when the girls started on each other in a series of exhibitions that amounted to pretty much full-on lesbian sex. I was shocked. I'd seen the blue film show in Hong Kong when I was on the ship but this was live and right 'in your face'. Literally if you were in the front row and were unlucky or lucky enough depending on your view, to be dragged in to "help out" as they put it. By this time I was a long way past aroused. Terrified would be closer to the truth but somehow I managed to get to the back and keep a low enough profile to avoid being called out. I noticed that Jack too had gone quiet and was not quite as up front with our friends as when we were in the pub. If I'm honest I was shocked at the behaviour of these 'respectable' business men as they hooted and cheered at every move.

If I thought that was it I was wrong again. The last show was a very artistic strip tease which I thought was actually quite beautifully erotic and very well done. But it was then thoroughly spoilt once the dancer was completely naked and she started doing unspeakable things with beer bottles before handing them back to the guys she had borrowed them from. I am not a prude but that was just a step too far for me and was the point at which I decided that enough was enough and that I would bring my drinking sessions with Jack to an end.

I didn't make a big thing of it but gradually started to ease myself out of the routine stop-offs.

v

Whilst I was in the mood for good resolutions and bearing in mind Mum and Dad's expressed concerns, I got to thinking about other things to do in my spare time that didn't only revolve around drinking and hit on the idea of joining the Specials. Despite the fact that I'd left the Met there were many aspects of the job I did enjoy and also felt it would be a way to put back a little something into society that I had thus far spent a lot of time taking from.

So with very little training due to my previous time in the Met I was taken on by Surrey and sworn in as a Special Constable and found myself patrolling my own home area which was a very different thing to working the anonymous streets of Lambeth. Fortunately I never did have to prosecute or arrest anyone I knew but I enjoyed going out on my beats and occasional tours in the local area car.

I made a bit of a name for myself one day when I came upon a building on fire. It was an old barn in Woodfield Lane, Ashtead and was semi-derelict but the timbers were dry as tinder and coated on the outside with tar for weatherproofing.

The smell of smoke was what I first noticed as I wandered by so went to investigate and found a small fire getting under way in a corner at the back of the building. Bearing in mind there were no personal radios in those days I ran to a nearby house and knocked up the occupant to call the fire brigade and then went back outside to where I had noticed a hose pipe lying on the ground behind the barn and started spraying the flames which by this time were licking up the inner walls and starting to get a good hold.

It was probably a bit stupid to actually enter the building but I thought that if I could just keep it damped down a bit until the fire service arrived the building might just be saved. And that was exactly what happened. It was probably about twelve or fifteen minutes before the fire engine arrived from Leatherhead by which time I was about all in although I'd also had some help from the neighbour. With their powerful hoses they soon extinguished the flames and as well as thanking me they gave me a good ticking off (despite my uniform) for putting myself at risk for the sake of an old building.

4 LOVE ARRIVES

i

It was around this time that Denise appeared on the scene. The first we heard of her was from Reg James who told us about a very pretty girl who worked as a secretary for his father. I can remember that Ken didn't need telling twice as news of an attractive new girl around was too much for him to resist and in no time at all it seemed he'd managed to get introduced to her and got himself a date. I had to hand it to him. He was very good in the 'lady stakes'. However their liaison didn't last long, probably because "she didn't do the business" as he crudely put it.

I'd met Denise a couple of times whilst she was going out with Ken but it was certainly a surprise when in May or June I received an invitation to her birthday party. Anyway I trundled along and was rather presented as her new friend. I deliberately don't say boyfriend because we'd actually only met a couple of times. There was guy called Melvin there who I discovered was a previous boyfriend that Denise had been engaged to and who was hugely jealous of my appearance on the scene. I wasn't that fussed but do remember wondering if I'd only been invited to wind him up. Whatever, I was pretty chuffed at the invite given my relative lack of success in the girlfriend stakes and the upshot was that we started dating.

I was overjoyed with the situation because Denise was a real looker. Whilst only short, she was extremely pretty with long black hair and the perfect hour glass figure. They say the best things come in small parcels and that certainly seemed to apply to her. If there were any shortcomings I certainly didn't see them at the time.

Ken however was far from delighted and displayed a real 'dog in the manger' attitude because although he didn't want her himself he certainly disliked the fact that Denise was now going out with me. He made various half jokey remarks about me picking up his cast-offs which whilst superficially hurtful, didn't really cut too deep as my attitude to girl-friends was very different to his.

Although I didn't need his transport any longer we still knocked about together from time to time but I saw him less and less over the following months and it was soon clear that our close friendship was over. For my part, I was completely besotted with Denise and our relationship went from strength to strength as we became pretty much part of each other's lives.

Denise lived at Chessington with her parents and younger brother Alan and as her boyfriend I was very much welcomed into the family. I used to spend several evenings a week there either watching TV together or going in for a coffee after we had been out somewhere.

It was certainly an interesting experience to get this pretty intimate insight into the workings of another family. Especially as it was the first time I had been so closely involved with a family apart from my own and it was soon clear there were many differences.

Her mother Marjorie was without doubt the dominant personality in the house and whilst pretty much always sweetness and light with me, she had a very cutting way with words when it came to things that upset her. One of which seemed quite often to be her husband Dennis.

Poor Dennis did come in for some stick, mainly because he was not great on the practical front so when it came to doing things around the house he struggled a bit.

Around that time there was a fashion for covering ceilings with white polystyrene tiles which were usually fixed in a diagonal pattern to create a quite attractive and interesting ceiling effect (or at least we all thought so at the time) Clearly we didn't know back then what a deadly hazard they are in the case of fire when they tend to melt on occupants and give off noxious fumes. But then, as I said – we didn't know and style was what mattered. Anyway, Marjorie decided she wanted to be in the fashion, and ceiling tiles it would be.

So Dennis was briefed to do the job which involved first marking up the ceiling to enable the tiles to be positioned accurately. Dennis was OK with this because if I recall correctly he had worked in a drawing office so measurement and so on was not a problem. The next stage was for the tiles to be dobbed with adhesive on the reverse and then pushed up into place on the ceiling. What he hadn't realised or considered was that the tiles were soft so that in order to avoid denting them they should be pushed up with something flat.

Well you are probably ahead of me. Yes. Job done; the only problem was that each tile bore the imprint of five fingertips where they had been pushed up by hand. The sad thing about this story is that I only remember this part and not the final outcome. Whether they decided to live with them or had to get someone in to re-do the job I just don't recall.

I was lucky to have a father who was very practical that I learnt a lot from so (with the exception of ceiling tiles) I had done or helped Dad to do a lot of things around the place at home. One such thing was to watch him pluck and clean a chicken when he had occasion to execute one of our hens that had gone off-lay. I never actually did do this hands-on but had watched several times which proved very useful one day at Denise's house.

Marjorie had sent Dennis out to the butcher to buy a chicken and you need to bear in mind this was before the days of shrink-wrapped oven-ready birds. So when Dennis arrived home with this (fortunately dead and plucked) but otherwise complete chicken she went up the wall at him for not asking for it to be drawn and dressed for the oven.

"How could you be so stupid Dennis?" she yelled. *"Now you'll have to take it back."*

I reckon that in the boyfriend stakes I must have rated very highly that day because I knew how to do the job and set about topping and tailing the bird in the kitchen as well as drawing its stinking entrails to everyone's disgust. Pretty much above and beyond the call of boyfriend duty but it was certainly a good point scorer with a future mother-in-law. Yes. I was starting to think in those terms although Denise and I hadn't actually got round to the subject ourselves.

I was so caught up with the romance of our relationship that I hadn't given any thought to our compatibility in more general terms based on things like education, experience, other interests or background, but then who does?. Basically we just fancied the pants off each other although that never did happen but as far as we did go things seemed to be working pretty well in that department.

I had certainly seen and done a lot more than Denise in my twenty-one years and had a good deal more confidence even in relation to things like finding my way around town. I recall once when we were in London and I decided to take a cab, she thought it was something quite out of the ordinary that 'people like us' didn't do. Made me smile at the time and I just felt so much the 'man about town'.

I was a bit of a poser though to be honest. I remember one evening when I had borrowed a little red MGB sports car from work and planned to take Denise down to the Brands Hatch Club where I was a member. I thought *"What could be better to impress a girl than a fast ride down to Brands in an open sports car?"*

Well the going down bit was Ok as indeed was the sophisticated drink in the bar. However, by the time we came to head home the rain came down and I had to hurriedly erect the canvas hood which made the car feel a good deal less exotic – very claustrophobic in fact. I then had a terrible drive back straining to see through the small rain-smeared windscreen all the way home in the peeing rain. If that wasn't enough to put Denise off the idea of a romantic evening out, attempting anything else in the confines of the little car with the gear lever and handbrake sticking up between us certainly was. Well you live and learn!

Denise's parents had some long-standing friends that they had known for years and with whom pretty much all of their social life was spent. There were two couples Nan and Arnold and Vic and Edna and known indoors as Aunties and Uncles to Denise and her brother Alan. What was not at first obvious to me, because I wasn't looking for it, was that there was something going on between Uncle Vic and Marjorie. Apparently it was known about within their circle because they had even talked about going off together and would have done so if it hadn't been for Edna's hysteria and threats of suicide.

The reason I mention this is because it was something so outside the experience of my childhood cossetted in the warm and loving relationship my parents shared. It took a long time for me to understand that such a situation could exist. Sounds naïve I know but that was me at the time. Events would prove that I should have thought a bit more about it.

ii

As 1966 arrived I had no idea what a momentous year it would turn out to be.

Life at the garage was trundling on very well and I had to a large extent managed to cut out my pub visits with Jack although by around this time whatever sort of extramarital affair he had going on had become quite established and I was still having to make excuses for his absence whenever Monica called. Definitely not a situation I enjoyed or felt comfortable with but Jack told me bluntly it was not my business. End of story.

I was still getting out and about with Dick and rather like Ken and I had once been we became another set of 'terrible twins' doing pretty much everything together in our spare time when I was not seeing Denise.

I remember late one Saturday afternoon on the way back from Brands Hatch I was driving the same little MG sports car. Presumably fired up by the racing we'd watched I was nipping along quite swiftly when I realised I was being followed by a little mini-van and it seemed to be developing into a bit of a race, which was fine and always a welcome diversion in those silly days.

We were zipping through the back streets of Bromley when Dick spotted a little blue police sign on the roof. *"Oh shit"* he said *"It's a bloody Police van."*

Well I backed off the gas straight away and was desperately trying to reduce speed by changing down and pulling on the hand brake whilst watching the van in the mirror that I went straight through a red light.

The good thing was that on that occasion we had not been drinking. The bad thing was that very deservedly I was reported for the traffic light offence and wound up at Bromley Magistrates Court. Fortunately for me, I couldn't be prosecuted for speeding as the mini van's speedometer was not tested or calibrated for speed offences.

Not exactly the best way to start a new year but there was more to come.

5 A STEP UP THE LADDER
i

It was not general knowledge among the staff that Ewell Downs had in fact been taken over in 1964 when in order to fund their individual pensions the directors had sold their interest in the company.

The buyer was one Horace Nutt, who owned a number of small garages and petrol stations in the South Midlands based around Royston in Cambridgeshire. As he could not easily be a hands-on owner he assumed the title of company chairman and only agreed to the take-over on condition that the directors continue to run the company for at least the next three years. There was clearly a reason for this although it was not obvious at the time but suited all concerned as the existing directors were approaching but had not quite reached retiring age.

Early in 1966, Geoff Welton's health gave cause for concern and he retired with Jack Moxley being appointed to the board as Sales Director.

This left the role of Sales Manager vacant which fell to me quite simply because Jack said so. He then moved into Welton's office leaving me with the day-to-day running of the showroom after which it soon became apparent that we probably needed another member of the sales team.

I must say I felt quite the business man as I set about advertising for the new member. To be honest I don't recall that much about the process but sufficient to say that Jack and I interviewed two or three applicants and appointed one Adrian Armstrong.

Arriving with newly printed business cards and styling himself as Adrian P. Spencer - Armstrong no less; Adrian set about learning the ropes and quickly became a useful member of the team. He was quite a character too. Despite his youth he had a way about him and an air of confidence which with a rather 'plummy' accent set him slightly apart.

I don't remember exactly how long it was but the fall came a few months later when I wasn't around for some reason.

You need to understand that we were all very young and completely car mad so when anything even vaguely interesting as in fast, exotic or different came within range we would be all over it like a rash. Such was the case when Adrian dealt with a guy who wanted to part-exchange a really pretty plum coloured Alfa Romeo.

On the grounds of checking the car over prior to valuation, Adrian went off round the block in it like a dog with two tails and then went bouncing into Jack's office to tell him about the potential part exchange and get a price to offer the client.

Well, he got the part-exchange figure which turned out to be acceptable to the customer. The necessary papers for the new car were signed and off went the Alfa man to await delivery of his car.

About two weeks later the new car arrived from the factory, pre-delivery checks were done and it was all polished up for collection. In due course the buyer turned up, completed the purchase and went off with his new car leaving the Alfa parked in front of the showroom.

I was in my own office at the time and had left the hand-over to Adrian to get on with whatever I was doing. A while later Jack emerged from his office and seeing the Alfa parked there went out to have a look and stopped dead in his tracks then turned around and came storming back into the showroom shouting for Adrian who was in the office at the other end of the showroom.

I could see Jack was furious *"What the hell have you done Adrian and what the fuck do you call that out there"*

Adrian, obviously shaken stammered *"It's the Alfa Jack. We spoke about it a couple of weeks ago."*

"I can bloody see what it is you prat. It's a bloody left-hooker and you've just cost us about a hundred and fifty quid too much in part-exchange."

Adrian went ashen as the reality dawned that in his excitement at getting the sale and also getting his hands on something a bit interesting he hadn't even thought about the difference that it being a left-hand drive would make to its value.

Jack didn't actually sack him but the air between them was so thick after that episode that the normally so bouncy Adrian was completely deflated and left of his own accord soon after. This of course left us one man down so once again we had to advertise for another salesman which was when I met Dave Cannon.

Dave was an extremely likeable and competent young salesman and in quite a short time we developed a friendship which was to last a lifetime. We did some very good business between the three of us as well as sharing 'chauffeur' duties collecting Jack from the various local hostelries more or less on demand.

Unlike many car salesmen of that era, I can honestly say that we never stepped over the legality line or got involved in fiddling mileages or any of that stuff. Occasionally a little economical with the truth perhaps, as in not exactly broadcasting the crash history of the car I came so close to getting killed in, but certainly nothing criminal or seriously dishonest. We were relatively big players locally so reputation was all important.

ii

Although my relationship with Denise was on-going and very nicely so, I was also spending time with Dick as it seemed important to keep a balance between doing things together and still keeping up with other friends.

In that context Dick and I were planning a camping holiday together in Scotland later in the year. We had never seen anything of what one might call 'wild' country so we thought a trip to the Highlands could fit the bill. However not being experienced at camping; we thought we needed a fall-back position so decided that a van we could sleep in if necessary could be the answer. As luck would have it a short time later we took the very thing in part-exchange at the garage.

This was a 15cwt Austin J2 van that had belonged to a firm of builder/decorators and certainly had seen better days. However it hadn't done that many miles and even better, we had allowed almost next to nothing for it against the new vehicle. I looked at the figures with Jack and he agreed I could buy it for £35. I know this sounds ridiculous now but it was fifty years ago when a pound went a lot further than it does today.

We were able to work on the van in the garage workshop at the weekend where we gave it a good check-over and were pleased to discover that the problems were mainly superficial and it was mechanically very sound. The floor in the back was pretty ropey where they'd been mixing cement and paint and whatever else so we decided to put another floor in. Dick managed to source some very thick carpet underlay which we then covered with sheets of hardboard cut to an exact fit and the whole thing looked dramatically better as well as much quieter. A coat of white paint inside completed the transformation.

Our holiday plans took a bit of a knock at one point when Dick managed to get himself disqualified from driving for exceeding the speed limit once too often and it wasn't just our holiday driving that he had to worry about. He was a sales rep and so his whole employment depended on being able to drive his firm's van. The positive aspect was that he was a very good salesman and was earning well enough to actually employ a chap to drive him for four days a week while he spent the fifth on paperwork.

iii

It was probably in April or May of 1966 that the big bombshell dropped on me. Mum was going to die, and apparently quite soon.

Following her hysterectomy a couple of years before when she was diagnosed with cervical cancer she had been sent home to recover and the medics were hopeful that they had "*got it all.*" Back then there was no follow-up chemo or radio-therapy as there is these days but simply a hope for the best.

Mum's abdominal discomfort had been building for some time and I imagine that with her own medical knowledge from nursing she must have known things were probably going seriously wrong although I have no idea how much she and Dad talked about it. Anyway she was admitted to hospital again and after an exploratory operation it was explained that the cancer had spread and was inoperable and she was sent home with a prognosis that she could live for weeks or months but certainly not years.

I never did know whether it was spelt out to Mum in so many words but I suspect not as she never spoke of it herself at least not to me. Whether she was in some kind of denial mentality or really didn't know the full facts or was simply trying to protect our feelings, I have no idea.

Obviously this news cast a huge cloud over the whole family and although we tried to carry on as usual – Mum being the most successful in this regard; it was pretty well impossible to think about anything else whilst still trying to maintain an outward appearance of normality. The cancer became the elephant in the room that was never mentioned but everyone knew was there.

Towards the end of June or early July she took a serious turn for the worse with a lot of pain and was taken into Leatherhead Cottage Hospital. Here at least they could control the pain if nothing else but it did mean that her awareness of our visits was patchy at best..

After a week or so in the hospital she was almost totally out of it with the medication and we used to just go and sit even though she was apparently unaware of our presence. One day I was there holding her hand and was bowed over weeping quietly when she put her hand on my head and in a very clear voice said *"Come on now Brian. Stop that nonsense. There's nothing to be done. You've just got to be strong for your dad and everything will be fine."* She then just lapsed back into unconsciousness.

A couple of days later I was at work when I had a call to go to the hospital but she had already gone by the time I arrived which was sad but at least I had that brief moment which was our goodbye.

Mum and Dad

6 MOVING ON

The holiday with Dick had been planned for around the end of July but after Mum's funeral I felt that I should stay around to support Dad although he thought differently.

"What's the point of us all sitting here looking miserable? We've just got to get on with things. I can manage perfectly well and you'd be better getting away for a distraction from all the gloom."

So that's what happened. Dick and I set off up the A1 as the southern end of the new M1 motorway was still under construction. We made the Lake District on the first day and then spent a very pleasantly distracting ten days or so meandering around the southern Highlands pitching the tent some nights and just sleeping in the van when we couldn't be bothered.

The van had a side loading door in the back and one day I was driving past this potato field when Dick said *"Stop."* He then hopped over into the back, grabbed a bucket and jumped out of the side door and over the bank into the field where he grubbed up a couple of plants and filled the bucket with lovely fresh spuds. About a mile further on I spotted a field of sweetcorn so we stopped again to add a bit of veg to our menu. Naughty I know but saved a few pence. Dick had also brought along his air rifle and was determined that we should try to get a rabbit for our meal that evening.

About four in the afternoon we saw a spot down by a lake with a stream running down into it and a level bit of grassy shore were we could drive the van down almost to the water. It was an overcast day but dry so we decided to actually give the tent an airing having slept in the van the two previous nights and set to getting it pitched and our little camp site arranged.

We'd noticed that there were plenty of rabbits about but getting close enough to shoot one was likely to prove a different matter.

The Great White Hunter had nothing on us as we set off from the van across the boggy moorland. As well as the air rifle Dick had produced a huge sheath knife and looked more as though he was setting out on some kind of big game hunt rather than a trying to pot a rabbit or two for supper.

It wasn't long before we spotted a few rabbits in a grassy hollow near a stream and dropped onto our knees to 'stalk our prey'. I had no idea what kind of shot he was so I was seriously impressed when crawling up to the crest of a rise Dick lay down on his stomach, took aim and hit one first shot. We didn't get a second chance as the others scattered immediately but unfortunately we could then see that the poor thing was only wounded as it was squirming around presumably in pain. I immediately felt sick with remorse.

"*Kill it Dick*" I said. "*Kill it quick.*" He shot it again but somehow it still wasn't dead. I was horrified but I just grabbed his knife and turning it round hit the poor creature hard on the back of the head and it stopped moving at which point I was almost physically sick. I'd seen plenty of dead animals before but it was the simple fact that we had taken the life that upset me. (It's todays classic hypocrisy isn't it? We are all happy to buy and eat our shrink-wrapped meat and fish so long as we don't have to see the animals meet their end.)

Well it wasn't the plumpest rabbit in the world but by no means the smallest either and although neither of us really knew how to prepare it for the pot we felt that one way or the other having taken its life we shouldn't just waste it. Though I don't think either of us had much appetite for rabbit at that moment either.

I suppose thinking back on it that given my experience drawing a chicken's innards I could probably have worked out how to do a rabbit.

However, as Dick had seen how apparently squeamish I was he said he would do it and set off down to the stream where he laid the little corpse out on a large flat rock beside the stream. He then skinned and set about it with his knife while I went off to sort out the 'kitchen'.

We had a little camping stove and kettle that we used to make tea and heat up the porridge, tins of soup, Irish Stew and baked beans that had been our fare thus far.

However as I felt we had moved ahead somewhat in actually sourcing our own food (ignoring the fact that the spuds and corn were stolen) I decided that we should cook it over a real fire. I assembled a small circle of stones and set off in search of fuel. There was no shortage of drift wood along the lake shore so I soon managed to assemble a good armful including everything from small kindling to quite substantial logs. My scouting experience had me searching for a couple of birch trees from which I took the paper thin silver bark to get the fire started and quickly had quite a little blaze in my stone circle.

It wasn't long before Dick returned with a surprisingly well cleaned and jointed rabbit which I'd already decided should best be cooked by adding it to a saucepan of Irish Stew that was by now simmering on a pile of glowing embers alongside four corn cobs toasting on the hot stones. Illicit spuds were scraped, chopped and added to the pot and in next to no time it seemed we had a tasty nutritious stew to eat as we watched the sun disappear behind the hills. The only mistake was that the sweetcorn was actually fodder corn and not sweet at all but it went down well enough with all the rest.

Such experiences, beautiful scenery and having to do all the driving kept me fairly well distracted from thoughts of Mum but I do recall that on several evenings I took myself off a little and let the grief surface. I remember one moment when the crying stopped and I sat there in the dark looking up at an almost jet black star-filled sky and somehow felt as though she was right there beside me. I was certain at the time that it was more than just an idea. There was a definite sense of presence and I felt very comforted as well as indescribably sad.

Dick was very kind in allowing me this space but then it was only a year or so previously that he had the similar experience when Anne died so he understood very well what I needed.

Overall the Scottish trip was a great success. We had fun, saw some marvellous scenery and did almost eighteen hundred miles in the old van without a hitch. Even better; when we got back we sold it at a profit, pocketed a few quid each and even got a refund on the road tax.

I called this chapter 'Moving on' and I must say it was quite surprising how much this little diversion helped in that regard. Obviously I was desperately sad over losing Mum but even at that young age I seemed to have this ability to rationalize the situation in a kind of logical rather than emotional manner.

Firstly there was nothing to be gained by prolonged and deep mourning and secondly I knew Mum wouldn't have wanted that. I was then still a fairly committed believer in the idea of 'the afterlife' and told myself that if there was another realm then she was distinctly better off there than in the pain she suffered while alive, and if not then it didn't matter anyway. So, it made sense to get used to the idea and move on holding on to the good stuff and letting the sad and bad just drift away which is after all pretty much what happens naturally over time.

7 WEDDING BELLS

i

Following Mum's death, life went on much as before and although I tried for a while to spend a little more time at home giving Dad a bit of support he made it clear that he didn't want me to, as he put it, *"hang around the house to keep me company"*.

My relationship with Denise was developing and early in 1967 we decided to get engaged with the idea of marrying later the same year. We managed to get away on a couple of brief holidays simply to spend some time together and actually away from our families in order to get used to each other at close quarters.

We had a great little trip up to East Anglia and Suffolk in particular as Denise wanted to visit the Woodbridge area which was where her father came from. Another trip took us down to the West Country where we stayed for a night in a bed and breakfast in the village of Mere in Wiltshire. This was a bit before en-suite facilities were the norm and the bathroom was shared with the owner. So when I got up around seven and shuffled off to the bathroom I was a bit shocked to say the least to push the unlocked door open to find our landlady on the throne.

Mortified with embarrassment, at breakfast time I again started with my apologies but she was unfazed. *"Lord save us"* she said *"If that's the worst thing you ever see in your life you'll be a lucky man."*

It was a strange scenario and so different to today because while we shared double rooms and beds when on holiday we still never went "all the way" as was said back then. So the truth is that as we approached our forthcoming nuptials, apart from the little experience I'd had with Theresa we were both hopelessly inexperienced in things sexual. And, as I had discovered with her, sexual compatibility is by no means a forgone conclusion.

Co-habitation was just not the done thing at the time although I wish with all my heart that we had as it would have made things so much easier. Although I guess we were not a lot different to any number of other 'nice' couples who decided not to start before the whistle and basically trust to luck on the big night. With the benefit of hindsight and a broader mind I think it was complete madness because of all things in a marriage that you need to know before you sign up, among the most important is your physical compatibility.

It was shortly after we'd been away that I had my final bust-up with Ken which was sad because although I'd seen less of him in recent months we had shared a lot over the years. And I still regarded him as a friend even though I realised he resented my ongoing relationship with Denise or Dee as he used to call her.

I think it was at a pub in Epsom where Dick and I were having a drink one evening when Ken came in, bought a drink and came to join us. We spoke about this and that for a few minutes and then he said *"How's the lovely Dee then?"* and I said she was fine and that we were getting married in October and then he said *"Yes I heard that. Bet you haven't got her into bed yet though."*

I couldn't believe what he'd said and just saw red completely. *"You bastard Ken."* I shouted. *"That's all it's about with you isn't it. Say that again and I'll bloody flatten you." "Oh Yea"* he replies *"You and whose army?"*

I came a so close to hitting him but Dick grabbed me and dragged me outside saying it wasn't worth getting in a fight over which I knew was true but the problem was I also knew in some ways he was right. Things seemed OK between us in that department but neither Denise nor I really knew for sure and I did feel a bit uneasy about it.

ii

Denise and I wanted very much to buy our own place from the start and began to look around for something we could afford. By this time my Sales Manager status meant I could use more or less any of our used cars that I fancied and I remember my set of wheels at the time was a bright red 3.8 Jaguar. As we set about our house hunting Dad quite wisely said *"Might be an idea to take a less flashy car or the house prices will be going up a bit."*

Surrey has always been a bit of a property hot-spot so when we couldn't find anything within our budget anywhere around our home area we eventually settled on a two-bedroom maisonette at Horley near Gatwick airport. It was going to cost the then 'astronomical' price (at least for us) of £3600. It was about sixteen miles from work but as I had use of a firm's car the distance was no big deal.

Victoria Road, Horley

The main issue was that we had virtually no money so whilst we could get a ninety percent mortgage we still had to raise the other ten which the mathematicians among you will have worked out was just £360. It probably seems unbelievable now but back then that took some doing as my part commission based income was a bit unreliable to say the least. As an idea of prices back then, a pint of beer cost about one shilling and ten pence which is the equivalent of less than ten new pence in today's money and a gallon of petrol cost less than five shillings (25p). A good average weekly wage would have been £21 which equates to a salary of around £19,000 a year today and that would certainly not be enough to afford a mortgage now.

In the event we managed to arrange a mortgage for the £3000 but also had to borrow a further £600 for the deposit and legal expenses which we achieved by taking out an additional life policy as collateral.

As Denise's money couldn't be taken into account fully this extra expense was going to stretch my income to the limit and although we both wanted children we discussed it and agreed that she would carry on working at least until this additional loan was paid off.

My own view regarding children was that it would be better to wait a while before starting a family in order to both get to know each other properly and give ourselves time to get more of a home together as well as maybe being able to afford the odd holiday. We were after all only twenty three and twenty two years of age. *"Loads of time."* I thought, before we should even begin to think about children. Although she agreed at the time as I was to discover, Denise had very different ideas.

iii

Something else rather unexpected happened around the same time. Despite the relatively short period of time since Mum's death – little more than a year, Dad had met and apparently fallen for another lady. Also by odd coincidence called Eileen and even more strangely she worked as a nurse at West Park, the same psychiatric hospital Mum used to work at in Epsom.

She was a widow of several years whose husband had been quite successful and together they'd had an active and enjoyable social life until his premature demise. Dad was a smart, upright and very presentable 60 year old widower and I guess she saw in him a way back to the social life she missed. So, it would be fair to say that around this time his thoughts were somewhat diverted from his son's forthcoming wedding plans. Not that I thought he showed a lack of interest but Denise did rather feel we and our plans were playing second fiddle to the new lady in his life.

To be honest, I never took to Eileen but was more than happy to accept her if that was Dad's wish although some of Mum's friends (also nurses at the hospital) seriously disliked her and were vehemently opposed to the relationship.

These friends refused to elaborate on their objections so I have never known whether they simply thought it was too soon after Mum's death or whether they knew something else about Eileen's background.

iv

Among other wedding-related plans the actual wedding venue and service had to be organised and as I was then a devout and practicing Catholic it was agreed that we would get married in the same church as my parents, namely St Joseph's in Epsom. This was chosen partly as it was conveniently half way between our addresses at Ashtead and Chessington but also because it ticked a huge nostalgia and good luck box for me to be following in my parents' marital footsteps. Denise, having no particular religious inclinations at the time was happy to go along with the idea.

One aspect we both disliked but had little option but to accept was the church's insistence that as we were not both Catholics we should go along to instructional sessions at the church. Here we were instructed (Denise in particular), regarding the Church's rules and beliefs, one of which was that any children of the marriage would have to be brought up in the faith. Being a believer I had no problem with that and I'm not sure that Denise was worried either way to be honest but I felt it was terribly patronizing.

I guess this assertion of my devout religious ideas sounds a bit hollow after my various – mostly unsuccessful – attempts at getting some sexual experience. Still, confession was a handy salve to that particular issue of conscience. (he said cynically)

Ever since school I had kept in touch with Father Peter Boulding who had been my physics teacher, my preferred confessor and also my friend and we agreed to ask him to officiate at our wedding which happily he agreed to do.

I'd had some difficulties reconciling the Catholic doctrines around birth control with the practical reality that in the modern world some kind of contraception practice has to be factored into a responsible relationship. Until this point in my life, following the faith had been easy. I'd been brought up a Catholic and it had never been any real hardship to trundle along with Mum to Sunday mass and just accept the teachings of the Church, believing, it must be admitted, at a pretty superficial level because the rules had never conflicted with any aspect of my life. Until then. Discussing the issue with Peter Boulding I was disappointed when the best he could say was *"Well you know what the Church teaches. All I can say is let your conscience be your guide."* I thought it was a total cop out at the time but looking back now I remember reading quite a lot about the number of clergy who were not just seeing the difficulty for married people but even beginning the think the 'unthinkable'.- The Church could be wrong.

Other things around the wedding plans included a reception and honeymoon. We booked a room at the Woodman pub in Ashtead for the reception which was not going to be overly large affair and for our honeymoon the most we could afford was a week away in The Lake District. As a little bonus Jack had said I could take a Sunbeam Alpine sports car as our honeymoon transport so I was a very happy bunny.

v

As life at Ewell Downs went on apace and the months ticked by, in no time at all it seemed October had arrived and the big day dawned. Friend Dick had agreed to be my Best Man and had me out drinking with a few other friends the night before so I was feeling a bit fragile to say the least. As we got to the church early with some time to kill we headed for the nearby pub which back in those days didn't serve coffee so an alcoholic 'hair of the dog' seemed the best bet and I must say a scotch and milk (a recipe picked up from Jack) did the trick.

We returned to the church in good time and took our place at the front to await Denise's arrived. A few minutes later the organ started with the wedding march and I turned to look. She looked so beautiful and absolutely radiant in her white wedding dress and veil and I must say my heart melted as she walked up the aisle on Dennis' arm to stand beside me at the altar.

Looking back on it, the service must have seemed a bit of a marathon to the majority of guests because Catholics were in the minority and the others would have found the rite of the Mass pretty unfamiliar. At least by that time most of the service was in English rather than the Latin of just a couple of years earlier. However Peter Boulding was lovely and made everyone feel really comfortable and before we knew it we emerged from the Church as man and wife for the photographs and then off to the reception at Ashtead.

We had arranged to spend our first night as a married couple at a hotel near Horley before setting out a day or two later for our Lake District honeymoon. So as the reception drew to a close we were seen off amid much waving and good wishes and set out for the relatively short drive to the hotel.

So far so good but a few minutes after we arrived Denise discovered that she had forgotten her make-up bag. Judging by the upset it seemed to be causing this was serious and so 'perfect gentleman' that I am I agreed to go and get it. Now the gods must really have been with me because despite probably being over the alcohol limit and certainly breaking a few speed limits I got safely back to her parents' place in Chessington and retrieved the bag.

This was turning out to be some romantic wedding night!

By the time I returned to the hotel it was quite late and Denise had gone to bed and apparently cried herself to sleep. Hopefully not out of regret but sheer exhaustion and frustration with events.

I guess I could have taken this turn of events as an ill omen for the future but I remembered my parents' story of their wedding night that also had a somewhat negative outcome.

They had gone to honeymoon for the few days of Dad's leave pass to the seaside at Broadstairs in Kent where they had booked a room at a small guest house. Apparently the room had a gas fire that needed the meter to be fed with coins so after sticking a few pence in the meter and in order to spare Mum's blushes as she made herself ready for bed Dad apparently said he would go for a short walk and a cigarette.

Walk he did, but short it was not. He lost his bearings and spent ages walking the blacked-out streets of Broadstairs trying to find his way back to their guest house. No mobile phones of course back then. Meanwhile Mum, suitable attired and perfumed I guess, sat and waited, and waited, and waited until the gas fire went out. So having no means of keeping warm or contacting Dad she like Denise went to bed alone on her wedding night only to be joined an hour or so later by her new husband.

So here was something else I had in common with Dad. Despite this rather dubious start I could only hope my marriage would work out as well as theirs.

8 LIFE GOES ON

i

The Lake District in October can be wet.

It was. Very wet, and we spent a fair bit of time watching the rain hammering down on the roof window over our bed in the little hotel room at Bowness on Windermere. Not that this was an altogether bad thing for a pair of newly-weds with love on their minds. We did emerge from time to time as the weather allowed and not just to eat but also to explore a bit. Lake District scenery is stunning but to be fair it is much better in the sunshine of which we saw little which was a shame so a week later we were back in our new nest at Horley to embark on married life proper.

I was still at the garage but of course I now had a slightly longer commute. Also, in order to help boost the income a bit during the period we were planning to pay off the to-up loan I was also working on the petrol forecourt on Saturday or Sunday and sometimes both if I could.

Denise had found a clerical or secretarial job at a firm in Redhill and so things looked as though they were panning out OK until only a month or so later when the baby issue emerged. We should probably have talked about it more beforehand but when the matter arose it was immediately obvious that on the subject of planning and timing the family we both wanted we were coming from very different places.

I was convinced that it made sense to wait until our financial situation was more secure regarding the extra loan. But more than that, as explained previously, I honestly felt it would be better to give ourselves time to adjust to each other and our life together rather than rush into starting a family. I also thought it would make sense to try to put a few pounds by for a rainy day as well.

It is incredibly easy to underestimate the maternal urge that can overwhelm a woman which is what happened to Denise. Despite our previous agreement, she couldn't have been clearer that the only thing that mattered to her at that moment was to start a family and I had misjudged it completely.

Talking around the subject or about waiting a while for the reasons mentioned above just wasn't going to happen. She made that quite clear. The sums were obvious to me. On my somewhat irregular money we were not managing that well anyway and a new baby was actually about the last thing that made sense.

Denise was convinced things would be fine. She could carry on working for most of the pregnancy by which time we would have paid of a good bit of the loan. I was still unconvinced but faced with a seriously broody wife and the potential to subvert our relationship almost from day one I capitulated but started making my own plans. I just couldn't take the risk of starting a family on the highly variable income from car sales and I knew then that sadly my motor trade days were numbered. But what to do?

I didn't actually get much time to wonder because almost as soon as we had agreed about the baby idea Denise became pregnant. Clearly nothing wrong in that department then – for either of us – but a bit longer trying would have been fun. With another mouth to feed due the following August I had to move things on.

ii

Christmas 1967 came and went. On the Ewell by-pass we were still selling cars but the general economic situation was not good what with the devaluation of the pound, inflation and lower industrial output. Also there were changes afoot that would bring about the almost total disappearance of most UK owned motor manufacturers over the following few years.

It would be wrong to claim that I fully understood what was going on but I definitely had a sense that things were on the slide and more particularly the unreliability of my own salary was already causing significant pressure on our domestic finances.

Something had to change but the problem was I didn't know what until one day at work I heard the sound of a police siren. Looking up saw a black police Jaguar carving its way through the traffic at speed. I thought *"That could be fun."*

I knew in that moment what to do. I would go back into the police. It was a job I knew and I had not left the Met because I hated the work but more because it didn't suit my then life-style coupled with anxiety over Mum's illness.

Now to say that my idea of re-joining the police arose from an urgent desire to fight crime and serve the community would be disingenuous to say the least. That's not to say I didn't believe in those things but it was the conditions of service that appealed to my primary need of providing a home and security for my family.

The salary for a probationer constable was not that great, in fact I would be earning less than I did selling cars but at least in the police the money would be regular and reliable. In addition to the basic salary there was the huge incentive that police officers were entitled to free housing or a rent allowance in lieu that could go towards the mortgage.

As we were then living in Surrey it made sense to apply to the local force which I did and in due course was interviewed at Guildford by the then Chief Constable Herman Rutherford. He didn't give me the hard time I expected about re-joining having left the Met. He was actually quite kindly and just seemed pleased I had decided to return to the fold albeit with a slightly wry remark about realizing which side my bread was buttered. Anyway I was accepted.

Re-joiners to the service were sometimes allowed to go straight back to duty with just a simple force-based refresher course but unfortunately the cut-off point for this was three years and as I had been out for four I would have to do the initial training all over again. This was bad news at home as it involved being away on the course for thirteen weeks and meant I would only just be finished in time for our baby's projected arrival in August. As it turned out, apart from the inconvenience absence from home, having to do the initial course again was going to work hugely to my advantage although I didn't know this at the time.

It was a sad and difficult decision to leave the garage because I really loved the motor trade, both the vehicles and the buzz I got from the commercial element of the business. Had I been single I would undoubtedly have hung in there and taken my chances along with the others. I may not have been the most natural of salesmen but I was bright enough to have held my own with most and run rings round quite a few and I suspect in time could have done quite well at a management level. However for the security of the family I'd decided it wasn't a chance worth taking.

It was with great sadness that I broke the news to Jack that I was going to leave Ewell Downs and he too seemed genuinely upset that I was moving on but said he understood completely why I had to. He then told me that my timing was almost perfect because although it was not general knowledge amongst the staff, he and the other directors were pretty sure that Nutt was planning to dispose of the company although nothing had actually been said officially.

Apparently the information had come through the back door from other contacts in the trade that a possible sale of the site to a major oil company was on the cards. He also asked me not to mention it to anyone which caused quite a division of loyalty. On the one hand I felt my main loyalty was to him for his trust, support and friendship over the last 4 years but I also would have liked to tip Mike and Dave off as to what was going on. Anyway I agreed and that was that.

So in April 1968 I left Ewell Downs Motor Services to return to life in the police service vowing to keep in touch with Mike Fahey, Dave Cannon and Jack Moxley which I am pleased to say I did. Indeed Dave remained a life-long friend and god-father to my daughter a few years down the line.

About a year later Mr. Nutt sold his interest, by then 99.6% of the equity, to the American oil giant Exxon Corporation, sacking the management and all but the most junior of the staff. Happily all the discharged staff were rapidly taken on by other motor traders in the area while all the directors apart from Jack went off to enjoy their pensions. The story went around that Jack left to manage a pub which although it would have been pretty apt was not in fact the case. He actually came off the drink almost completely and was taken on as office manager / accounts person by a local building firm in Leatherhead.

Dave and Mike, who were both far more natural salesmen than I ever was, eventually found their feet again and went on to great success including happy and long-lasting marriages. Mike got into double glazing and in due course established his own company producing double glazing and conservatories. Dave apparently took a leaf out of my book, went off and did a spell as a steward with P&O having apparently been inspired by my own experiences.

This was followed by a short time working as a DJ on the Costa Brava before he returned to sales. Initially this was office machines for Canon. He later moved on to Ricoh where he became UK sales manager before retiring to South Africa where he bought a piece of land, built a beautiful house and set up a successful B&B enterprise overlooking the Indian Ocean. Later when his boys married, he and Barbara eventually sold up and returned to the UK to play with the grandchildren.

9 A CONSTABLE ONCE AGAIN

Monday 22nd April 1968 and I join the Surrey Constabulary at Guildford.

George Ball, the recruiting officer had the unenviable job of knocking us into some sort of shape during this first week before we headed off to the District Training Centre. Whilst all forces had their own in-house training departments, the initial training of new recruits took place at one of six centres in different parts of the country. Contributed to by each police force on a per capita basis these Home Office Central Services as they were known included in addition to the training centres, the National Police Forensic Science Service. Bramshill Police College and the Police National Computer, Regional Crime Squads (and probably others I don't remember)

The main tasks during this first week included getting our uniforms measured and issued, hair trimmed to regulation length, and various other bits of kit issued including all the text books for our initial training. Once uniform was in good order we were photographed individually for our warrant cards and official records. We were then given a bit of drill instruction in an attempt to help with our bearing and general presence as guardians of the law. There would be more, much more of this we were told which was a bit worrying for the inevitable individuals who seemed to find marching difficult and somehow managed to drop into a peculiar same arm/leg motion.

Our intake was about ten individuals from a variety of different backgrounds. Most were about the same age as me – early twenties, a couple of very fresh-faced ex-cadets and one older guy who like me had seen previous service but in an overseas force.

Probably the most impressive was a former guardsman who was almost a head taller than most of us and who really looked the part in uniform. However we were not apparently all destined for the same training centre. Five of us would be heading for Sandgate in Kent while the others were off to Eynsham Hall in Oxfordshire. Unlike my first days in the Met four years earlier, this time I was the one in the know having done it all before which conferred a certain amount of status from day one that I must say I enjoyed. But I had never been to the Sandgate training centre before and would have to admit to a certain apprehension for all my outward experience and confidence.

I think it was on the Thursday that we were sworn in. Having been through this before, I knew what was coming when we were ferried down to the Guildford Magistrates' Court to take our oath. Known as Attestation the brief ceremony involves the new recruits standing before the bench and, either reading from a card or in our case repeating the words of the Clerk as follows:

I do solemnly and sincerely declare and affirm that I will well and truly serve our sovereign lady The Queen in the office of constable without favour or affection, malice or ill-will and that I will, to the best of my power, cause the peace to be kept and preserved and prevent all offences against people and property; and that while I continue to hold the said office I will to the best of my skill and knowledge discharge all the duties thereof faithfully according to law

The interesting and worrying thing was that having been sworn in we then had the status and powers of constables but without the knowledge (apart from my own case) to apply them. We were also issued with warrant cards but strongly cautioned against attempting to make any use of the powers we now had until our training and knowledge was complete.

So, on the Friday, duly kitted out and briefed we were dismissed and instructed to report to our respective district training centres on the Sunday afternoon in order to begin our thirteen week initial course on Monday 29th April 1968.

I can't remember how much, if at all, Denise and I talked about the negative implications of me re-joining the service. But looking back on it, I rather suspect I presented her with a fait-accompli, with me focusing narrowly on the need to secure our financial position and assuming she understood.

In my defence, I was entirely driven by the impending arrival of our new baby. So desperation on the one hand to earn a more reliable income whilst being qualified for very little else; and on the other, by the existence of something I knew I could do that was extremely secure.

Thinking back on it I suspect that this initial training course and my forced separation from my new wife was probably the first stage in what for her, (although I didn't recognize it at the time), was her gradual disengagement with the idea of me as a police officer. Realistically it was asking a lot of my twenty two year old wife who was five months pregnant and now living at some distance from her family and friends.
Insensitive –Yes. Understandable – I hope so. Forgivable – I also hope so.

Apart from a few trips to Brands Hatch, and a caravan holiday in Swalecliffe near Whitstable, I'd never ventured far into Kent so the A25 east of Sevenoaks was not really on my radar. Over the next three months it was to become depressingly familiar. What a nightmare road it was back then because it was not only narrow but almost all single carriageway and as twisty as hell so if you got behind a lorry which was virtually inevitable you were totally stuck for miles. Seventy two miles of misery. Even now Google Maps gives it as two hours ten minutes without traffic. On Sunday afternoons when we travelled down there was always some lorry traffic but on the Friday afternoons as we tried to get home it was far worse and could be closer to a four hour run so weekends were a bit curtailed to say the least.

There was another guy travelling from the Redhill area who was half-way through his course and George Ball the recruiting office had put us in touch so we managed to arrange a car share on an alternate week basis which made life a bit easier. I quite often think back to those journeys now as I speed along the M25 which has on occasion become the new nightmare road but even on a busy day is infinitely easier to drive than the old route.

10 SANDGATE

The No.6 District Police Training Centre at Sandgate near Folkestone in Kent was an impressive Victorian mansion known as Enbrook Hall and dating originally from the 1850's but with various later extensions. Subsequent to occupation as a residence it had been in use as one of the Star and Garter convalescent homes for servicemen between 1919 and the 1940's when it became a police college.

The contrast between this and the Met training college at Peel House in Westminster couldn't have been greater. Perched on a hill above the town with park-like grounds and panoramic sea views this was more like a luxury hotel. An elaborate entrance porch known as a 'port cochere' and designed to cope with the arrival of a 'coach and four' led into a long central hallway with polished herringbone parquet flooring that reflected the light pouring in through the rooms along either side. On the left there were student sitting and reading rooms with doors out to the terrace whilst on the right was the main hall where we were to take out meals. This was also the venue for the end-of-course dances with nurses from Folkestone hospital bussed in as dancing partners for those whose wives and girlfriends couldn't make it.

Breakfast and lunch were relatively relaxed but dinner was more or less formal and if I recall correctly at the end of the meal an announcement was made that *"Gentlemen you may smoke"*. Yes it was gentlemen only as female recruits went to another centre. I was going to say unfortunately but perhaps it was just as well!

Sleeping accommodation was on the first and second floors. True, the accommodation was still dormitory style but they were spacious and enjoyed even better views at that level. There was a gym in an adjoining building and a bar in the basement.

View from my dormitory over the croquet lawn to the parade square and beyond that was the sea.

Having said I felt comfortable and familiar with the introductory process at the Surrey HQ I felt a bit less so at Sandgate simply because it wasn't Peel House. I expected much of the process to be the same or similar which it was but I was also mindful of the fact that in the four years I had been out there had been a few significant changes in the law I would have to bone up on.

The course was programmed to last for three months of intensive training and at the end of each four weeks there was an exam, with the warning that the marks would not be allowed to drop below a set level after the first attempt. Thereafter any back-sliders would be in danger of being returned to their forces to be either discharged or re-coursed to do the whole procedure again. It certainly kept us on our toes. New definitions were dished out daily and had to be learnt by heart and repeated orally or in written tests every day and once again woe-betide anyone who started to fall behind here.

I hadn't particularly noticed it at Peel House but as the definitions and legal stuff like powers of arrest were covered I realised that I already knew them and they would come back almost instantly without having to re-learn them. I seemed to have an almost photographic memory (not so these days I'm sorry to say) and especially for this type of material. I found I could just close my eyes and literally 'see' the written words of the definition etc. in my head. As a result I soon began to pull ahead of my colleagues in the tests and in a short time had become a bit of a star turn which was both satisfying and embarrassing at the same time. Nobody loves a 'smart arse' do they?

One area where I did have to work a bit harder was in relation to the newly introduced Criminal Law Act of 1967 and the Theft Act 1968. As well as re-defining such things as theft, burglary, robbery and other property related crime, the former felonies, misdemeanours and other offences were re-classified as Arrestable or Non-Arrestable offences. This in turn produced a whole raft of new definitions and powers of arrest which had to be learnt by heart. Here I found I could also deal with new material almost as well as the stuff I'd learnt four years previously. It really was quite spooky.

The other significant new area of law around that time was the revised legislation around drinking and driving. This was embodied in the Road Safety Act 1967 and saw the introduction of a statutory blood alcohol limit and the introduction of the road-side 'blow-in-the-bag' style of breathalyser and associated powers of arrest. I was certainly pleased it hadn't been in force a couple of years previously during the worst of my boozy motor trade period.

There were periods of drill, physical fitness training, and a style of unarmed combat based on Aikido where police holds were taught together with a milder form of self-defence using our batons. There were cross-country runs and the sheer torture of swimming lessons in the cold water, open air baths in Folkestone – real brass monkey stuff. Swimming was obligatory, and we were told that no one had yet left Sandgate without learning to swim and without obtaining a life-saving award into the bargain. I got mine.

Our Drill Sergeant was one Bill Squires who was absolutely mustard hot on the drill square and soon had us marching around as smartly as his own regiment the Coldstream Guards. Bill took absolutely no prisoners with regard to any misbehaviour or chatting on parade and one of his standard punishments for anyone who stepped out of line was to make the miscreant run a number of circuits of the parade ground. However, Bill also had a heart of gold. One day he had sent one of the squad off on a few laps but the lad tripped and fell over and in doing so wrecked the shiny toecaps of his carefully bulled-up boots.

Bill helped him up and saw the state of the boots. Knowing the work it had taken he said *"I wouldn't have had that happen for the world son. Bring them downstairs later and we'll do them together."* So that evening in the little room behind the bar that served as Bill's office the two of them set to and brought the boots back to parade standard.

Bill Squires also ran the centre bar and sometimes at the end of an evening he'd have a lock-in with a few of us and with the doors shut we'd sit and drink and tell a few yarns. I'll never forget one evening when Bill was in full spate with some story or other. Presumably he suddenly needed to pee and without pausing for breath or interrupting his story he stood up wandered over to the sink, turned on the tap and calm as you like, peed in the sink, let the tap run a bit then turned it off and carried on with his story as if it was the most natural thing in the world. Well it probably was for him but quite amusing though it was to watch I never felt quite the same about my evening pint in the bar after that.

So as one month crept into two I emerged as top of the class pretty consistently but what I didn't know was that I was being talked about and word of my supposedly 'outstanding' marks had reached the Surrey HQ.

We had tutorials with our class instructors and mine was a Sergeant Ray Pilbeam from the Kent force. He didn't beat about the bush but told me that on my present performance if I kept my head down during my probation I should be able to pass the Sergeant's promotion exam and could very well line myself up for a crack at The Special Course. The what? I had no idea what he was talking about but as I didn't want to appear dumb I just nodded enthusiastically and said *"Yes Sergeant. Thanks for the advice."* And then it just went out of my mind.

Meanwhile the domestic situation was a bit tricky because with Denise by this time six months pregnant she was planning to stop work shortly which meant even longer days by herself to dwell on her situation. Consequently my very short weekends were spent trying to support her both physically by doing stuff around the place and psychologically by just being together and trying to calm her understandable anxieties. This was also against a background of the pile of homework I brought back with me to be either written up, revised or learnt by heart for the next week's test.

The prospect of Denise stopping work also raised again the spectre of our dwindling financial reserves. Reserves would be a serious overstatement. We had a bit of money but I knew it wasn't going to last that long once the new baby arrived in August. A further difficulty was that police recruits didn't get an increment until their two year probationary period was up and their appointment was confirmed. As a constable my pay was now going to be regular but taken across a year it was likely to be less than I had earned in my last year at the garage. I wondered how we would make it but right then with two months of the course still to go I had more immediate things to worry about.

About half-way through the course the training officers from the various forces made what were called welfare visits to the centre. The idea was to ensure all was well with their individual students as it was not that unusual for some of the younger students to be suffering homesickness along with other welfare problems. Situations like mine with babies due or sick family members also came within their remit.

One afternoon a Chief Inspector from Surrey (whose name I can't unfortunately remember) turned up at Sandgate and I among others was called out of class to see him.

"I gather you're doing very well." He said. *"Carry on like this and you could turn out to be a bit of a flyer if that's what you want"*. He too then started on about The Special Course and on this occasion I confessed that I had never heard of it.

Apparently The Special Course was the start point in an accelerated promotion programme designed to get a new crop of capable younger officers in position to fill the higher ranks in the service. It had been recognized that the current tranche of senior officers was likely to be depleted in the next few years as those who had joined or re-joined the service after the war came to the end of their time. As I read up on the situation it became clear that there was also something of a sub-text to the idea.

This seemed to be about trying to change the organizational style of the service from the somewhat militaristic imported by so many ex-service personnel to one more in line with modern management ethos.

Constables were eligible to take the sergeants' promotion exam once the two year probation was completed. Passing the exam above a certain level guaranteed appearance before an in-force selection board who were then able to refer candidates on to a three day extended interview for selection to the course itself which was held at the Bramshill Police College in Hampshire. Selection for the Special Course came with the temporary rank of Sergeant which on successful completion of the course was made substantive. A year later officers who continued to perform were promoted again to the rank of Inspector. So in theory if the dates all fell right a capable young constable could progress to the rank of Inspector in little more than four years. In normal circumstances promotion to sergeant somewhere between about six and ten years would have been regarded as fairly good going with Inspector taking perhaps another five or more years if ever.

The more I thought about the possibilities the more fired-up I became, and what's more, people who mattered seemed to think I could do it. With my preoccupation about security and earning enough to give us all the life I aspired to, the possibility of really 'flying' through the ranks became my dream, ambition, obsession almost.

At the end of July 1968 the Sandgate course came to an end and I did indeed come out as top student winning the Book Prize for that course (although I can't remember for the life of me what the book was). In the last week of the course I had also been notified of my posting. I was going to Reigate division (which was just as well as we were living there).

11 REIGATE DIVISION

i

By the time I eventually got back to Victoria Road it was less than a month before our new addition was due to arrive. So there was a fair amount to think about and to be honest, by that stage heavily pregnant, Denise needed all the help I could give her just around normal domestic activity.

At one level I felt quite guilty for having left her at such a time when we really should have been together planning and looking forward to the new baby. If I could have done it differently I surely would have.

However, on the other hand there was a bit of me that felt cheated. Cheated out of continuing in the job I really enjoyed and out of the time I had hoped to spend enjoying each other and laying the foundations of our future life. And all because motherhood apparently couldn't wait. You could say that this was not an ideal frame of mind and while I was not exactly eaten up with resentment I cannot deny its existence.

A further factor at the time was Dad and his new relationship. Denise's parents had been able to support her by regular visits during my absence and she also spent time back in Chessington with them. However, I know she had anticipated that along with her new husband she would be getting a father-in-law who might be equally excited at the prospect of grand-fatherhood.

This didn't happen. Not, I am sure from any deliberate intention to hurt or snub us as I don't believe Dad could have been capable of such thoughts. Quite simply, he was fully engrossed with his new wife, who also being a mother, had her own priorities too so I guess his loyalties were almost impossibly divided and we were further away and came off worse. Although I didn't relish the situation I did understand. Denise however did not and nurtured her hurt for years.

ii

So having arrived back from Sandgate I had almost no time to unpack my bags before starting work on 3rd August 1968. My first posting as a new member of the Surrey Constabulary was to the Reigate Division which had three sub-divisions, namely Reigate, Redhill and Horley which included the land around Gatwick Airport. There was also a small police office at Salfords as well as a number of police houses dotted about the division in places like Outwood, Smallfield and Charlwood from which local home beat officers provided what in effect was a more or less twenty four hour service. The general public pay no heed to rest days, weekends or even the wee small hours even for the most mundane and non-urgent of enquiries.

The divisional headquarters in Chart Lane occupied a former private detached house of Victorian vintage that following the amalgamation of the Surrey and the old Reigate Borough force had been converted for use as the police station. The building housed a number of offices most of us never had reason to visit as well as a public enquiry office, switchboard, Pc's room and further offices occupied by sergeants, inspectors and CID respectively. There was also a yard and garage/workshop where the divisional mechanic was based and where routine maintenance of the very few locally based police vehicles was carried out. Those in use at the time were a Hillman Husky which I think the sergeant used, one or two Morris Minors for CID and then the white Mini Panda cars. However my posting was to Redhill so for all practical purposes I rarely visited Reigate nick.

In Redhill the constabulary occupied what was the former fire station converted to use by the police and was situated on the A23 just to the north of the town centre. It still had the large garage doors and even the pole down which the crews used to slide from their rest room to clamber on board their fire engines.

Redhill nick was a bit of a 'make do' set-up with the various offices including the public counter more or less tucked in where they could be made to fit. The guys, and the one or two women officers there were a great crowd and I was made very welcome and quickly began to feel my feet. As in the Met I was attached to a more experienced constable for a 'beat learning' period of what should have been about four days if I remember correctly. And that was shorter than normal based on the fact that I was a re-joiner who supposedly had some idea what I was doing.

Actually my familiarization only lasted about an hour after which the sergeant said *"Well you might as well go and explore a bit and try not to get lost."* and then I was on my own. However it wasn't so much the outside work that caused difficulty as the need to find my way around the building and get to know who was who and where they could be found. And then there was the paper work which whilst pretty similar in purpose came in a very different range of booklets, paper colour and form numbers.

I hardly had time to develop any familiarity at all before Denise went into labour and I was given some leave to be on hand and do whatever new fathers do. We had plans for me to attend the birth which was the coming thing around that time and I was very keen to be present. Unfortunately, although we had told the doctor of our wishes this had either not been passed on in the notes or dare I say the midwifery staff at Crawley Hospital weren't that forward thinking. Anyway in the flurry of the final moments before Denise went into the delivery ward, the 'too difficult' light came on, excuses were made about them not being prepared for me and I was excluded.

Our son Robert arrived on 21st August 1968. Writing this I can hardly believe I have a son who is now almost fifty years of age. Where did those years go? Stick with me and I'll tell you.

He was a lovely baby and we were obviously delighted and ridiculously proud and besotted. Life took on a new meaning and brought a bunch of new and hitherto unimagined experiences and challenges we were determined to enjoy as much as possible.

We did have one drama shortly after Robert was born which whilst a bit scary at the time was in retrospect quite hilarious.

Did I say we had a cat? Well, we did and a budgie too. The cat used to sit on the back of a chair for hours simply staring at the bird in an almost mesmerized state. It never went any further than that but it was extremely funny to watch and was a perfect recreation of the cartoon characters Sylvester the cat and Tweety Pie the canary. *"I tawt I taw a puddy tat."*
Actually that is by the by but the story does involve the cat.

One evening I was about to have a bath but needed first to sit on the loo so I reached over and turned on the hot bath tap to run whilst I cogitated. Hot water in the flat was provided by an Ascot wall-mounted gas heater in the kitchen so when I turned on the tap the thing fired up and produced the water. Having sat on the loo for a few minutes mulling over this and that I reached over to turn off the hot water. Well the water stopped running but what I didn't know was that the gas valve had jammed and the burner was still going.

Suddenly there was an almighty explosion from the kitchen. I came running out of the bathroom with my trousers neither up nor down. Denise screamed, probably at the sight of me as I ran into the kitchen.

The room was full of steam and the heater was hanging off the wall with mains pressure water pouring from a ruptured pipe but most impressive of all, in retrospect if not exactly at the moment, was the cat. Obviously terrified, the poor thing was literally running around the walls about halfway between floor and ceiling in much the same manner as the fairground 'Wall of Death' or the modern movie super-heroes who run up buildings and leap huge distances. It could only have been sheer speed that overcame gravity.

I managed to turn off the water quickly enough and fortunately the gas valve had shut down so apart from a fairly big clear-up job it was not the disaster it might have been if the gas hadn't shut off. If I recall correctly, Robert slept through it all. A skill he has managed to retain all his life especially when needed for some task around the house.

Ours was the ground floor maisonette and the one above was rented out to a couple of air stewardesses who worked at Gatwick and it saw a fair bit of action. Frequently when we were in or just heading for bed ourselves we'd hear footsteps on the outside staircase accompanied by loud stage whispers or fits of giggling as one of the girls and latest boyfriend arrived back.

The floors weren't terribly thick so we could more or less follow their movements upstairs which included the kitchen as a kettle was boiled for coffee, the sitting room for half an hour or so usually accompanied initially by more giggles gradually subsiding into quietness with the occasional creaking of the furniture. This was followed by hurried steps to the bedroom immediately above ours. The next sound was usually two bodies landing on the bed, four thuds as footwear was discarded followed by the unmistakable sound of fairly athletic copulation rising to a crescendo of pants and moans and creaking bedsprings. I was telling the guys at work about it one day and someone suggested we might give them a round of applause. It was a fun idea but we never had the nerve to do it. They'd have been mortified if they knew how much detail passed through the floor to us below.

Paternity leave not existing as it does today, I was back at work within a few days and resumed my daily travel to duty at Redhill. Because I was a bit older than some probationers and had been in before and also perhaps because I had this 'potential flyer' label I was given a driving authorization after only about two weeks on station. Or it may just have been because they were short of 'Panda' drivers. This was by no means a driving course, simply a test to see if I was safe behind the wheel.

It made a huge difference to me though. Apart from the couple of town beats, Redhill subdivision was largely rural in nature and car patrols made it possible to actually patrol and respond more quickly and with fewer officers which at the time I arrived there was the problem. So I became a Panda driver with my little white mini, a POLICE sign on the door and blue lamp on the roof. Talk about the 'bee's knees'. I was loving it, and then on 14th September the rains came.

It rained and it rained and then the flooding reports started to come in and these were not just little floods. Apparently, according to the press the flooding across the county was on a scale only reckoned to be likely every thousand years. I don't know where they plucked that statistic from but it certainly seemed like it.

The principal impact for me was that the A23 became impassable so I couldn't get to work whilst a PC who travelled daily down from Redhill to Horley faced the same problem. Our postings were then reversed and Horley became my new station. Seems only common sense now and I can't imagine why no-one had thought of that before I was sent to Redhill in the first place. I guess the guvnors had their reasons.

It was a bad time though with people marooned in isolated houses (at least as far as one can be in Surrey), power supplies failed, streams and rivers overflowed, roads and railways were either blocked by water or mud slides, shops ran out of stocks and chaos reigned (or should that be rained). I also learnt how by keeping the revs up in my Mini and the speed down it was possible to drive through quite deep water until just before the point at which the car began to float, which it actually did a couple of times.

Talking of floating cars; while all this was going on I heard from Dave Cannon at the garage that Jack Moxley had had a lucky escape. He was apparently going down Bridge Street in Leatherhead driving one of the company's demonstrator cars which would have been virtually brand new when he saw the road ahead was flooded and the bridge was partly under water. Knowing the area, he thought he could turn right before the bridge and go round behind the fire station where, although this was also flooded, he thought he could actually get through. WRONG. The water was quite deep and he managed to stall the car so had no choice but to get out but as soon as he did, with his weight out of it the car began to float. Not only did it simply float but because of the current it actually floated away and was last seen disappearing off down the river Mole towards Fetcham. On balance he was lucky to bail out when he did even if the firm did lose a nearly new car. As it turned out it didn't much matter because shortly afterwards the garage was sold and everyone was out of a job anyway.

iii

I rather liked my new station at Horley. They were a great crowd and I settled in very quickly. The station, in Massetts Road was only a short walk from home so there was no commute and it also meant I could pop indoors sometimes for my meal breaks depending which beat I was working.

I drove a Panda here too but as the non-Panda beats were larger areas and more rural than at Redhill the Sergeant told me I needed to get a bike. Well by some lucky coincidence (or cunning plot on their part) the sergeant also knew that Wally Heap, the Salfords Pc was looking to sell his.

"Oh Great." says I, and made contact to have a look at said machine. It was a very traditional bike; very sturdy, very black with a large saddle-bag and in pretty good nick as far as I could tell. So I paid my seven quid and set off to ride it back from Salfords to Horley. Not a problem as a good part of the way back was along the A23 which was mostly slightly downhill or flat but I did notice though that the couple of slightly uphill sections were quite hard going but then I was not exactly cycling fit.

An old Hercules like mine

Once home I had a better chance to look at my new steed. It was a Hercules and like Steptoe's horse of the same name, no lightweight. Actually it was very heavy and about a trillion miles from the cycles of today that can be lifted on a couple of fingers. Indeed I had a job to lift this thing with both arms. However there were clearly plenty of miles in the old fellow yet and I was destined to put in quite a few of them losing a few pounds in the process. Had I re-joined a few months earlier I would still have been working my beats in the manner I'd become familiar with in the Met in 1964. This was the point system and was at the time the only way patrolling officers could be supervised or contacted once they'd left the station.

Points were locations around the area where individual officers were instructed to be at given times during their period of duty. Usually these were at public telephone boxes or in London they would also have been at the blue Police Boxes which were phased out with the advent of radio and re-incarnated as the TARDIS of the Doctor Who TV series. Sometimes however in more rural areas there were neither police boxes nor public kiosks so a point might just be on the junction of road A and road B.

The idea and purpose was that if it was necessary to contact an officer on his beat he could be called on the phone at the planned location or met by a supervisor. This brings me back to the cycle beat and the need to keep very much on the good side of your sergeant. It was far from unknown for a vindictive supervisor to set up points at such a distance or at such times that you had to pedal like mad between locations to be there on time or risk being on report. These were known as "arse-stretchers" for reasons that will be obvious if you think about it.

By the time I arrived in Surrey, mobile communication via personal radios had just been introduced and should have rendered the old point system unnecessary but due to the radios' unreliability and poor coverage they didn't. One is also tempted to suspect that a few of the 'old soldiers' among the supervisory ranks were inclined to hang on to the former system because they found accepting change difficult or perhaps they even liked the power the point system provided them.

To be fair, early personal radios, usually known as PR's were not that great. The very first we saw in Surrey was the Stornophone; large and heavy and almost the same dimensions as a brick. They were cumbersome and carried in a kind of holster or harness slung over your shoulder with a telescopic aerial about three feet long that had to be pulled out to use it.

The next incarnation was the two part Pye Pocketphone. This had a receiver unit with a spring clip that allowed it to be tucked and quite neatly retained in the tunic pocket or lapel although in all but the quietest location they had to be held to the ear in order to hear anything. However the worst thing about this model was the transmitter unit that had a press-to-speak button on the side which also activated a short spring-loaded aerial that popped out of the top and has caught many an unwary officer a sharp jab up the nostril.

A further disadvantage of this was the fact that not being in any way attached to the person as soon as you put it down it was easily forgotten

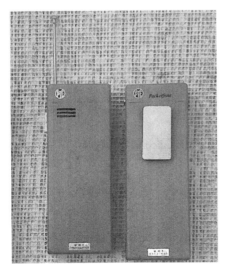

and there were any number of officers who having stopped a motorist had to watch half their radio set disappearing in the distance on the car roof.

The PR system worked on the UHF wavebands and was very much 'line-of-sight' so coverage was often limited in built-up or heavily wooded areas or by the topography. Control of this network was from local police stations while the county-wide 'main scheme' radio system as it was known was the VHF fitted to police cars which were controlled by a central operations room at Headquarters. As might be imagined this could cause untold confusion with unknowing left and right hands trying to manage and direct personnel.

Over the next few years both personal and main-scheme vehicle radios got much better and with the further development of sophisticated comms systems the service of today as far as I can understand it is very well equipped.

Once again I think the sun must have been shining on me because, unusually for a probationer constable I was allocated Area Car duties which meant being one of a double crewed Ford Cortina covering the whole subdivision rather than just a small Panda beat. I know Cortina sounds a bit naff now but it was much better than Panda driving when you often spent a lot of time carrying out relatively mundane enquiries or ferrying post around the division. In addition to having our locally based personal radios the area car was also on the county-wide VHF scheme so was far more likely to be assigned to more serious and therefore interesting incidents such as crime reports and road traffic accidents. A further significant benefit to me was that I was crewed with older and more experienced colleagues so was able to pick up a lot of knowledge and practical tips.

It was only my second day on the Area Car when we were sent to my first 'sudden death'. Apart from my mother who died in hospital and a mortuary visit during my Met training course I had never seen a dead body so to say I was apprehensive as to what we might find would be quite an understatement.

Police are routinely sent to reports of sudden death because it is their role to provide the liaison between the death and the Coroner whose duty it is to investigate all sudden and unnatural deaths. It's the system our society has created to ensure we can't just go bumping each other off willy-nilly. Unless it is obviously a serious crime scene in which case a police pathologist will attend; for what we might call apparent 'natural cause' deaths a local doctor will usually have certified a person dead. However if the doctor has not seen the person recently or for any other reason is unable to state with certainty the cause of death they must notify the police who then report the circumstances to the Coroner.

On the day in question we had started at six on a dark and frosty morning and got the message around half past. The call had come from the warden of a local gypsy (now we would say traveller) site in Salfords. His lodge was located by the entrance and he was at the window awaiting our arrival and came out to direct us to the caravan concerned. Police were not usually very welcome on the site and had it been later in the day one of us would probably have had to stay with the car to ensure all wheels were present on our return. However there was little sign of light or movement from the nearby vans so we both decided to go in.

We knocked the door and someone said *"Come in."* Inside we were faced with a woman of about sixty sitting up in bed under a pile of blankets pulled up to her chin and drinking a cup of tea. Initially she appeared to be alone until she explained it was her husband who had died and he was apparently still there under the blankets beside her. It all seemed a bit surreal at first but then as we spoke practical reality dawned. She had woken around five to find him apparently dead and having no phone had to knock up the warden for help and the doctor had been called.

Despite the output of a small gas fire the van was freezing so she had done no more than cover him up, made a pot of tea (which she offered us) and then hopped back into bed to keep warm. The procedure on these occasions was for someone – usually the next of kin – to identify the deceased by name and relationship. Usually the bereaved relative would be in another room suitably distressed and comforted by a neighbour or friend while the officer would be discreetly writing the deceased's name on a label and tying it to a toe or finger for the benefit of the undertaker or mortuary attendant.

Well this still had to be done and it was the most bizarre situation going through the procedure watched by the apparently unconcerned widow. I expect the grief came later as I learnt over many years that it is actually not so unusual for next of kin to be apparently unmoved initially only to collapse later. This was why in our initial training we were advised if possible to find a neighbour to come in and sit with a person until family support arrived.

Over the following weeks with my experienced colleagues I was sent to numerous burglaries, umpteen road accidents, domestic disputes and several punch-ups. One thing you learnt about intervening in fights is that it is usually better not to rush. This is particularly so when you know the location and the individuals likely to be involved which is where local knowledge comes in very useful. For example if someone is reported being attacked in a street, in the absence of other information it normally requires an urgent response. However if the fracas is reported at a pub known to be unruly or frequented for example by the gypsy fraternity it is probably better not to rush for several reasons.

Firstly, the landlord can very often sort the problem out himself and generally prefers to do so rather than put his licence at risk by creating an incident report. Secondly if a bunch of gypsy lads or other local kids want to fight it is often better to let them get on with it than wade in straight away because this usually results in both parties turning on the police or doggedly refusing to make a complaint or even acknowledge that anything happened at all.

Christmas at Horley came and went and I became more and more familiar with the patch including the outlying areas, one of which was the service area at Gatwick airport. Whilst the airport was strictly the responsibility of the BAA Police we were always welcome around the place as any additional security patrols were seen in a positive light. We did have a slightly ulterior motive though.

Our night-time 'security visits' included one of the airline catering companies where in addition to a friendly chat and cuppa we could usually guarantee walking out with a tasty packed meal that made the ideal snack for our 2 or 3 am meal break. These were packs that had been taken off flights and were destined for the bin so we never had any qualms about accepting them although I am sure that someone could have dug out a police regulation that would have labelled it an 'improper and corrupt practice'.

I must say that as I began to settle in to county style policing I was delighted to find that if you made the effort it was quite easy to develop a rapport with locals who were more than happy to see the uniformed presence and also provide snippets of information that was all grist to the local intelligence mill.

Lory's Farm at Charlwood was also a regular daytime stop and there, in addition to passing the time of day it was an ideal opportunity to buy a tray of cracked eggs. Being even slightly cracked the shops wouldn't take them but for just a few pence they were wonderfully fresh and perfect for a few days' breakfasts.

Having got to know Charlwood and the area immediately surrounding the airport I feel enormously sad at the prospect of a new runway at Gatwick that would obliterate the village and its community beneath tons of concrete. You dear reader may well know by now what the eventual outcome was or is to be – Gatwick or Heathrow. I fervently pray it will be nowhere as I think we have enough airport capacity and if anything should be looking at ways of reducing air travel and the use of resources it takes.

iv

Gatwick Airport has a very good safety record but its most serious accident occurred in the early hours of 5th January 1969. A Boeing 727 of Ariana Afghan Airlines was attempting to land in fog and crashed short of the runway at Fernhill to the east of the airport. The aircraft damaged trees, house chimneys and then swept away an entire house before breaking up and erupting in a fireball killing forty-eight of the sixty two people on board plus two occupants of the house. Miraculously a baby in the house survived beneath an upturned cot and was rescued by my namesake Pc Keith Simmonds who together with other officers received awards and commendations for their efforts in pulling people from the blazing wreckage.

Photo by Bob Catt

By comparison my own involvement in this incident was trivial but very interesting and informative for all that.

An incident room and Casualty Bureau were set up at Horley police station and a temporary mortuary in a hall opposite. I was posted to the incident room where I worked with then Chief Inspector Chris Atkins. Our job was to collate all records pertaining to the incident, in particular the casualties with the ultimate objective of identifying the fatalities.

As bodies and body parts arrived at the mortuary as much detail as possible was recorded and ideally would include gender and description plus details of clothing and property. It was an awesome job for all concerned and we were receiving cards on which the only words were "charred mass".

I went over to the mortuary once after the post mortems had begun and could hardly bear to look. "Charnel House" would not begin to describe it with blackened corpses laid out beside isolated limbs and parts of torsos. The smell of charred flesh was appalling and I could only feel immense admiration for those working for hours in that place and even more so for the colleagues who had so bravely risked their own lives at the scene a couple of days before. I often wondered how I might have performed. Not so well I suspect.

There are few experiences in life from which nothing can be learnt and one thing very few of us down in leafy Surrey knew about at the time was Asian culture and naming systems. There was initially no passenger manifest available locally which meant we had not even a starting point in the identification process. Eventually the London office of Ariana Airlines managed to get hold of one and in order to save time; I was dispatched by train from Horley to collect it. The first thing that was apparent was that most passengers had one of two surnames which were either Singh or Kaur so where did we go from there? My next task was to find out how the name system worked which basically is that adherents of the Sikh religion are required to take the name Singh for males and Kaur for females and the rest of the identity is found in the forenames. I can't recall the full details now but it certainly took some unravelling.

I remember someone coming into the office one day. looking at the passenger list and saying *"Blimey. They're all Ram-Jam bloody Singh."* This was not in any sense meant to be disrespectful but just expressed quite graphically the frustration we faced with this seemingly impossible task.

Chris Atkins was brilliant, an absolute model of calm efficiency and organization. He had that very special ability to relate to people at all levels and could be talking to me almost as an equal and then the next minute talking on the phone to the Chief Constable as though he were his brother-in-law. He was also brave and honest enough in his final report to contradict Chief Constable Peter Matthews' assertion that he was among the first on the scene which the record showed he was not. Interestingly the appendix listing arrivals was removed from the final report at HQ and prior to circulation so you can make what you like of that.. I always had great admiration for Chris Atkins who went on to become one of Surrey's longest serving Assistant Chief Constables and it was my privilege to work quite closely with him later in my career.

As probationary constables we had to attend weekly classes at Reigate where we continued our instruction in law and police practice although in progressively more depth than at the initial training centre. There were still definitions to be learnt and tests to be passed which I'm pleased to say I was still finding quite easy.

Following the information I'd discovered about the Special Course I was determined to keep my head down in the books and take the Sergeants Promotion exam as soon as I possibly could after my probation ended. Promotion is what I wanted and if others thought I could do it then I was determined to go all out for it myself.

12 DORKING DIVISION

i

Overall we were very happy. Me with my new job and both of us discovering the joys (mostly) of parenting. Robert was growing fast and providing new delights every day.

The only, but quite significant cloud on the horizon was still our financial situation. At least my money was now regular and included a rent allowance which went a good way towards the mortgage. However the cost of the new baby and absence of Denise's income meant that the bit in red at the end of the bank statement was getting gradually larger each month.

Police Discipline regulations are very specific about officers getting into debt and the last thing I wanted either from that aspect or from that of our own comfort and well-being was to let things get out of hand. Although the mortgage payment was only twenty two pounds (how little that sounds now), that was almost exactly the amount by which our overdraft was increasing monthly. As a probationer there was no increment in view until my appointment was confirmed and that was more than a year away so to say I was worried would be an understatement.

The only way I could see around the problem was to sell the maisonette and request a police house which would be free and then hope to jump back on the housing ladder later. So that is exactly what we decided to do and 148 Victoria Road went up for sale at an asking price of four thousand pounds and I served notice of my wish to apply for a police house.

If I recall correctly there was immediate interest and in no time it seemed we had accepted an offer of three thousand nine hundred, a whole three hundred more than we had paid. We felt rich. How naïve we were. And how little we knew about the property market because within a couple of years house prices would explode and with them our hopes of getting back into the market any time soon. Not that we could have done anything different if we had known. We just didn't have the assets.

My request for a police house was granted but when I saw the address I couldn't believe my eyes. 11A Gladstone Road Ashtead. The road I had been born in just under twenty five years before. How bizarre was that?

The only problem as I thought about it was that Gladstone Road was an unmade stony road of Victorian semis so I really wondered what we had let ourselves in for until we went to have a look. The road was now made-up and 11A was one of a pair of almost new semi-detached police houses built just a few years previously on the site of an old orchard where I used to play as a toddler. I don't know if I still believed in guardian angels at that time but it certainly felt as if someone was looking out for us.

The regulations around police housing included a removal allowance towards such items as curtains and carpets but only if the move was directed by the force so in our case we didn't qualify.

Consoling ourselves with the fact that we would at least have our three hundred pounds profit we relaxed until the final completion statement arrived showing that after deduction of our costs and fees we might just about come out with about forty or fifty pounds.

So as moving day approached we embarked on a practice that would become familiar over the following years; that of pulling up carpets and taking down curtains and cutting them to fit the next house. I became quite a dab hand at carpet fitting and using a sewing machine.

I didn't remember much if anything about the three or four years I had actually spent in Gladstone Road as a child. However I did know the road quite well as had often visited my aunt, uncle and Nan there over the years and so it felt comfortingly familiar to be unpacking and settling in there.

We moved into Gladstone Road in March 1969. The house was great, especially when compared to the maisonette. Fairly standard in layout, there was a kitchen with adjoining dining room at the back and an interconnecting door to a good sized sitting room. There were three bedrooms and a bathroom above and a very nice sized and private garden at the back. A drive ran down beside the houses to a pair of single garages. A couple of concrete coal bunkers in the back garden held fuel for the living room fire and anthracite for the little boiler in the kitchen that heated the radiators. Central heating for the first time in my life. We did feel pretty well off and it wasn't costing us a thing. Result? I should say so.

This was the first time we'd had our own garden so I soon set about digging us a veg plot and getting everything ship-shape. I loved that but then I guess that here I was very much following Dad's example as to what good husbands did. At least by watching him over the years I knew how to go about it.

I had brought Hercules with me and on the first day of duty set off to pedal the mile and a half to Leatherhead police station. I was getting astride Hercules outside the house when a voice said "*Hello young Brian.*" I turned to see and elderly man standing on the edge of the road smiling broadly. He said "*I don't suppose you remember me.*"

I said "*I'm sorry sir. You're right. You have the advantage.*" He laughed loudly. "*Hark at you mister policeman. All hoity-toity. I'm Arthur Stenning and you used to hold my hand all the way down to the allotments and help dig up spuds when you were just two or three years old. You used to call me uncle Arthur*"

Now it was my turn to laugh. He told me the bush telegraph had the information about my pending arrival almost two weeks previously which must have been about the same time I found out. And I thought the police was supposed to be a secure outfit!

ii

Situated on the corner of Kingston Road and Kingston Avenue, Leatherhead police station looked like an Edwardian terrace of three or four houses at first sight and did indeed incorporate one or two police quarters but the major portion in the centre accommodated the operational part. A gabled entrance porch led into the front enquiry office where the public counter was manned 24 hours a day. The ground floor also accommodated the PC's room where we were briefed before duty and sat to do our writing; the sergeants' office, CID offices, charge room and cells as well as a large parade room used for larger meetings, briefings and so on. The typist's office, women police and rest room were on the first floor

It was a Chief Inspector station commanded by a dour scot by the name of Alfred (Jock) Hay) He was a bit in the old rather militaristic school but also had a gentler side to him when the need arose. The two Inspectors were Brian Silver and Bob Short.

The subdivision also included Ashtead, Headley, Bookham and Fetcham and as at Horley we operated round the clock shifts based on walking or cycle beats. Panda car beats covered the more outlying parts with an area or crime car patrol superimposed over the lot.

There was also a divisional motorcyclist considered by many to be a plum job due to the freedom it gave you. Quite a lot of the time the motorcyclists found themselves acting as postmen but that apart they were pretty much at liberty to patrol wherever they felt inclined. The manoeuvrability and low profile of the bike made it ideal for carrying out traffic stops and they were often top of the league when it came to the number of reports submitted.

The county was also divided into three traffic areas based at Godstone, Burpham and Chertsey and this is where the 'raspberry split' traffic patrol cars were based. Their main role was to look after 'traffic' matters by patrolling main roads, detecting vehicular offences and dealing with more serious accidents that local patrols were not up to for lack of equipment, signs etc. Some Traffic Department officers were also authorized vehicle examiners who had the power if appropriate to put a vehicle off the road and we lesser mortals had to call them in to help us deal with more serious or complex offences.

In those heady days before the force started flogging off police buildings, notionally on the grounds of efficiency but mainly to balance the budget; there were small police offices at Ashtead, Bookham and Horsley with adjoining police houses plus further police houses dotted singly or in clusters around the subdivision.

In my initial months at Leatherhead I was often posted to beats in the Ashtead area so could sign-on by phone from the little office in Craddocks Avenue which was also a useful bolt-hole in bad weather on the pretext of 'report writing'. It was here that I did most of my initial research about local intelligence, convicted individuals, potential offenders, vulnerable property and so on. All the stuff that was meat and drink to the conscientious and ambitious constable which is exactly what I was.

One day whilst in the process of browsing through some local records in the Ashtead office I came across a record of a good friend who to my amazement had a conviction for indecent exposure when he was about sixteen and although he received a conditional discharge it was nevertheless a conviction. Frankly I was amazed because whilst he was as red-blooded as the rest of us I just couldn't imagine him doing anything like that. The sad thing was that at that time the rehabilitation of offender legislation didn't exist and in the event of a serious sexual assault occurring in the area he would almost certainly have come into the frame as a suspect based on what was probably some minor teenage hormonal aberration. Fortunately such an event never happened and he. like me, went on to marry, have children and live a normal honest life.

In addition to my cycle beats around Ashtead I also worked the Panda patrols out of Leatherhead for a while and I remember one job which turned out to be a bit more than I expected.

A woman came into the nick in a state of high excitement and worried about her boyfriend. They lived in a caravan up at Headley and she explained that he'd got in tow with some London criminals to whom he owed money or some sort of debt and they had threatened to come down and either collect or 'do him over'.

He was apparently terrified, started drinking and popping pills and locked himself in the caravan with a shot gun and was threatening to blast anyone who came near. The station sergeant who was Trevor Foxall listened to her story and then turned to me and calmly said *"Here's one for you young Brian. Pop up and have a chat with him. See if you can't sort him out."* And good as gold like a lamb to the slaughter I toddled off.

It wasn't until I was about halfway there that it dawned on me that this might just be a bit risky. What would I say? What steps could I take? Bloody great big ones if I had any sense, but of course I just kept going thinking *"Thanks for nothing Sarge."* The woman had said the boyfriend's name was Heseltine which rang a bell as I'd sold a car to a client of the same name but I didn't recall a Headley connection. Probably none.

Anyway, I arrived a few minutes later, left the Panda in the track to the kind of farm or stable yard where this caravan was parked. I could see the van on the other side of the yard and called out

Hello. Mr Heseltine. Are you there?" No reply.
"Mr Heseltine Can I come in?"
"Go away. I've got a gun"

"Mr Heseltine. It's the Police and I need to come and talk to you" Silence
"Mr Heseltine I'm coming in now. the Can you open the door" No reply so I started walking towards to van and knocked on the door. *"Go away"*

"Come on." I said. *"Just open the door and let's have a chat. See if we can't sort a few things out shall we."* And I knocked the door again. I heard some movement in the van and thought *"It's now or never if he's going to shoot me."*, and stepped back a bit as the door opened a couple of inches.

Well obviously I wasn't shot and to cut a longer story short I talked my way inside where I could see this shot gun barrel just sticking out from beneath a bed quilt. I didn't make a big thing of it although I did sit on the bed where I reckoned I could probably grab the gun first if I needed to. It turned out that it was the same chap that had bought the car so at least he knew me. Although I did say a brief prayer of thanks that the car had been OK or he might have blown my head off anyway for selling him a duff motor.

After a few minutes chat I persuaded him that guns weren't going to solve the problem and perhaps he'd better give it to me which he did and then came with me back to the nick. I suppose we could have locked him up and charged him with something but no harm was actually done. He was in lawful possession of the gun so we sent him off with his girlfriend, hung on to the gun for a few days and told him to give us a call if the bad guys turned up which to the best of my knowledge they never did.

It may well have been a bit foolhardy but looking at the incident through today's eyes I shudder to think what the outcome might have been. Without doubt a Firearm Support Team would have been deployed and had the poor bloke opened the door with the shotgun in his hand there's a fair chance he would have died. I had more dealings with police firearms later in my service and whilst I know you don't mess about where guns are involved I do sometimes wonder if we aren't in danger of precipitating problems by an excessive response on occasions.

As usual in any organization there were quite a few 'characters' and individuals who had their own way of doing things. Sadly perhaps, the changes in organizational structures and management over recent years have resulted in something of a homogenization so that these interesting individuals are rather 'kept down'. This probably makes organisations safer and easier to manage but in my view significantly less interesting. I met quite a few of these individuals during my time in the police and will chat about them a bit more along the way.

One guy at Leatherhead, whilst not of the 'loose cannon' variety but very interesting because of his experience and the way he told his tales was a Pc Jim Camber. I mentioned previously how dealing with a sudden death for the first time can be quite a trying experience for younger officers and it was this situation that Jim exploited to wind up newcomers to the nick.

You'd find him in the canteen with a couple of probationers listening open-mouthed to his stories of sudden death experiences and one of the one's I liked best was along these lines.

"We didn't always have it easy like you lot you know what with your radios and Coroner's Officers, typists and so on. Blimey, when I started we hardly had electric light and before Coroner's Officers we had to do everything ourselves including preparing bodies for the pathologist. That meant undressing and washing them down which was a bit grim at times especially if they been in an accident or lying around a while.

I remember one day when we had this 'sudden' on a late shift and the body had been taken to the mortuary. Not the posh one over at Epsom hospital. No, the old Leatherhead mortuary was down by the river next to the fire station.

It was a funny little brick building, probably Victorian; all white tiled walls with just the post mortem table in the middle and a single light in the centre.

Anyway, the following morning I had to go down there and sort out this body. It was still more or less dark and the mist was rising off the river and wafting up the bank so the surrounding streets were a bit like a snapshot out of the old Whitechapel and Jack the Ripper stories. You can imagine the scene. I parked my bike by the wall and fished out the key to the mortuary and with the help of my torch managed to unlock the door.

I switched on the light which as I said was just a single bulb high up in the centre of the room directly over where this fat old man's body was lying on the post mortem table. I shut the door and turned round to make a start getting his clothes off when the light went out. God! I didn't half jump and swear if the truth be told.

I guessed the bloody bulb had gone but didn't know if there were any spares or where they might be. Also I'd put my torch down somewhere so had to go groping around and eventually found it between this bloke's feet on the table.

I found a little cupboard under the sink and there actually were a couple of spare bulbs but just as I was getting them out there was this terrible groan from the body. I nearly shit myself, dropped my torch and then banged my head on the top of the cupboard.

Bodies do that sometimes. They fart too. It's the internal gasses fermenting. Anyway I got the bulbs and then realised that the only way I was going to get to the light was to climb up on the table with the corpse. I had my torch in one hand and a bulb in my pocket as I got up on a chair and then got astride the body.

I needed both hands to get the bulb out so I tucked my torch in the top of my tunic and reached for the light at which point the torch slipped out and clattered to the floor. Trying to grab it I lost my balance, fell onto the dead body and then onto the floor in the same movement dislodging the corpse which fell off the table on top of me and pinning me to the floor just like that.

Here Jim bangs his hand on the table frightening the shit out of the two recruits before leaning back in his chair, picking up his sandwich and saying *"Still, all in a day's work I guess"*

I saw him do this on several occasions and it was almost word perfect each time which is why I can pretty much remember it word for word even now.

We had another Pc at Leatherhead called Tony Begbie. Whilst not exactly a 'character' in the same way as Jim Camber he was interesting and very much one of a kind. Tony was an electronics and radio enthusiast. He lived next to the office at Ashtead and was mostly allocated to cycle beats in that area.

Well as I said, we had the personal radios which were not always that great but Tony never had a communication problem. I don't know if he doctored his own PR's but apparently he had a battery powered VHF radio set in the saddle bag of his bike which was more than a match for those fitted to the police cars. I was told he had even managed to install a miniature flashing blue light into the top of his helmet. That story may be apocryphal as I never saw it but it certainly would not have surprised me.

Tony Begbie's reputation as being good with radio had even spread to HQ because when, following the Gatwick air crash, Peter Matthews bought two ex-military ambulances to be converted into mobile major incident vehicles, Begbie was seconded to Mount Browne to design the radio installations.

iii

At home, we had settled down very nicely and felt happy and secure with our ten month old son Robert when Denise started to talk about perhaps having another baby. I can't say I was that excited about the idea to begin with but on thinking about it I came round to the idea because I certainly wanted Robert to have a sibling and having got all the baby kit together it rather made sense to get the child rearing done at this time of our lives while we could be young with the children. It would also mean that as they grew up we would be able to perhaps do some of the things together that we'd missed out on while they were young.

Well we must have been a very healthy young couple because it seemed that no sooner had we talked about it than Denise fell pregnant again and we learnt that all being equal we could expect to be a family of four by the spring of 1970.

By this time too things with Dad had started to settle down a bit and we had visits from him and Eileen quite often at Gladstone Road and it was lovely to have him dropping into the grandad role more fully. He found it really odd given his history in the street but he did enjoy making contact with some of the locals he still remembered including old 'Uncle Arthur'.

Whilst Dad's visits to us were never a problem, for Denise there was clearly an issue with her around visiting Dad and Eileen at their home in Chessington even though we were quite often over there at her parents. It was very difficult to get to the bottom of it but eventually she explained.

When Dad and Eileen got married we had met Eileen's daughter and son-in-law. Denise had immediately recognized him as a man she'd been out on a date with when she was working at a factory in Leatherhead where he also worked as a toolmaker. After she had discovered he was married and heard all the *"My wife doesn't understand me."* lines she didn't see him anymore but felt terribly awkward about the risk of running into him again.

Having decided to go ahead and increase our domestic head-count it was probably not the ideal time given what was going on at work because I had further absences from home in the offing. In August '69 I had to be away for a month on my continuation course which was held at Nutfield near Redhill. Not a million miles away but it was unfortunately residential and required pretty intensive work on my part to ensure that I passed the final exams and got confirmed in my appointment at the end of my probation.

Following this in the October of the same year I had my standard car course which was another couple of weeks away from home at Headquarters. It was a brilliant course especially for someone as keen on cars and driving as I was. The police driving system is all about observation and anticipation and making 'progress'. Basically this means driving when necessary as fast as is safe for the prevailing conditions which was right up my street. With my motor trade background I was a pretty cocky little devil to begin with until my instructor Colin Highton deliberately let me, even encouraged me to do it my way one day. This resulted in me making a complete hash of things and he said *"Now perhaps you'll listen, learn and do it my way instead of yours. The road is not a race track. Fast is good when appropriate. Stupid isn't."*

My own car at the time was a 1958 Morris Oxford. Quite a lumbering old tank, but by the end of the course and by applying 'the system' I could make the old thing sings songs compared to how I drove before. In the end I passed out well enough to get a grading for traffic department which was very satisfying but didn't feature in my career plan. So what was my plan?

Having been encouraged to see myself as a potential 'flier' in the service I had decided to really go for it and the first step was to pass the sergeants exam as soon as possible and with the highest possible marks thereby ensuring at least a Special Course interview. I had also looked at a number of other people who seemed to have progressed well and achieved early promotion. Seeing what departments or specialisms they had under their belts enabled me to formulate my own intended career path. I decided a period on CID was a box to be ticked as was a period in headquarters to get my face known and training department seemed to have served a number of people well in terms of career advancement.

Looking back on it I must have been quite a difficult partner because I spent so much time studying that in those early years I'm afraid Denise and baby Robert were somewhat short changed. I can remember her saying *"Do you really need to keep a pile of law books in the toilet?"*

What with my studying, shortage of spare cash and the demands of a young baby, home life was a bit humdrum and I'm sure Denise felt it too although as I said many times the effort was not just for me but for all of us in the longer term.

There was a certain amount of social activity within the Dorking division which revolved around functions at the divisional social club and bar at Dorking nick, although that wasn't exactly on the doorstep for the Leatherhead families. There were also the personal relationships I developed with colleagues at work some of which involved going round to each other's homes for dinner or drinks. I seem to remember 'cheese and wine' parties were starting to be the thing to do around then. Apparently they are coming back into style now a bit like the fondue sets of the same period which are also trending again. It was such a slow eating process that all I recall was getting terribly drunk waiting for the oil to heat up or the blessed cheese to melt.

These social contacts were particularly important for Denise who was pretty much house-bound looking after the baby. We had lovely neighbours at Ashtead in Roy and Muriel Auger who also had youngish children so at least she had a friend there. It's tough for house-bound mums especially when money is limited whereas the husbands do at least get out and in my own case my job was far from routine so I was also growing in knowledge and experience.

Shortly after completing my driving course, and again unusually early in my service, I was allocated to permanent Area Car duties with an experienced colleague by the name of Maurice Elliott. He was great to be with because he had been there and done it all. He was a former Guardsman and very tall so when he started to get out of the car he kind of kept coming until he stood up to his full height. Just the sort of partner to deter the bad guys and give me a bit of additional confidence.

We developed a great working relationship and I learnt a lot more about the local area, one of which was that the first port of call on an early shift after leaving the nick at about half six was a 'bacon buttie' at Clarks Café next to the bus station. Perfect start to the day.

Maurice also had a great eye for suspicious circumstances, people or vehicles. We used to sit beside the A24 at Leatherhead watching the traffic go by and he'd suddenly say *"Let's have a look at that one."*

He seemed to have a kind of sixth sense because very often we'd pull up a vehicle and discover not just road traffic offences like vehicle defects but disqualified or uninsured drivers and even on a couple of occasions the policeman's dream – a boot full of nicked gear.

Vehicle checks were a high priority in those days because at the time car theft and burglary were rife and Surrey with its relatively affluent population was a prime target area for travelling professional criminals. They came down from south London to break into houses and so our brief was to make it a high probability that drivers would be the subject of random 'routine checks'. This was acceptable and understood by our law-abiding local residents and over time we learned on the grape-vine that Surrey was regarded as a bit of a high risk destination for those with criminal intent whether locally or London based.

Back then, before the computerization of vehicle and driver records it was much harder to confirm for example that a person driving the car we had stopped was actually the owner or in otherwise lawful possession. In the absence of direct access from police cars as they have today a vehicle check involved a radio call to the local police station who then telephoned the vehicle registration office; Tolworth in the case of Surrey vehicles. They then had to do a visual search of a written records to tell us the registered owner. Unwieldy? Just a bit, but at night it was even worse and you hesitated to put it into train unless you were seriously suspicious because this required a call to Kingston police who then had to take their key round to the licensing office and do the search themselves. Often it was easier just to lift a person on 'suspicion' and sort it out at the nick. Although it was seriously embarrassing if you were wrong.

Within a few years it was possible to get a registered owner check done over the air so you knew before you stopped a car who the owner was. Nowadays it's even better with details of ownership, insurance, MOT, disqualification etc. available in a few moments from the road side. I smile sometimes when I think my computer is a bit slow and remind myself that the speed with which we can access almost any information today is like lightning compared to just a relatively few years ago.

Having said all of that, we had to run quite fast to keep up with the changing tactics of visiting burglars who were not about to abandon such potentially rich pickings just because there were a few more police cars about. Professional criminals are not stupid; they simply took to the back roads and even public transport. Surrey responded by setting up the Burglary Squad which was a group of CID and uniformed officers patrolling back roads and residential areas in unmarked cars as well as targeting known active criminals who they would follow from their homes. It was very 'cat and mouse' and to be honest, despite quite a few excellent results, overall we probably lost.

I recall one man that was caught but not until he had had a very successful run travelling to and from his chosen locations by train. His practice was to visit areas by car and just drive around spotting potential target properties by any number of giveaway signs. Empty houses almost scream out that they are unoccupied by their total silence. It is a matter of a moment to stop outside a house with the car window open and notice the absolute absence of any living sounds. A radio playing, a dog barking, a door banging or a child crying. The absence of these plus the parcel or milk bottles on a doorstep, open garage doors, and total darkness, pretty much guarantees the property is empty.

Having selected a few potentials he would return the next day by train, smartly dressed, and walk to the house knocking the door to 'ask directions' just to confirm all was well. Then if no-one was in he'd be round the back and in via a variety of means ranging from the quite technical to simple brute force. It was usually easy enough to find a suitcase which he then filled with 'loot'. After which, this particularly cheeky chap used to phone for a taxi back to the station and who on earth would think to challenge a smartly dressed man arriving by taxi to catch a train.

In more recent years greater public education, Neighbourhood Watch Schemes, more sophisticated security systems and CCTV have made vehicle theft and high value dwelling house burglary a bit more of a challenge for the criminal fraternity. However don't expect these guys to give up anytime soon. They just change their tactics and develop new subterfuges to con people out of their possessions and of course nowadays that includes sophisticated technology and computer crime.

One aspect of Area Car duties was the fact that being on the main force-wide radio we were frequently directed to attend road accidents. Non-injury accidents were OK, quite interesting in fact especially if one or both of the drivers was clearly at fault and we were able to compile a dangerous or careless driving case to put before the court

Injury accidents were a different thing altogether as more often than not we wouldn't know the seriousness of the situation until we arrived. Police were usually called after the ambulance although sometimes we might be first on the scene and have to provide first aid until their arrival and to be honest I wasn't that good with blood. Somehow the adrenaline kicks in though and you just get on and do what's required.

I only ever went to a few fatal accidents and never got used to it. It was somehow easier when there was a bit of blood because you almost expected it to be a fatal. But it was terribly weird to find a person sitting in a smashed up car, dead with their eyes wide open but with no apparent injuries. It was only after attending a few post mortems that I understood the massive trauma to vital internal organs sustained in such situations.

There was one day when I had just dropped Maurice off for his meal break and resumed solo patrol that I got a call to a 'serious accident' at Headley Heath and as my bad luck would have it on this occasion I was there before the ambulance. An Austin Healey Sprite soft-top sports car had lost control on a bend, shot off the road and into a tree.

My heart sank and knees trembled as it dawned this could well be a fatal and I was on my own. Leaving my car with the blue light flashing I crawled into the hedge and under the wreckage of the soft-top I found the driver unconscious. The tubular steel frame of the hood was twisted and disappeared beneath his jacket looking for all the world as though it had pierced his chest. With huge trepidation I lifted the jacket to see that it wasn't through his chest but under his arm and at which point he came round and opened his eyes. He was incredibly lucky and got away with a broken leg and not a lot else.

On another occasion I dealt with a fatal accident and had to go to the house to tell a woman her husband had been killed. I only ever had to do this on three occasions and it doesn't get any easier.

A week or so later I went back to see the widow and return some of her husband's property. She was a bit more collected by this time, made me a cup of tea and just wanted to talk about him, in the course of which she told me he had been an enthusiastic artist and showed me some of his work. I said how good I thought they were and she then did no more than asked me to choose one as a gift for dealing with the situation so sensitively. Strictly speaking it was against the rules to accept gifts but I felt it would have given more offence and hurt to turn it down so I chose one of the river Mole explaining how I used to fish there as a child. She was delighted and wrote in to the Chief Inspector to further express her thanks but fortunately did not mention the picture.

Because sudden and sometimes violent death is something that police find themselves dealing with quite frequently; in common with the other emergency services there is tendency to build something of a 'shell' around yourself to protect your own emotions. This can from the outside sometimes seem a bit cynical or even disrespectful and it is important that as far as possible the public don't see it. On occasions this 'defence' can even include seeing a funny side to something sad or tragic and I remember one such occasion myself.

I was dealing with the death of a man found dead at home following a call from a neighbour and the body had been removed to the mortuary. My next job was to arrange for identification and on this occasion the person agreeing to do it was not a very close relative so there was none of the usual emotion involved as I drove her to Epsom. We simply made polite conversation touching on how she knew the deceased.

Here I need to set the scene slightly. In the little chapel at the mortuary there was a raised catafalque on which the body rested at about chest height to someone standing and it was normal for the body to be positioned with the feet towards the door.

OK. We arrived and the mortuary attendant asked the relative if she was ready then opened the door to let her into the chapel. A very sombre moment you'd think. It should have been but as the door opened the only thing I could see was this guy's nose. It was absolutely enormous. Two great black holes almost at shoulder level and not unlike looking down the Blackwall tunnel. I had to bite my lip so hard, it was all I could do not to burst out laughing. I hadn't noticed it before because I hadn't seen him from the same angle but now; well you couldn't not see it, in fact it was the only thing I could see for a few moments and all this while the relative was looking sadly at her departed great uncle or whatever he was.

Another thing I found quite challenging as a young police officer was the fact that many people live very different lifestyles to what I was accustomed to. I had seen some pretty squalid homes in and around Lambeth during my brief time in the Met but I have to say that some of the houses I was unfortunate enough to visit off the Kingston Road in Leatherhead were worse. It is almost certainly a lot different now but at the time Cleeve Road and the surrounding area was a bit of a sink estate where it seemed a high proportion of our local 'known' individuals lived. The trouble is that these areas get a negative reputation and somehow bad seems to beget worse so that in the end a kind ghetto of poverty, unemployment and criminality develops. It was never the 'no-go' sort of area that existed in some inner cities but it was a bit grim.

I remember visiting a house one day where the electricity meter had been broken into. I wouldn't have kept pigs in it. There was a carpet of sorts on the floor but it was almost invisible under a thick layer of rubbish that included discarded bottles and beer cans, general litter, dog excrement and soiled nappy liners that had simply been left lying about. The doors and bannisters had been cut down and used as firewood and there was half a bag of coal and a rusty bike frame in the bath. The occupants were not especially anti so I was asked in, invited to sit which I declined and then believe it or not offered a 'cup of tea' served up in a jam jar. I passed on that too. I was and still am at a total loss to understand how anyone can live like that but I guess if a kid, and there were four, can survive that they must develop the immune system of the Incredible Hulk.

It is not just about the area, the deprivation or the unemployment and neither can it be laid solely at the door of local authorities. It is about people and their attitudes because in the house next door there was a couple with one child and it was a little palace. They weren't well off but did have enough self-respect and pride in their home to keep it and themselves clean. As they told me *"We don't have a lot but a tin of emulsion paint and a broom don't cost that much."*

My probationary period ended in April 1970 and as if to confirm it our daughter Maria was born on the 9th. We were now four and as far as Denise and I were concerned we had our 'pigeon pair' and that should probably be enough. We were once again besotted new parents and absolutely delighted with our lovely daughter.

Dad with new-born Maria at Ashtead

The fact that my appointment was now confirmed made me feel more secure in my employment and short of seriously blotting my copy book I could look forward to a thirty year career ending at fifty two years of age with a golden handshake and an index-linked pension. All seemed very well sorted and I felt much more able to relax and spend time with the family.

Around the same time I took the Sergeant's promotion exam passing with the top marks in the county and winning the Barlow Cup. This was a trophy presented annually to the officer gaining the highest marks in the sergeant's exam and had been presented to the force by the widow of a former Superintendent Basil Edward Barlow. I immediately applied for a Special Course interview.

Peter Matthews presenting me with the Basil Barlow Cup

iv

It was also around this time that I was first introduced to the police use of firearms. Applications were invited from officers who wished to be trained as 'authorised shots' as they were called and given my high level of ambition and enthusiasm for everything I jumped straight in, without, if I'm honest, giving much thought to what it might entail.

We went in small groups to the army ranges at Pirbright and here met Sergeant Arthur Crawford, at that time the force firearms instructor and an expert and enthusiastic shooter in his own time too.

I remember he pulled us up very short in his introductory remarks when he said *"If there is anyone here who objects on moral or religious grounds to killing another person, even as a last resort, now is the time to leave."*

Well, as I said I hadn't actually given it that much thought and his remark certainly did give me pause for consideration. As he explained it the use of lethal force must always be the last resort but in a situation when our own or an innocent person's life is in danger and no other means are appropriate we must not shrink from that responsibility.

"Make no mistake." he said. *"Like it or not, this is about killing but it's not that we want anyone to die. However, your objective if you draw a weapon is to stop a person doing what they are doing or about to do and we do not have time to think about shooting at arms or legs and so on. To be effective you will learn to aim dead centre and if you are a half reasonable shot the person is likely to die. So I say again, now is the time to withdraw if you can't handle that responsibility."*

I did stick with it and over the few days of that, and what were to be many more courses, I learnt how to shoot and must say I absolutely loved it. Although it's true that after blasting away at cardboard targets it is easy to forget the seriousness of the whole thing and the fact that one day there might actually be a living breathing person in your line of fire.

The idea around the training was that in the event of an incident possibly requiring an armed response, local 'authorised shots' would be issued with the limited number of Smith and Wesson 0.38 revolvers held on stations. They would then be under the direction of whoever was in command of the incident and who almost certainly had absolutely no knowledge or experience of firearms or their tactical deployment. So not an ideal scenario which would fortunately change dramatically in the following few years but that's the way it was then and for a while to follow.

After that first introduction I was so entranced with pistol shooting that I decided to take it up as a hobby myself. Arthur Crawford helped me crystallise my thoughts around choice of weapon and I also joined the same club that he belonged to near Guildford.

I didn't know it then but I was destined to be much more involved with shooting in the job over the coming years.

13   I'M A DETECTIVE

i

In June the same year the next step of my plan came about when I was accepted for what was known as a CID Learner. This was a six month attachment for both the individual and the department to test the water so to speak with a view to being considered for a permanent CID posting.

I loved it and despite being once again at the bottom of the heap in terms of knowledge and experience of detective duties I had a few results that built my confidence and I soon began to feel part of the team.

The Criminal Investigation Department on the division was headed up by Detective Chief Inspector Philip (Paddy) Doyle, Detective Inspector John Carr and in my office at Leatherhead my immediate boss was Sergeant Jock McLachlan. The DC's in the office were friendly and supportive and once I had shown that I could down a few pints with the rest of them I knew I was accepted.

I know that shouldn't have been the case but CID in the early 70's was very similar to the stereotype portrayed in the Life on Mars television series. We were 'the lads', a cut above our lesser uniformed colleagues referred to unkindly by some as the 'woodentops'. It didn't take me long to slide into the mould as my hair got over the collar and the sideburns lengthened. I was a detective and poor Denise didn't half know about it.

Hours of duty were very different being based largely on an eight hour day which was either normal nine to five office hours or a late turn which would be a two till ten. However detective duties benefitted from a detective allowance that assumed a certain amount of overtime would be worked over and above the basic eight hours a day, so in order to qualify for this we had to put the time in, often more or less regardless of whether we actually had anything to do. What this meant in practice was that we put ourselves about in the haunts of the local low-life, visiting clubs and pubs and notionally cultivating informants and eliciting useful intelligence.

Well, that was the theory and whilst a certain amount of that went on, fundamentally we went out drinking. To cap it all the force even paid for some of it as we were allowed to submit 'reasonable expenses' for such things as buying drinks for informants. The upshot of this for Denise was that she got to spend a few more evenings alone at the end of which I turned up smelling all beery. Although to be fair to myself I had usually only had a pint as I certainly didn't want to find myself on a drunk driving charge.

One morning I came in to find a local youth had been detained overnight on suspicion of ABH – that is assault occasioning actual bodily harm. I'll call him Terry Springer. Apparently he'd hit a guy on the head with a bottle in some sort of fracas as a result of which the victim was in hospital with a cut scalp but fortunately *"no bony injury"* as the medics put it.

I went to interview him in hospital, got his statement and went back to the nick to interview the prisoner. The incident was one of those in which all bystanders miraculously happened to be looking the other way at the moment in question which meant we had no independent witnesses to the assault. Now I wasn't about to tell Springer this and although I didn't actually say there were witnesses which would have amounted to a lie, it was not my fault if he seemed to assume there were.. So he admitted the incident blaming the fact that he'd had a bit to drink and misinterpreted a remark the victim had made. After taking a statement under caution in which he repeated his admission of the assault I completed the usual process by taking his fingerprints in the old fashioned way with mucky black ink rollers and so on. In consultation with Jock McLachlan we decided the injury was enough to justify a charge of Grievous Bodily Harm and Springer was duly bailed to appear at court about a month hence. End of job or so I thought.

The following afternoon I was working a late shift when the bush telegraph let us know that the DCI was coming over to Leatherhead. Cue to look busy or go out somewhere. As I had a few ends to tie up with the Springer file I was still there when Paddy Doyle walked in.

"Who's dealing with Springer?" he asked. *"Oh that'd be me Sir."* I said, all cock sure and happy to be in the boss's eye. Paddy raised an eyebrow.

"Oh that'd be you would it?" he said with a hint of sarcasm. *"Well you're now the officer in a murder enquiry."*

I went weak at the knees and must have blanched because he smiled and said *"Not by yourself you daft bugger, but you are still nominally the case officer as you've dealt with everything so far and well enough too as far as I can see."*

It turned out that the victim had died overnight in the course of an epileptic fit and the logical conclusion had to be that this was precipitated by the crack on his head.

My next task was to attend a post mortem at Epsom Hospital in order to identify the deceased to the forensic pathologist who turned out to be Professor Keith Mant, one of the country's most eminent and well regarded in his field. To be honest I wasn't very keen to stay for the p.m. but Mant said *"Hang on and we'll be able to give you the exact cause of death for your paperwork."* So I felt I had little choice.

I must say it was a bit hard to stomach seeing the initial part of the process taking place on someone I had been speaking to barely twenty four hours earlier but once it got under way and with Mant in full flow it was absolutely fascinating. He was a brilliant teacher and clearly loved imparting knowledge as he carefully dissected a large gall stone to expose and explain its internal structure. Further examination revealed that the victim had a cyst in his throat which when he inhaled sharply in the course of the fit had (to use Mant's words) *"just plopped back into his windpipe and choked him"*

So the conclusion was that while the assault may have triggered the fit, he did have an epileptic history and there was in the pathologist's view insufficient evidence to connect the blow with the fit and therefore with the cause of death which was suffocation.

Unfair though it seemed it was very lucky for Springer because without an independent witness and in the absence of a victim and now with a dubious cause of death we had no alternative but to drop the charge.

I mentioned earlier about letting my hair grow into the on-street style of the seventies but just, it seemed, to stop me getting too full of myself I had the hair event to end them all.

There was a little device around at that time called the "Comet Safety

Hair Cutter". Advertised on TV, it was a kind of four sided comb with a blade built in that according to the way round it was used could "cut, trim, groom or style to perfection."

One Saturday evening I had washed my hair and decided that a gentle trim was needed. So standing with my back to the bathroom mirror and holding up a hand mirror to see what was happening I took a careful stroke down the back of my head and felt something heavy fall on my shoulder. Changing the angle of the hand mirror I was horrified to see that high up towards the crown of my head was this great hole in my hair where I had damn nearly gone down to the wood.

I was distraught. My carefully coiffed and nurtured barnet was basically wrecked. I couldn't believe what I'd done and now what the devil was I going to do about it short of taking a month's leave which wasn't an option. And then I remembered Doreen.

Dave Hancock, a colleague on CID lived adjacent to the nick and his wife Doreen was a hairdresser, so 9.30 sees me knocking on their door for help and advice. Not surprisingly they both thought it was hilarious which was a million miles from how I felt and then Doreen put her professional head on and started to think about it.

She said the only choice was a regulation short back and sides and although it would be pretty short she felt sure she could cut it to disguise what had actually happened. So that's how it was. I was sat in a chair in the CID office with a roller towel from the toilet around my shoulder while Doreen lopped off my hair.

I was the butt of a lot of teasing for a while, quite a while actually but eventually it grew back and became history but an experience I'll never forget.

My learner attachment to CID finished in mid-December 1970 but just six weeks later I was back on again; this time not as a learner but Temporary DC.

In October the previous year the body of 24 year old Barbara Mayo was found in Derbyshire. She had been raped and strangled whilst hitch-hiking to the north to collect a car for her boyfriend. Information suggested that she had been seen getting into a Morris Minor Traveller at a service station and a decision was made to have every owner of such a car interviewed. There were a hundred and eighty-five thousand such vehicles across the country and it was this job I was brought back on to help with. The department couldn't afford to allocate a full time DC to the job but the DCI had said it needed someone with a bit of CID experience and I turned out to be that person.

I can't remember how many such vehicles were listed in the county but it was at least couple of hundred I think. I went back into civvies and was paid mileage to drive my own car around the lanes of Surrey completing pro-forma interviews of all the owners. It was pretty repetitive but interesting for all that and always with the need to keep alert for any signs of guilt or unease among the owners.

In 1990, with the continuing advance of scientific investigative techniques, information came to light suggesting a positive link between the murder of Barbara Mayo and eighteen year old Jackie Ansell-Lamb whose body was found in the same area. In 2007, one Peter Tobin was convicted of murdering a young woman with two more convictions added in 2008 and 2009. His MO was strikingly similar and he remains a strong suspect for Barbara Mayo's murder but until now that has not been conclusively proved.

This aspect of the investigation was similar to one that had occurred in Leatherhead a couple of years before I went on the department there. In April 1968, fourteen year old Roy Tuthill had disappeared on his way home from school. He had broken his bus journey from Kingston to hitch-hike the rest of the way in an effort to save money for a new bike. His body was found three days later on the Cherkley Court estate at Leatherhead. He had been indecently assaulted.

It was discovered that Roy had been seen by a bus driver talking to the driver of an Austin Westminster car that had also been sighted near the location where the boy was discovered. Back then, provincial forces weren't always able to muster enough officers with the experience and knowledge to carry out a major enquiry and would often call on the Met's Murder Squad for assistance. Indeed there was a considerable incentive to do so as this assistance came quite cheaply if not actually free when called in the early stages.

As in the later Mayo case a decision was made to interview the owners of eighteen thousand such vehicles countrywide. But in this case too, despite the assistance of the Met's Murder Squad, whose main skills in those days appeared to be long beery lunches and smoking large cigars, the trail went cold.

It was not until thirty three years later that detection and amazingly a conviction was achieved after all that time. This was due entirely to Paddy Doyle's refusal to admit defeat and after the Met had walked away he had all the evidence reviewed and forensic samples carefully preserved against the day sometime in the future when science could do more to help. That day came in 2001 when a motorist was stopped in Birmingham for a drink/driving offence and a routine DNA swab was taken. Entered into the national database the connection was made with forensic material carefully preserved from the scene of the boy's murder.

A compelling case for an obligatory national DNA database? Or is that an infringement too far of our human rights? There is of course the argument that *"if you have nothing to hide, you have nothing to fear"*. But still, the argument might go *"it is a free country not a police state."*

Personally I swing between the two viewpoints although I'm sure most serving officers frustrated by dead-end investigations would be well in favour. *"But personal liberty is everything"*. Try telling that to the grieving parents of a beautiful daughter raped and strangled almost before her life has begun. A tough question.

ii

Just towards the end of my time on CID at Leatherhead the interviews for The Special Course were held at Headquarters and I was called to attend having automatically qualified for the force board by virtue of my exam marks. Success at this first hurdle would see me go forward to the three days selection process held at Bramshill.

I have always hated formal interviews and in those days they tended to be very formal. Since then it has been realized that a more relaxed approach helps to put candidates at their ease and elicits a better result. That's not to say that a relaxed style of interview necessarily achieves less of an insight into the individual, indeed it probably achieves more.

I mentioned earlier that part of the rationale behind the Special Course was to try to move the service away from its rather militaristic style. This also included, on the part of many senior officers, an attitude of elitism such as existed in the services between the officer level and other ranks. Unfortunately using these same individuals in the interview process rather tended towards the selection of people in their own image and perpetuation of the problem

If this is beginning to sound like the justification for my failure at the board that would be exactly right. I did fail and have always felt cheated because this was how it went.

The panel comprised Chief Constable Peter Matthews plus either the Deputy or Assistant Chief Constable and a divisional Chief Superintendent. All gentlemen of a certain age and background and very much 'old school'.

To be fair they were very positive and complimentary regarding my success in the promotion exam and my end of probation report and I started to feel a little more relaxed. We talked then a bit about my education and the fact that it had rather stopped short at the age of sixteen and had I never thought about going on to university? I explained that a chance would have been a fine thing if I'd had any idea about university and the opportunities it might have offered. But my family were not academic and hadn't the background or knowledge to even consider the possibility.

The temperature began to cool and I endeavoured to compensate for my lack of academic background with my mind-broadening experience at sea and in the Met. I also made the point that surely my exam results indicated that I could learn and retain complicated material. I felt I had gained a little ground and we moved on to talk about my family.

I was and have always been intensely proud of my father. I felt that for a man of relatively lowly beginnings, who having risen to quite a high position as a regional manager of a major supermarket chain, he had done well. I can't remember which member of the board said it but the words *"You mean he's a grocer then?"* hit me like a bolt and I responded *"Yes he is and what's wrong with that. We'd all be in a pretty stew without them."*

The room went very quiet and I knew at that point that I clearly wasn't special enough for their precious course. A few platitudes concluded the interview and as expected I heard a week or so later that I wasn't going any further.

I remember reading some time later a very 'tongue-in-cheek' account of The Special Course by an academic who had been on the staff at Bramshill. He described the major benefits of the Police College as learning how to get pissed with style; port is passed to the left and that it's better not to eat peas off your knife.

Perhaps I didn't miss out on so much then.

14 GUILDFORD

i

Following my time on CID at Leatherhead I was asked if that was the direction I wanted my career to go. I obviously said it was; they didn't need to know that it was only part of a bigger plan. So after a brief return to beat and area car duties at Leatherhead, in July 1971 I was posted to CID at Guildford in the old police station between Woodbridge Road and Leapale Lane.

This obviously entailed a move of house and we were allocated a police house on an estate at Slyfield Green on the outskirts of Guildford. Being an ordered move we were entitled to the removal allowance which went a fair way to providing some new curtains and carpets but certainly not all. The location was not actually that great being a row of six police houses on the edge of a council estate. Added to which it was only a short distance from the local sewage works and although not a problem most of the time there were occasions when the weather conditions were right that a foul-smelling morning mist would drift across the fields to our front doors.

We had a nice bunch of neighbours including Pc Bob Taylor and his wife next door and Brian 'Taff' Evans who also worked on the department at Guildford..

Guildford CID was a large office run by D/C/I. Ian McGregor who went on to eventually become Assistant Chief Constable with the British Transport Police. Our immediate bosses were Detective Inspector Les Haynes and DS's Wally Hammond and Ron Briggs. Les was every inch a stereotype of the television D/I Gene Hunt so ably portrayed by actor Philip Glenister. Apparently some of the older uniform colleagues had given Les the nickname 'Eliot Ness' and us detectives The Untouchables after the 1930's Chicago Prohibition Agents. However, we certainly weren't about prohibition. Quite the contrary, as much of our time seemed to be spent sniffing out where we could actually get a drink which often included the fairly newly opened Cinderella's night club and the Silver Birch Club off the High Street. We were usually welcomed with open arms in both locations ostensibly because they were very pro-police (which they actually weren't) but most likely because they wanted to keep in with the local Old Bill on the basis of *"keeping their friends close and their enemies closer still"*

Television programs in recent years depicting the sixties and seventies have often characterized detectives of the period like the Gene Hunt character as sexist and racist bigots and I am ashamed to say that they are not so very far adrift. I think it would be true that a proportion of the police officers back then did unfortunately fall into that stereotype but certainly not all. Much more recently the police service and the poor old Met in particular has been criticized as being institutionally racist and sadly I have no difficulty in accepting this may well be so. You cannot wave a wand and make bigotry and discrimination simply disappear. It needs concerted effort over years, generations even. All of that said, having spoken to many serving officers over the twenty odd years since I retired, I feel confident that any problems, where they still exist, now lie with the minority

Life on the department at Guildford was pretty much run of the mill for a junior detective like me. My work tended to revolve around attending local shops to arrest and process detained shoplifters, and dealing with a variety of burglaries of which there were many, ranging from garden sheds through gas meters to warehouses and high class dwelling houses. Following perhaps on the initial attendance of a uniform officer a DC would then trundle along with the scenes of crime expert (SOCO) to take further details and collect lists of property stolen etc.

Detection rates for burglaries were extremely variable depending on the type of target. What we called *'good class dwelling house burglaries'* were not easy to solve because as I mentioned earlier they were more often than not committed by skilled professionals from outside the area who knew what they were doing and left very little in the way of clues to follow. By contrast there was quite a sizeable group of known local 'breakers' who were often extremely amateurish in their MO, identifying themselves either by the type of property attacked, method of entry and type of property stolen. In some cases the MO was almost a calling card and you could scoot round to the person's house and not uncommonly find them still in possession of stolen property if not actually sorting it on the kitchen table.

Weekends brought the usual rash of assaults ranging from the very minor to serious and often involved military personnel owing to the proximity of army barracks at Pirbright and Aldershot. I am pleased to say though that I never again found myself close to another homicide.

Children and women were, I found, the most difficult to deal with because even caught red-handed they would sit there and swear their innocence because logic and the obvious just didn't seem to compute. Whereas by and large, male offenders would usually see when the evidence was against them and put their hands up. I never did hear anyone actually say *"It's a fair cop Guv"* but that's what it amounted to.

What you might call 'professional criminals' were intriguing and I met a few who in other circumstance you'd have said were pleasant enough guys. They had this interesting philosophy around their criminal activities, tending to see it simply as their 'job' and the fact that their job happened to conflict with mine was simply unfortunate. I got this in a conversation with a burglar I was escorting to prison one day and he explained that if a copper ever caught him in the act he'd probably be prepared to *'give him a slap'* in order to get away but there would be no personal malice in it and would never use serious violence or a weapon. He also regarded periods in prison as an occupational hazard or even as a bit of a break.

The rules around dealing with suspects were very different then, being based on procedural guidelines drawn up and reviewed over time by senior judges. Known as The Judges Rules they provided for the way in which suspects were questioned, cautioned and so on and the latest version applicable at that time was enshrined in a Home Office Circular in 1964. To say they were meticulously observed might be to stretch a point and there was to some extent both flexibility and laxity in their application on occasions. However I was never once aware of any serious breaches or downright 'fit-ups' of the sort often alleged and indeed proven against the Metropolitan Police and which resulted in the major anti-corruption efforts by Sir Robert Mark in the early 70's

An amusing story used to circulate in the office about a local thief who stood up in the Guildford magistrates' court and complained that he'd been hung head first by his ankles out of the upstairs CID office window until he confessed to which Lord Hamilton, Chairman of the Bench apparently said *"Utter rubbish. Take him down."* I often wondered about that and could well appreciate the frustration of knowing a person is guilty but being unable to prove it. I hope it didn't happen but could almost understand if it did.

The Police and Criminal Evidence Act (PACE) came into effect in 1984 incorporating and strengthening the Judges Rules into law which police often felt hamstrung them and provided excess protection to offenders who quickly learnt to play the system. A further unintended complication arising from PACE was the number of successful appeals against conviction based on the failure to follow the principles and rules of PACE during investigations and interviews carried out before the new law came into effect. I never did understand how this came about.

A couple of the more interesting investigations I was responsible for whilst on Guildford CID included a fraud at the Yvonne Arnaud Theatre. The restaurant manager had a great little scam going and whilst I don't recall the exact details it enabled him to lift significant amounts of cash from the till whilst somehow keeping the books to avoid discovery.

Anyway it wasn't so much the technique that interests me in hindsight but the response of the management. Sufficient to say the crime was suspected and a trap was set which resulted in the man's arrest and a subsequent search of his house. This was filled with all manner of things including home electricals, hi-fi and clothing that his basic income could never have supported which was all seized and admitted to be the proceeds of his fraud. However the management were so embarrassed and fearing the negative publicity they declined to support a prosecution and also refused to accept all this property which we then had to dispose of through the police auction system.

The other job was reported whilst I was on a temporary internal posting to Godalming. We received a report from a woman in Dunsfold that her female tenant in a cottage beside the house was in possession of some suspicious property.

Exercising her right to inspect the property she had entered in the absence of the tenant and discovered the strangest collection of stuff. There were multiple similar item including three Slendertone vibratory massage belt machines, hairdryers, two foldaway home offices, portable typewriters and several electric footbaths among other things.

The tenant had only quite recently arrived from a tenancy in Witley and it transpired that her little game was to order all these item from a variety of different mail order catalogue companies like Littlewoods.

She used to give a slightly wrong address in an attempt to conceal her true location. For example in her dealings with the companies she gave her address as Tree Road, Witley which doesn't actually exist but thanks to the diligence of the Post Office and Royal Mail they found her eventually at Yew Tree Road, Witley.

Once in possession of the items that she never intended to pay for she would decamp to another address and then proceed to rent the items out on a monthly basis thus developing a nice little revenue stream for no more effort than was required to deliver them in her car and pop round each month to collect her hire fees.

She was duly arrested and admitted the offences but in this instance too it was the devil's own job to get the mail order companies to press charges as they explained *"It's honestly not worth our time and effort to get involved and anyway the publicity would only give other people the same idea."*

In December 1971, just five months after joining the CID office at Guildford I was allocated a place on the Initial Detective Training Course which was held at that time at Peel House in Westminster. This was serious nostalgia time as it was Peel House where I'd completed my initial police training to join The Met the first time round in 1964. Another location for training was at Wakefield in Yorkshire but I was more than happy to be relatively close to home as I was conscious that yet another course involving a couple of months away was likely to go down like a ton of bricks indoors.

The course wasn't residential and this was the only time in my life I was ever a commuter in the normal sense and joined the lemming like rush to Guildford station every morning for the crammed half-hour run to Waterloo. This was followed by a very pleasant twenty minute walk over the river to Regency Street. Days were long with the travelling but the studying was less intensive and so evenings (what was left of them) and weekends were still family time

Not a lot had changed at Peel House apart from the fact that there was not a uniform in site. Run by Commander McIver as Commandant, all the instructors were experienced Detective Inspectors including one Freddie Luff whose claim to fame was being the officer in the case of the Oz trial at the Old Bailey which was going on at the time. Oz was one of the forerunners among a number of underground magazines being monitored by the Obscene Publications Squad and charged with corrupting public morals by publishing gay contact ads on its back page. How times change!

I'm middle row – second from left

I was the only Surrey officer and ten of the other seventeen were from the Met. It was certainly a bit of a revelation once we started exchanging experiences and I realized what a sheltered life the provincial forces have compared to the big cities.

I'd heard tales that I'd assumed were apocryphal, about some of the stunts Met detectives were said to get up to in order to keep their arrest figures up. One such story was that pairs of learner detectives would take up observation positions on the street in order catch offenders; the most used charge being the now infamous 'sus law' offence of acting suspiciously in preparation to commit a crime. (my paraphrase) The story went that frustrated with the lack of suitable 'suspects' they would agree *"Ok. The next bloke in red socks"* who would be arrested, taken in and charged with a trumped up set of 'evidence'

I laughingly mentioned this to a couple of the Met guys expecting a clear denial and was amazed at their reply along the lines of *"Well maybe sometimes you just need to show the flag."*

A couple of the other Met guys were with the Special Branch at Heathrow and proudly told how on a couple of occasions they'd had to *"Stop that aircraft."* Apparently it is incredibly expensive to bring a flight back from what's known as the threshold. That is, on the point of take-off. I'd love to do that. What power, but my goodness you'd have to be sure of your facts.

Not too far from Peel House was a pub, the name of which now eludes my struggling grey cells but which was very popular both at lunch times and in the evenings due to its scantily clad and occasionally topless Go-Go dancers. Walking fast we could get there in less than ten minutes, down a couple of pints, top up with erotic dance and a steak pie and be back in class for the afternoon session.

Evenings were even more tempting as the potential for a longer session was strong. I only ever succumbed on a Friday though and can recall tottering back towards Waterloo in time for a late train to Guildford all fired up in my head by the tasty ladies but suffering the unfortunate effects of excess alcohol if I was tempted to follow my fantasies through at home.

I enjoyed the course tremendously and the comradeship that it engendered was of a very different type to my initial course, given I guess, that we were all much more experienced and had some credibility. The end-of-course celebration (OK - piss-up) was at the Anchor pub on the riverside by Tower Bridge where the Met guys were well known and got us a very good deal for the evening meal and drinks.

After that in mid-February 1972, it was back to Guildford and the 'same-old, same-old'. However on the 22nd a bomb exploded at the Officers' Mess of the Parachute Regiment's barracks in Aldershot killing several people. It was all hands to the pumps and together with a number of colleagues from the Guildford CID office I went over to assist the Hampshire guys. As I recall we were mainly involved in local enquiries and following up leads and taking statement from potential witnesses. Being a crime scene there was no immediate attempt to 'clear up' any debris which included bits of human flesh blown some distance by the blast. I remember seeing part of a human face hanging in a tree. It really was the stuff of nightmares. As in my experience of the Gatwick air crash I was grateful not to be more 'hands on' but had huge admiration for the scenes of crime people, pathologists and so on who were more intimately involved.

ii

Whilst work was keeping me very busy and interested I knew that Denise was finding it hard going. I was working quite long hours so our time together was pretty limited. The children were lovely though. Robert was coming up to four, bright as a button and interested in everything. Maria, rising two, was the light of our lives and such a pretty child but then I guess every parent thinks the same about their kids.

We did manage a couple of holidays though, one of which was a week at a Warner's Holiday Camp at Camber Sands. Much as the thought of such a holiday horrifies me now it actually worked pretty well at the time. There was plenty to entertain the children and a 'baby-watching' service allowed parents at least a couple of hours for a drink and a dance in the evenings.

Relationships with our respective parents and my stepmother were fine although we saw more of Denise's parents than my Dad and Eileen for the reasons already mentioned. At a personal level our relationship was really no better than OK due to Denise's growing discontent with the impact of my job. To my mind she was failing completely to understand that my ambition, whilst a bit difficult in the here and now, was all about us as a family and our greater happiness and prosperity in the future but then I suppose I would say that. With hindsight I guess I did make it a bit tough and the lack of spare money for any extras to sweeten the pill didn't help either. Police pay was not great and it was to be another seven years before the Edmund-Davies Review dramatically improved things.

Around this time the rules changed to allow constables who had passed the Sergeant's exam to go ahead and take the Inspector's rather than waiting until promoted to sergeant. It made huge sense to be able to continue studying and get both hurdles out of the way, but it did mean another year of further study and a further demand on my family. In the event I passed the exam and once again came out with top marks in the county. Then I relaxed. Well, as far as the study was concerned.

From this point on things at home improved a lot as I became less bogged down in the book-work. Although I was still putting in the hours to justify the CID allowances when I was at home I was spending much more time with the family.

Unfortunately the social life at Guildford was nowhere near as well organized as it had been on the Dorking division. So not only had the move cut us off from most of the friends we had made at Leatherhead but there was little or nothing to look forward to in the way of socializing with colleagues. This was a undoubtedly a difficult time for Denise and the contrast between our daily lives was stark. I was getting out to work and continuing to grow in experience every day. Meanwhile her own days basically revolved around housekeeping and the care of two small children, and with few local contacts or other interests to stimulate her, she probably felt her own world was getting smaller.

We were still in touch with both David and Michael from the garage although as that had now closed they had both moved on to other things. I think Mike was married by this time and David had a long term relationship so we did the usual dinner party thing from time to time with them coming to us to save us having to get baby sitters in.

And so due largely to shortage of money for entertainment life trundled on for us at a relatively mundane level as it does for many until quite out of the blue in November 1971 I got the call to go and see the Chief and was promoted to uniform sergeant at Guildford.

I was over the moon. Ecstatic even, because this was a very early promotion at just over four years and confirmed to my mind that the 'officer with potential' tag still existed despite being turned down for the Special Course.

On the subject of The Police College; shortly before I heard about my promotion I had been invited to assist with an exercise to be held at Bramshill called 'The Right Man for the Job'. The Inspectors' course at the college was learning about interview techniques and they needed 'stooges' to practice on. The scenario we had to act out was as constables appearing at interviews for promotion to sergeant in another force. As I said earlier, I had limited experience of interview situations and so was very pleased to have been asked if for no other reason than the benefit of the practice.

This was the first time I had ever actually been to Bramshill and I must say it was impressive. Not far from Hartley Wintney, it is a fine Jacobean mansion sitting atop a rise in the Hampshire countryside surrounded by hundreds of acres of park-like grounds at the end of a mile long drive. Despite my pique at not being selected for the Special Course I couldn't help being impressed and wished heartily that things had panned out differently on that front as I imagined it being the most wonderful learning environment. Not that Denise would have been very impressed and certainly would have had difficulty seeing how absence for yet another year was in any way a good thing. Sad though.

The exercise was very straightforward, we just had to be ourselves despite the temptation to ham it up a bit for our own amusement. The interviewing students were clearly working to some sort of script and when a previous interviewee told me what his last question had been I immediately know what my answer would be.

As expected at the end the concluding question was
"Tell us Pc Simmons, what will you do if you are not successful here today?"
I said *"To be honest Sir I'll not be that worried as am just about to be promoted in my own force."* Their faces were a picture.

15 PROMOTION

i

It was unusual to be promoted on the same station as it can create quite difficult situations with a newly promoted supervisor having to manage former colleagues. However in my case, having been on CID I didn't have the same problem moving back into the uniform branch at the same station.

Newly promoted Sergeant Simmons

The normal set-up on a shift or section as it was known would be that two sergeants would be responsible for running the team of maybe up to a dozen constables on a large station although, unlike my brief time in the Met, at Guildford we rarely had the luxury of more than six or seven at most. We had no women officers on the section as in those days there was a separate Police Women's Department whose specialist role related to issues around missing children and offences involving women and girls.

We were answerable to a shift Inspector and the two sergeants alternated between the roles of Station Sergeant and Patrol Sergeant the titles of which are pretty self-explanatory.

As Patrol Sergeant I was responsible for briefing the section of PC's, allocating their beat or patrol areas and ensuring they had everything they needed in terms or equipment and information. The responsibility continued throughout the shift with a requirement to be out and about, meeting individual officers to monitor their activities, continue their training, supervise incidents and frequently help out in a hands-on way as required.

One of the beats covered the High Street and it took me a while to cotton on to why Pc's seemed to vie with each other to work it. This was particularly so in summer when all the short skirts came out and after the first time I walked the High Street which is on quite a steep hill I understood completely. Boys will be boys I guess. (Me too!)

Apart from their talent spotting potential, the town beats were more interesting because there was so much more going on both day and night and for the younger and keener officers they were the obvious choice. Outer beats were by that time mostly covered by Panda patrols and whilst their mobility did mean they could get quite a variety of jobs it also meant that they could find themselves heading out with sheaves of enquiries and statement to be taken about, for example, road traffic accidents or offences for other forces which could become quite a drudge.

The Station Sergeant on the other hand was responsible for the supervision of one or more station office personnel who might comprise one (or very occasionally two) station constable manning the public counter and a communications officer working in the comms. centre behind the scenes. He (or she) could also find himself directing resources over the local radio system in response to incidents and calling in support from other departments as required or requested by his Patrol Sergeant colleague or other officers on the ground.

A further responsibility of the Station Sergeant was the physical security of the station and dealing with persons arrested, ensuring correct procedures and deciding whether to charge or release according to the evidence presented.

The surprising thing however was that for some reason or perhaps oversight, two brand new sergeants were appointed to the same section whereas the usual practice was to pair a new sergeant with an experienced colleague. So I found myself working alongside likewise newly promoted sergeant Terry Ashcroft and to be honest it really was pretty much a case of the blind leading the blind. But it was huge fun for the most part and we managed without too many serious cock-ups.

I think one of the most important things to learn in life is that no-one knows it all and that one should never be afraid to admit that. Nor does anyone like a self-styled know-all and all they want to do is see them take a tumble. So I always felt it was easier, safer and more diplomatic to acknowledge that whilst I might have been responsible I had no monopoly of knowledge, experience or flashes of brilliance and that I was never above asking an experienced constable for his or her view.

My favourite sounding board in this respect was PC Gary Hyldon, a very experienced constable and former Guardsman. Gary was extremely knowledgeable, unflappable and reliable and had pretty well been there and done it all before. The even better thing was that he had huge respect for the rank structure, always referred to Terry and me as Sergeant rather than "Sarge" or "Skip" and whilst obviously perceiving our inexperience was happy to contribute a view without being in any way patronizing. I came to respect him and his judgement immensely and although I didn't know it then, would find myself alongside him in a very different role within a year or two.

Once the dust had settled a bit on our appointment Terry and I soon established a good arrangement and I think we both learnt a lot about running a team and finding that fine balance between being a supervisor and 'one of the boys' Terry was certainly more inclined to the latter than me. I suppose I would class myself as more introvert than anything which has been born out in various personality tests I've completed over the years. For myself I think that a degree of reserve is appropriate in a manager but that said *"team player"* seems to be a sought after characteristic these days and I'm afraid that's not really my style.

We did have a few laughs at Guildford, one of which was about me learning some of the bolt-holes my PC's could disappear into when the short skirts on the High Street became too much, the rain came or they quite simply needed a cuppa.

As patrol sergeant I was in the practice of calling up on the radio to arrange to meet this or that beat officer, ask his location and fix a place and time. It was a while before it dawned on me that the reply, quite often and particularly on night shifts was likely to be *"On Castle Street Sarge"* So I'd drive round to Castle street and there somewhere along the road would be PC 'Whoever' and we'd have our supervisory chat or drive around for a bit.

One day I decided to try to discover why that location seemed so popular so I took myself to Castle Street and called up the town PC. Sure enough the reply came *"Castle Street Sarge"*. *"That interesting"* I said. *"I'm here too but can't see you."*

A minute or so later an embarrassed looking young PC emerged from a yard entrance buttoning up his coat. It transpired that the bakery behind The Corona Café was the favourite stop, particularly at night which was when the best of the cakes and pastries were produced. It soon became a haunt of mine too.

Another fun event was New Year's Eve. The practice back then was for everyone to spend the evening in the town pubs and then tip out onto the High Street just before midnight to hear the Guildhall clock strike the hour.

In December 1972 I happened to be the outside sergeant on New Year's Eve and just before midnight along with the town beat PC we had positioned ourselves up on the doorstep of the Town Hall or a neighbouring building to get a slightly better view of proceedings. As the final chime struck, a great cheer went up, impromptu groups gathered to sing Auld Lang Syne and then I heard a female voice shout *"I want to kiss a policeman."*

Suddenly I saw this girl, not unattractive it has to be said, making a beeline for us. She got in first and then the idea seemed to catch on and we spent the next several minutes being snogged by dozens of mostly inebriated young women. *"Well let's hope that's set the tone for the new year."* I thought.

Sadly it hadn't and we spent the next hour or two sorting out the odd scuffle and dragging the paralytic back to the nick to spend the first few hours of their New Year sobering up in the cells.

To be fair, we were full of seasonal good cheer as well and I think out of a number arrested only a couple who wanted to fight us got charged while the remainder just slept it off and were then kicked out.

ii

Assuming I could now expect to be spending some time at Guildford I asked for a transfer at our own expense to a much nicer police house at Shalford. It was older, probably about 1930's and was a substantial semi-detached property situated in a small close in quite a pleasant residential area. The only slight downside was that it was just behind the train station and as the sub-soil was sandy it tended to transmit a bit of vibration from passing trains. It was never much of a problem though as the trains weren't that frequent. We liked the house which had a lovely private rear garden and was just a short walk from the few local shops and only a few minutes from either Guildford or Godalming.

With studying out of the way for the present and with a regular eight hour shift pattern established life at home became far happier. Denise was never keen on me doing night shifts. Nor was I come to that because they played havoc with my digestive system and unlike in the Met where we worked three weeks of nights and my body had a chance to get used to it, in Surrey the shifts changed weekly which was much worse. However they were an unavoidable part of the job at this level and there were compensations.

I rarely slept beyond about one o'clock so we could go out together as a family during the afternoons and with everyone else at work it was often the best time to go to the coast or wherever. I was around at home either in the morning or afternoons and the shift pattern also included a long weekend off every month which was great for developing some quality family time.

Overall I began to feel that life was settling more into the pattern I had hoped for and now we weren't so badly off either. Not exactly flush because with young children there is always a call on any available funds, but not so bad really.

With neither of the children yet in school Denise still had her hands full when I wasn't there but I was around much more and started to be the father I'd always wanted to be. I spent as much time as possible with the children thereby enabling her to get a few more breaks when she could visit her mother or friends.

Dad with Maria and Robert at Shalford

I was still attending regular three monthly pistol training sessions at Pirbright ranges and in addition also managing to put in a bit of practice time with my own gun at the Worplesdon Rifle and Pistol Club. With Arthur Crawford's advice I had bought a Smith and Wesson Model 17 0.22 revolver because of its similarity to the 0.38 calibre weapons used by the police.

Notwithstanding the much improved home-life situation, the master plan was still lurking in the back of my mind, the next stage of which I hoped would get me into the training department at Headquarters. With this in mind I applied for a Student Instructors Course and rather surprisingly given my short time at Guildford, I was allocated a place in March 1973, Unfortunately, and here I go again; this was a two month residential course at Ryton on Dunsmore near Coventry. We could come home at weekends but this was to prove probably the most intensive training course I've ever undertaken – before or since.

16 I BECOME A TRAINER

i

Like so many steps I initiated during my time with the police my application to become an instructor was probably not thought through or researched as much as it should have been. My main focus all the while was advancement and the experience boxes I needed to tick to improve my promotion prospects and our prosperity.

Apart from having been on the receiving end as a student, in reality I didn't have a clue what the work of a trainer involved other than standing in front of a class nor whether I was even temperamentally or intellectually suited. I just went for it and what a shock awaited me. Understandably I guess the view from the home front was predictably low key. Denise was far from delighted at the prospect of me on yet another course despite my assertions that it should enhance my promotion prospects in the long term.

The truth is I am not a natural extrovert, quite the contrary in fact; preferring to work either alone or as part of a very small team. So standing up and making myself the centre of attention was not natural or that comfortable for me. However it is remarkably interesting how stimulating it is to be terrified and then overcome those fears to move forward and then in an almost masochistic way actually to enjoy the process. This is what I quickly discovered the next two months were going to be about.

In more recent years, teaching, training or whatever you want to call it has become far more student-centred and ideally should involve quite a lot of dialogue and discussion between teacher and student which develops a deeper understanding of a subject.

This was most certainly not the case at the time I went to be trained as an instructor. We were more in the world of the lecture. *"Pin back your ears, listen and learn and tomorrow we'll test you."* This was the style we aspiring trainers faced and the one we were expected to develop ourselves.

A relatively short time was spent on the psychology of teaching and learning and quite a lot about how motivation aids the learning process. Another skill we had to develop was to seamlessly incorporate a technique of getting feedback to check understanding. However the point was made that for the most part our job was to present the facts of the law clearly enough for it to be remembered and understood. Teacher training these days usually requires at least 2 A levels followed by several years at university to get the appropriate degree. So it can be appreciated that the idea of turning us into teachers in two months was ambitious in the extreme. I have to say that this attitude was pretty much the standard approach to most police training back then.

"Demand the impossible and you'll often get it." And by and large they did.

Once the fundamentals of teaching theory had been presented the remainder of the time was devoted to lesson preparation and presentation. Depending on the topic we were assigned to teach the first thing to do was to mug up the subject ourselves as it certainly couldn't be taken for granted that our current knowledge of the law around a huge variety of subjects was still up to speed.

Then came the task of preparing lesson notes – ABSOLUTELY NOT TO BE READ AS A SCRIPT. These were solely for use as a lesson plan and prompt to keep ourselves on message but most importantly for the timing. The most heinous crime was to find yourself out of time with only half the topic presented.

These were no nine to five days and every evening would find us either walking back and forth across an empty classroom practicing our presentations or teaching our allotted subject to a small group of colleagues who acted as students. Eleven o'clock was a fairly early night and there was rarely any time for visiting the bar.

About three quarters of the way through the course we had to do a week's teaching practice with real students at one of the District Training Centres and I was sent to Sandgate where only a few short years previously I had been a student myself. Notwithstanding plenty of nerves initially I eventually got into my stride and the sessions went well enough at least that's what the monitoring instructors who sat in on the lessons told me. *"Not perfect but then it's early days"*

By chance my week at Sandgate coincided with the formal end-of-course dinner and dance for the new constables leaving that week. As by that time my week there was also nearing its end I was feeling relaxed enough to attend myself, enjoy a few drinks and I thought *"maybe a dance or two"*

There were a number of nurses invited to the evening to provide company and dancing partners for officers whose wives were unable to attend. All very seemly and above board of course and the Sandgate dances had over time become quite popular and something the girls looked forward to. To be fair it was probably the best night out in Folkestone at the time where they could go, have a fun evening and come away without having to fight off the groping of some drunken sailor. The police recruits were far too closely observed to misbehave so the girls knew they were safe. (Apart from predatory Sergeant Instructors. No I'm joking – honestly)

However the class I had been teaching had their own plan for me and set me up a treat. I was standing chatting to a group of them including several nurses when one of the nurses decided to drag me onto the dance floor. Well that was OK. I liked dancing and we jigged about for a while to some faster stuff and then came a slow ballad and the girl moved in on me to carry on dancing. That was OK too. She was pretty, smelled lovely and the whole experience was frankly delightful. So I let myself go with the flow and we carried on smooching to several slow numbers in what was now a more darkened ballroom.

Then the DJ said *"Is everyone having a good time?"* and the crowd responded with a loud *"Yes"* I was more or less lost in the moment to be honest until the DJ said *"And is Sergeant Simmons having a good time?"*

At this point my world exploded in light as two spotlights fell on me and my pretty nurse and I looked up to see that almost everyone else had left the floor and were gathered around the edge of the dance floor laughing and clapping at my embarrassment.

I had no option but take it in good part and why not. After all, no harm done. My little nurse gave a very warm kiss goodbye which had I not been a faithful married man I might have been seriously tempted to follow up. Life is full of 'what might have been' isn't it.

That course at Sandgate was probably one of the last to be held there as the whole South-East District Training operation was moved shortly afterwards to Grosvenor Hall in Ashford, a centre recently vacated by the Met Cadet School when it moved to its new premises in Hendon.

ii

Returning to Guildford nick after the course I was now a qualified instructor and something of a wasted asset locally so within a couple of months I found myself transferred to the Training Department at HQ.

Here. to my enormous surprise and pleasure I found my old probationer training sergeant Owen Allard who having completed his service had found himself a great little niche as a civilian. Owen was responsible for producing visual aids of all types, not only for us trainers but also for anyone else (more often than not the Chief Constable) who had some sort of presentation to do and needed OHP's or handouts for support. Nowadays of course we'd be using Powerpoint or some similar computer-based tool but this was long before such aids existed.

I was in Owen's office one day when I noticed a poem on the wall which made a real impression on me. It's called the Indispensable Man.

Some day when you're feeling important.
Some day when your ego's in bloom.
Some day when you take it for granted
You're the best qualified in the room.
Some day when you feel that your going would leave an unfillable hole,
Just follow this simple instruction and see how it humbles your soul.

Take a bucket and fill it with water.
Put your hands in it up to the wrists.
Take them out and the hole that remains
Is a measure of how you'd be missed.
You may splash all you like as you enter, stir up the water galore,
But stop and you'll see in a moment, it looks just the same as before.

The moral of this is quite simple.
Do always the best that you can.
Be proud of yourself but remember,
There is no indispensable man.

It would be disingenuous in the extreme to claim this became a guide for my life but it has been something that has almost always been floating just below the surface and has undoubtedly helped me to keep things in perspective from time to time. It reminded me of the day I was station Sergeant at Guildford. The former Chief Constable Herman Rutherford was in the practice of parking in the police station yard while he went shopping and then wandering in like he owned the place to chat to Ron Hagley the Chief Superintendent. He walked in one day and as he disappeared towards Hagley's office the young station officer said *"Who's that old bloke think he is?"*

I said *"A yesterday man but he hasn't realised it yet."*

So there I was. A training sergeant at force HQ. *"Stage two complete."* I thought smugly. I could now expect to settle down there happily for a couple of years maybe, to consolidate my position. Then I could begin to think about how I might push myself into position for the next promotion step to Inspector. The Fates it seems had another plan and not one that was going to please either me or Denise.

I had been working in the training office for a couple of months when we were asked to provide a volunteer to go on the staff at the Ashford Training Centre in Kent to which the general reaction was along the lines of *"Stuff that"* I wasn't entirely sure why no-one seemed to want the job but I certainly didn't as I'd had more than enough family disruption so I kept my head down too.

The next word came direct from the Chief's office and was along the lines of *"I will have a volunteer or I'll come up and nominate someone"* Apparently there was a Kent police house available near the coast at Hythe which was only about a thirty minute drive from the centre.

Still nobody volunteered but several were looking at me and the Chief Inspector suggested it might be quite nice for me to go and build up my experience and *"Wouldn't a year down by the sea be nice for the family?"*

I was being manoeuvred into a corner with the arguments that I had only been in the office a very short time and so far had no regular classes of my own. I wasn't in my own house and my children were not yet of school age so *"Surely you wouldn't mind a spell on Central Service and the experience will look good on your record."*

I should really have stuck to my guns on this one but there was merit in what he said on both counts. Central Service experience was something that several successful colleagues had under their belts and the idea of living by the sea for a while was not unattractive so I went home and talked it over with Denise.

I was pleasantly surprised when she agreed, even seemed quite keen on the idea so I put my head up and a month or so later in September '73 we moved to a Kent Police house on the western edge of Hythe near Folkestone. The sea was only about four hundred yards away – once you'd walked through the army ranges (when the red flag wasn't flying).

The house was absolutely fine, a fairly tidy three bed semi with a garden. There was a bus at the end of the road for the five minute ride onto Hythe itself for main shops but within a few minutes' walk there was a small local centre for convenience shopping including a chippy.

We were easily able to get Robert into a primary school. It was in Hythe but as Denise had the car it was easy enough to do apart from the fact he didn't like the nuns. They scared him. Maria, our delightful little daughter was growing up fast but still only three years old so not ready for school.

So a few days to settle in and I went up to Ashford to do a kind of pre-visit and introduce myself to the Commandant, Chief Superintendent Jim Kirk who was also a Surrey man on secondment to the centre. He was a really nice guy, extremely smart but very chilled, in fact the day I was ushered into his office he was in civvies which included jeans and a pair of 'cowboy' boots up on his desk. I thought *"I think I might like this sort of regime."* especially when he started to tell me about the staff volleyball team that he also played in and the generally relaxed set-up he ran for the staff once away from the students.

The bolt came when he told where my room was. Room! What room? The room I would apparently be living in and hadn't I realised the post was residential? I told him absolutely not and that this was the very first time anyone had intimated such a thing. Having been given a Kent house for my family it seemed reasonable to assume I would be living with them.

Jim Kirk was furious I had not been told and we both concluded it had been a 'convenient' oversight to get the post filled with the minimum of disturbance to the training branch back at Surrey HQ. I felt so totally stuffed and could see that he was sympathetic although he clearly didn't want his tenure as Commandant to me marred by a big bust-up with Surrey HQ so he explained how things worked and talked me through some options.

Instructor posts were residential for two good reasons. One was that they were expected to develop a rapport with their class of students and to be available for tutorials and welfare or problem solving sessions out of class hours. The second was that there was a duty officer rota in order to ensure that for safety and emergency reasons there was always a responsible member of staff on call. Well I could see all that but not that it helped my own situation.

Jim then said that in the circumstances and if it were kept unofficial, he would be happy for me to go home one night mid-week if that would help me and Denise to at least try it and see how things panned out.

The other available option was to cry 'foul', kick up a big stink and demand to be returned to Surrey forthwith claiming misrepresentation and imagine what that would do to my future prospects. This was not said at all as a threat but simply suggesting I take a reality check and at least just give things a try.

Denise was predictably and justifiably incandescent. Wasn't it bad enough to be down here with the kids in the middle of nowhere, away from her family and now she had to live by herself. Why couldn't I just be a guy that did a job like anyone else and come home at the end of a day and play with the children?

She had a point and I said we could turn it all around and go back if that's what she wanted. She said of course that was what she wanted but was also very aware that it would probably be disastrous work-wise especially with no guarantee of whereabouts in the county we might be dropped down. So both very disillusioned with the whole scenario we agreed that we would try it. She could drive me back and forth as necessary but at least that way she had the car to use.

17 ASHFORD

i

Grosvenor Hall was lovely. A classic red brick Victorian mini-mansion set in some fifty acres of grounds that had once been gardens and an arboretum. Like a number of other police establishments I visited at different times it had seen several incarnations over the years. Originally called Bockhanger Hall it was built in 1875 for a local banker in Ashford and occupied as a home until 1913 when it became a TB sanatorium with patients being transferred from other premises known as Grosvenor House in Sandgate, hence the name change. It was curious too that almost all the police students and staff there would also at some point have spent time at Sandgate for their initial training as I had and also just a couple of months previously for my teaching practice.

Developing antibiotics in the fifties rendered the old style sanatoriums largely redundant so it became a conference centre for several years. The Met Police took it over in '61 as their Cadet Training school installing new accommodation blocks and superb sports facilities including the gymnasium and pool complex. Sadly most of the gardens disappeared under the parade ground and playing fields but happily most of the specimen trees were preserved.

In '73 the new Met Training Complex opened at Hendon and Grosvenor Hall was once again redundant but not for long. Police continuation training in the region was being done at Nutfield in Surrey which was no longer adequate for the numbers involved so that all moved to Ashford the year before I did.

And so it began. I was one of five or six sergeant instructors drawn from different counties including Mick Wayland from Surrey, two from Kent and another from Hampshire. There was also an Inspector and Chief Inspector plus a Superintendent as Jim Kirk's deputy.

Other staff included a PTI from the City of London and a Drill and First Aid instructor also from Surrey. They were a happy well-knit team and I felt comfortable almost immediately with one small niggle. One of the guys from Kent did actually live at home because he was in a police house in Ashford that was just a few minutes away so I guess it was fair enough but it rankled all the same. He also had a room at the centre where he laid his head on his 'duty officer' days.

Being an inexperienced newbie I didn't have a class of my own initially but sat in on classes with other instructors to get the feel of things and spent the rest of my time ploughing through the curriculum and preparing reams of lesson notes that I would need for my own class who would be arriving on site with the next intake in about three weeks.

In order to assess my ability and confidence the Inspector got me to teach several classes for which I had notes prepared and sat in the back as an observer which was really nerve-racking.

What I didn't know was that my colleagues next door in the instructors' office were also keeping score. But for them it was the number of laughs I got or the jokes that fell flat. I discovered my score was minus two after the first session but it did get better as I found my feet. Given what I said about not being a natural extrovert it was surprising how much I enjoyed the experience.

It's all about control. You have to be sure of your subject and remember that no matter how lacking in confidence you feel, you always know more than the students do. (If not, you certainly are in the wrong place) And it gets better with time too as you learn the script so that after a while it just becomes one big ego trip. You are the star of the show, you know it all and you have them laughing at your jokes and hanging on your every word. What could be better? Not a lot really.

For the first few months all our students were male constables because the girls went to a segregated training centre at Ryton where I had done my instructors training. That too was 'rationalised' and also complying with the move away from treating male and female constables differently they were all brought under the same roof. Dormitories were still very separate of course. That would have been far too risky but I understand not impossible. Hormones are powerful chemicals. Enough said I think.

The arrival of women in the classes was quite a challenge for the instructors though. With a class full of male students it was not so necessary to watch one's language or be too politically correct (not that I remember the phrase even existing at the time). But with the arrival of the new breed of 'liberated and emancipated young females' it was a bit like walking on egg shells to begin with until we realized that far from being shrinking violets most of them could trip out a pretty rich vocabulary themselves.

Of course the arrival of women on site did raise another issue, namely fraternization between the sexes. I think it was more or less assumed that things would happen between students and while it was notionally 'off-limits' at least if we had laid out the ground rules then we had rather passed responsibility over to them. However, the big issue we were all warned very seriously about was inappropriate relationships between staff and students.

Most of these were horny confident twenty somethings and it happened regularly that word would get back to us that this or that female had the hots for her instructor. Now if that wasn't a situation ripe for exploitation I don't know what was so we had to be very careful about not allowing ourselves to get in a situation which could suggest anything improper was going on. We were all very clearly advised that any such behaviour was sure to put us on 'the nine o'clock bus' back to our forces. Well dabbling with the affections of student police officers was one thing but the guy whose feet certainly did not touch the ground was found *'in flagrante'* with his tongue down the throat of a very pretty teenage girl who unfortunately for him happened to be the Deputy Commandant's daughter.

Although we were there on duty for the basic eight hours or so it was hardly an arduous existence because our own students were often taught by other specialist instructors or they would be having drill, first aid or any of the other things that meant we were not required for an hour or two at a time. Initially as I said, I had lots of preparation to do but after a while we could almost be at a loose end. This is where the sports facilities came in useful. It was great to be able to go off for a swim or a run during the day and sometimes Jim Kirk would wander into the office looking for someone to play squash or badminton. Followed up by a sauna and shower it really was a pretty ideal working scenario.

There was a very comfortable staff lounge in the main house where we all went for morning coffee, a doze after lunch or a few hours of TV in the evening. We certainly made a point of being there on Thursday evenings. As you can imagine, a bunch of guys away from their partners were more than ready for our weekly dose of Pans People, the beautiful and sometimes not so subtly provocative Top of the Pops dancers with legs up to their armpits.

I think the continuation courses were four weeks and there were always two courses running. The Junior and Senior, which meant that every couple of weeks there was a passing-out parade. On the night before, the centre used to put on a formal dinner and disco for the departing course with the junior course doing the necessary menial setting-up and clearing-down afterwards.

These were on Thursdays but the meals were served early enough for us to get back to the lounge for Pan's People before re-joining the students for their disco.

Some of the instructors, me included, used to pop into the bar on the odd evening for an hour or so during the course just for a sociable half pint with the students to prove we weren't totally aloof. End-of-course dances though were a bit different. Our responsibility was almost over with the departing lot so we felt we could relax a bit and naturally our students always wanted to buy us a thank-you drink or two.

My poison at that time was gin and tonic after a meal and there were several occasions when I turned up in the bar to find not just a couple but six or seven lined up waiting for me. I drank a few of course, too many probably, but it is surprising how adept one can become at 'circulating' and in the process disposing of surplus liquor into the odd pot plant, into a fire bucket, out of the window or even someone else's glass.

Sometimes Denise would come up but it wasn't very easy to find someone to babysit the children and not much fun when she then had to leave me there for the night only to pick me up again on Friday. Although on a few occasions if I wasn't duty officer I did go home and drive myself back early in the morning. It was a bit of a performance though so eventually she stopped coming to the discos.

ii

So that was how it went for a few months with me getting home midweek and doing my best at weekends to make up for the time away by doing as much as possible with Denise and the children. She was far from happy at the set-up and frankly I didn't blame her and actually suggested after about six months that we should pack it in and ask to terminate my secondment early. We both knew this would do my career prospects no good at all and to give credit where due it was Denise who said *"No. Let's see it out and hope it's worthwhile eventually."*

Having said earlier that the house was fine, well so it was but the location, whilst convenient, had its issues. Located on the western edge of Hythe, it was a bit out on a limb and the back of the house faced out onto the flat open space of Romney Marsh. Lovely for sunsets but very exposed. The wind seemed to gather its forces around the power station at Dungeness and accelerate howling, across the marsh to our back door. And if the wind wasn't blowing, the military were up at the end of the road on the ranges shooting their machine guns until late evening.

So, all in all not an ideal situation but she had agreed to come in the first place and also to stay. Our relationship was suffering though without a doubt which was hardly surprising. We're all different I know and need different things from our relationships. Some wives seem quite self-sufficient and able to deal with running the show whilst their partners are away. Thousands of military wives are an example of this although that's not to say they exactly like it. Unfortunately my wife was not one of those.

One weekend I was at home when I saw some photos on the table that I didn't recognize showing the children enjoying fun-fair rides. They told me 'Uncle Melvin' had been to visit and taken them out. Melvin was the former boyfriend who it turned out had been around a few times over the time we'd been together and whilst I was away.

Nothing to worry about apparently according to Denise. Just an old flame who was now just a friend. Obviously I couldn't say it was otherwise but must confess to a certain unease, not least because she had chosen not to mention it, and I made even greater effort to make my time with the family more meaningful.

Unfortunately, although I was enjoying the work a lot and feeling pretty confident in my instructor role, things at home didn't really settle down. Denise became more unhappy and depressed so that in August 1974 I put in a request to cut short my posting to Ashford and return to Surrey citing my wife's unhappiness at my absence from home and separation from her family and friends.

Although nothing was actually said I understood only too well having seen it with other officers, that my card would now be marked '*domestic issues*' which would undoubtedly take some getting over if I was ever to return to the favoured '*officer with potential*' status. However for the time being the main concern was my wife and children.

We were offered a choice of a couple of police houses and chose one in West Horsley which was a lovely rural location with a large garden and only half an hour or so from our respective parents. Work-wise, I was to return to instructor duties at the HQ training department.

The house was really nice but needed a bit of decoration and the garden was a quite overgrown. In fact on the day we moved in I was wading through the long grass when a bee went up my trouser leg and stung my thigh which resulted in me running indoors yelping and pulling my trousers off as I went which had the children laughing and Denise looking at me as though I'd lost it completely.

Located behind Cranmore School at West Horsley, it was one of four police houses and our neighbours included dog handler Pete Morley, traffic officer John Hoey and immediately next door was PC Dave Wilson who worked on the Horsley section. Both Dave and John had young children for Rob and Maria to play with which was a further improvement on Hythe.

I was still quite firm in my religious beliefs at that time and wanted to adhere to the promise we'd made to bring the children up in the faith and so we found places for them both at St Thomas of Canterbury Primary at Merrow. It worked very well and a bus picked them up each morning at the end of the lane although in retrospect if they had gone to school in the village Denise would have become part of the school gate gathering and got to know a few more people.

The garden at Hythe had been quite small which was just as well with me not being around to do what was necessary but our new one in Horsley was a decent size so we set to work and over time had quite a productive vegetable plot as well as plenty of space for the children to play. Because the move was for so-called welfare reasons we had qualified for removal allowances so new curtains and carpets appeared in the main rooms whilst those dragged from Hythe were once again hacked about and cannibalized to fit elsewhere. As I have always been reasonably practical with skills picked up from Dad I set to and decorated most of the house inside which gave it a significant lift and in quite short order it seemed we had settled in and established a nice comfortable home in what could only be described as a really lovely semi-rural situation. How great was that?

18 LETHAL FORCE

i

So after just a year I found myself back in the Training Department at Mount Brown where, because my return had not been anticipated in the staffing plan, I found myself a bit of a spare part.

Being an extra pair of hands I got the dogs-body job which was the production of General Order Amendments. The force General Orders was similar to the Metropolitan Police Instruction Book which we'd had to study so hard when I joined the service first time round. Described to us then as a catalogue of a thousand cock-ups – probably many more actually; this was the book of orders or instructions for any given situation. Written ideally before but more often after the event when someone has done it all wrong; some wise guy in an office with the benefit of research and time to think writes an instruction for how it should be done right. Hindsight, as they say is a wonderful thing.

At a user level GO Amendments were a pain too. Everyone had their own personal copy of this two inch thick tome (just to ensure nobody could ever say *"I didn't know"*) and it was your individual responsibility when a fist full of amendment sheets fell in your tray to painstakingly go through the book either replacing pages or amending text as required. Supervisors then had to check it had been done which was pretty time-consuming all round. I'm describing this simply to illustrate at least one positive benefit to the introduction digital communication and the paperless (which it still isn't) office. Today, instead of there being some two thousand bible-like tomes sitting in cupboards or propping up table legs and needing amendment, there are NONE. There is only a digital version (plus a few back-ups if they're wise) sitting on a computer file and available to every member of the force intranet at the click of a mouse thus removing all the costs associated with the printing, distribution and supervision required under the old paper system.

So, the production of these routine amendments was the job everyone hated but was supposed to contribute to more or less equally although in reality most people managed to be too busy apart from the newbie in the office or me on my return from Ashford. However it didn't last long as an escape route presented itself almost immediately and I jumped at the opportunity.

By this time Arthur Crawford was no longer doing the firearms training which had been taken over by Inspector Dave Smith occasionally assisted by Sergeant Dave Stone, one of the other instructors. It was felt a further instructor was needed for when either one of them was not available and being keen on shooting both in the force and as a hobby I popped my head up and got the job.

The first thing I needed was a reclassification shoot just to confirm I could still do the business after which I then started assisting with the instruction which took place on the army ranges at Pirbright. We had a great relationship with the military and it was the matter of a moment to get me issued with a set of NATO fatigues in the classic green/brown camouflage pattern which was eminently more suitable for lying around on the ground than my police uniform or the horrible oversize and much used blue boiler suits our trainees had to wear.

The police use of firearms has been much in the news over the years, more often than not when something has gone wrong. From all one hears it would seem that the physical and psychological selection of police marksmen as they are now generally called, at least in the media; is taken very seriously. However it certainly wasn't always so at the time I first became involved.

Local divisional commanders were like mini Chief Constables and guarded their autonomy jealously in all matters including the appointment of their divisional firearms officers. You might think this was as it should be but it is also important to recall that none of these senior officers were authorized themselves and at that time none had received any training in the tactical deployment of armed officers.

Who then, in the event of an armed incident, was running the show? A very good question and one to which at that time it was difficult to give an answer. It was true that some senior officers had military experience but the military and police contexts are so different as to make that experience virtually irrelevant.

The upshot of this situation was that as instructors we were not uncommonly faced with having to train someone who for one reason or another we judged unsuitable.

We always gave the same introduction I described previously being given by Arthur Crawford about the serious risk of perhaps having to take a life and gave people the chance to opt out on moral grounds. That was not a problem as a divisional senior officer could hardly contest a conscientious objection. I only ever knew of one person who did. The police back then was a very macho organization and very few would have wanted to look weak

However some, and not just younger officers, were clearly not appropriate because they were either too headstrong, excitable, frivolous, unable to concentrate and take instruction, excessively nervous or simply couldn't hit a barn door at ten paces. We even had one student who would turn the gun on himself and look down the chambers to check how many shots he'd fired!

Because of the rank structure it was very difficult for us to tell a divisional commander whose reaction was more likely to be *"I selected the man, now you train him. That's your job"* Fortunately, being a headquarters based department we had access to the very senior hierarchy so it was a relatively simple matter to put a word in the right direction for the problem to be solved but it was something we tried to avoid because going over someone's head usually leaves a bit of resentment that can fester.

A well-established tenet of command theory is that commanders need an overview that it is hard to see whilst getting involved at ground level and for that reason the senior officers of the force were not firearms trained as they were never expected to get their hands that dirty so to speak. This is a practical view and not as cynical as it may sound but there were exceptions as there are in all organisations.

I referred before to the way in which the service tended to throw up some highly individual characters and one of these was Maurice Jackman, the Chief Superintendent at Woking whose division covered the Guards

Depot at Pirbright. Maurice was a larger than life individual; very much a man's man, popular with his officers, loud-mouthed and extremely likely to call a spade a f**king shovel which made it the more surprising that he was often to be found dining in the Officers Mess at the Depot. Whether it was for his entertainment value or because he was truly liked I've no idea but he was very well connected there. Come to that so were we and the police instructors could always guarantee to eat in the Sergeant's or officers mess if sandwiches from the tea wagon out on the range didn't appeal.

One day when I was at Pirbright, in addition to the expected batch of constables and sergeants expected, Maurice Jackman turned up to participate on the grounds, as he put it, that he should be able to do everything his men were asked to do. Sounds reasonable and just the sort of comment to appeal to the canteen culture back at Woking nick so one up to him I guess. But Jacko fairly predictably had to do better than that. He'd been to the armoury where he had been given a military issue Browning automatic for his own use but in addition he had persuaded one of the army trainers to bring a couple of machine guns to the range so we could see the damage they could do and maybe have a go ourselves.

Well we did have a go and enjoyed it hugely and I suppose it was useful in illustrating the devastating damage such weapons can wreak and thereby discourage any silly heroics. But it also put our class back by the best part of an hour which was annoying. However, fair do's to Jacko, he listened to instructions, observed range discipline and safety practice and went ahead and qualified despite the fact he would be unlikely to ever draw a weapon operationally.

During the year I was away from Headquarters there had been much discussion around the further development of the police use of firearms. The impetus for this had been the wave of terrorism and hijacking of the early seventies including the attack by the Red Army Faction on the Israeli Olympic team at Munich airport in 1972.

As the Surrey force area included Gatwick at that time questions were being asked about how we would respond to such an event. This together with the realization that a few policemen with pistols (effective practical range about 40 yards in the hands of a very good shot) was probably inadequate in a heavily armed terrorist confrontation. There was much discussion about how we could deal with, for example, a terrorist threatening a hostage at the top of aeroplane steps a couple of hundred yards away. If that offender had to be 'taken out' we had neither the equipment nor skill to do the job.

It was decided that there would be a force sniper unit when, quite coincidentally, local boundary changes meant we lost the airport to the Sussex force at almost exactly the same time. On the basis that airports were not the only possible venue for terrorist incidents the training went ahead anyway and I found myself as one of those nominated for the course. Frankly we were pretty well punching in the dark around the whole subject and there was nowhere really to go for reference as most forces were in the same predicament or even further behind so the whole thing was more or less made up on the hoof.

The first thing that happened was the purchase of appropriate weapons which was also pretty much guesswork. The force eventually purchased half a dozen Parker Hale Safari, heavy barrelled 0.762 mm rifles. Basically they were target rifles; the weight making them very steady if a bit difficult to move with and they were also a favoured weapon for military snipers. These had an effective range of up to 900 yards so in theory a shot of 200-300 should be well within the capability of a trained marksman.

The next thing was the training which involved two weeks lying out on the ranges at Pirbright honing our skills. The sun shone and despite it being October it was a very pleasant interlude altogether. There were a dozen of us to be trained and the idea was that we would work in interchangeable pairs, one acting as shooter and the other spotting the target and reporting the hits or misses as appropriate.

To my delight I found myself partnered with PC Gary Hyldon who had been one of my constables on the section at Guildford. What I hadn't known then was that he was a highly experienced marksman and member of the British Deer Society with one of the very few 'open' firearm certificates issued for stalking and culling in any part of the country. The boot of his car was like a small armoury with heavily secured racks for up to about four rifles all of which he explained had a different purpose.

His knowledge and skill was consummate and I could not have had a better partner. In this context rank ceased to be an issue and as a pair we were on first names which I think at first he still found a bit awkward but I insisted.

"Gary if we're likely to get shot at together the least you can do is call me Brian.
"Right Sarge, I mean Brian." He replied

Rifle and pistol shooting are very different skills especially in the police context. Going along to the local gun club and shooting circular targets is all about careful sighting and high scores. Combat shooting with a pistol on the other hand, being a close quarters skill, is rarely about sighting at all but more about developing mobility and an instinctive point-and-shoot rapid fire ability.

Working as a sniper is also a very different experience for two reasons. Firstly with regard to the skills and knowledge required; to get a good shot at two or three hundred yards is certainly not simply a question of aim and shoot. Bullets at that range do not fly straight. Gravity comes into play and they have a falling trajectory which has to be understood and allowed for. As does the effect of side wind which has to be judged by observing such things as cloud direction and speed, how a plume of smoke drifts or the movement of leaves. It is a very precise skill which might have to be brought into play very quickly in an urgent situation and can only be developed by hours and days or ideally months of practice which realistically we were never going to have.

The second difference about the sniper role, for me at least, is that it is a very deliberate process. Looking down a telescopic sight at a human target in the cross-hairs you cannot help but be conscious of the fact that, all other things being equal, when you squeeze the shot off that person will almost certainly die a fraction of a second later. That does rather concentrate the mind. Perhaps the fact that I am even saying this means I am temperamentally unsuitable. Can a Special Forces sniper in Afghanistan for example afford such thoughts or do his targets cease to be people at all? For me the only way to rationalize it was that lethal force was always a last resort and could only be justified in protection of another innocent life. Fortunately I never had to make that decision but I think I could have.

We did quite frequent re-training and then one day were sent on a Tactical Sniper course. This was all about how to get into a good firing position which meant being able to move with your rifle and I'm not talking about standing tall and ambling about from one place to another. No this was covert movement with a three foot long lump of steel and wood hanging around your neck.

It was physically very difficult but also hilarious to see us learning to do the elbow crawl through tussock grass and muddy ditches as we tried to keep our heads down whilst allowing enough space beneath us for the guns to hang. We found muscles we never knew existed. And God help anyone who managed to stuff the end of his gun barrel with mud. This was not just about care of the weapon because if unnoticed a blocked barrel could have lethal consequences for the shooter.

These were very interesting and happy times for me as both trainer and student but in honesty it was a bit of a pantomime. I'm pleased to say that today the police use of firearms has become a highly specialist operation with a very broad range of equipment and intensively trained personnel who do a great job on our behalf.

ii

The significance of all this firearms training was accentuated by the occurrence of the much written about Guildford Pub Bombings on 5th October 1974 which was actually while the initial rifle course was going on. We had absolutely no involvement at the time as it was run as a major incident by operational personnel from Guildford on the day and subsequently by CID as a major crime investigation with the unhappy results that need no further discussion here. Apart, that is, from a related experience I had a few weeks later.

I was back home in Horsley one evening and about to jump in the bath when a knock came at the door which I opened to find one of the Horsley officers there with a message that I was to report immediately to Guildford police station for an armed operation. This was the moment you hope will never come because for all the expertise and confidence you gain blasting away at cardboard cut-out villains nothing really prepares you for the feeling that *"This time it's for real"* and the further thought that *"It's just possible I might not come back."*

I headed off to Guildford nick where I joined a bunch of other authorized firearm users to be issued with our revolvers and spare ammunition. There were quite a few of us plus several busy looking CID officers and some senior ranks from HQ that I recognized and some that I didn't that I guess were probably Special Branch or military intelligence. As there was no room in the building large enough to do the briefing we were told to gather in the bar and await instructions. There were the usual wisecracks aimed at relieving tension mostly related to taking the chance to grab a drink as it might be our last etc. but for the most part people seemed content to wait quietly. The issue of firearms was not exactly run of the mill in Surrey and looking around I couldn't see a single officer who I knew had ever been on a live call-out like this. I knew what I was thinking and I guessed most of them were in the same place.

Half an hour went by before we were joined by several senior ranks including the Deputy Chief Constable who did no more than bought everyone a stiff drink *"to settle us down."* he said, and someone else said *"Fucking hell. We're not coming back."* and everyone burst out laughing. Well, you'd have to laugh wouldn't you? Dish out a load of guns and then give everyone a drink. Sounds like a perfect strategy! I sincerely hoped the bosses had a better plan than that.

Tension broken we got on with the briefing. It transpired that following intensive combined enquiries by the Met, Surrey CID and SB, information had come to light indicating several addresses where suspects for the bombings could be hiding. Most were in London but I think a couple where elsewhere and the intention was to raid them all simultaneously to see what we could turn up. We were divided into smaller squads and I was with a group of about twelve who were going to London.

It was something like a small army on the move as we left Guildford around one in the morning in a raggle-taggle mix of cars and mini-buses and a variety of clothing ranging from uniformed sergeants and pc's like me to some very stylish looking detectives with classic seventies hair styles and a couple of military types from the bomb squad.

We arrived at Brixton nick in the small hours where there followed a further wait for an hour or so whilst the bosses discussed tactics I presumed. Eventually my group was split into three sub-groups with two shooters in each. And then, 'Joy of Joy' I learnt that the property my small group was heading for was believed to contain a couple of bombers who had vowed never to be taken alive, promising to blow themselves and all round to kingdom come. Just what I wanted to hear! I thought *"Why on earth had I ever got involved in this daft shooting business?"*

About four am. and we move off again in our van. The 'two musketeers', Detective Superintendent Ron Underwood from Surrey, a Met D/I , a couple of DC's and a Major from the Bomb Squad who is the explosives and booby trap expert. I sincerely hope so. We park up on a corner and on the stroke of 4.30 set off up the stairs of this tenement building to arrive on a landing outside the target flat.

"*All ready then?*" says Ron; a nod of assent all round and we're off. None of your modern ram-type lock breakers back then. No, a good old-fashioned drop-kick by the D/I but unlike the doors in the films this one stands firm while the D/I bounces back, arms flailing and smacks Ron Underwood in the mouth so we have blood drawn before the door is even open. Another kick does the business and we are into a long unlit hall. The major's in front with me and another shooter on his shoulder as we inch our way along the hall eyes straining along the tunnelled beams of our torches.

Suddenly a sound to our right and we drop to the standard crouch firing position as a door begins to open and together my partner and I shout "*Armed Police. Stand Still.*" Ever so slowly it seems the door continues to open revealing what at first appear to be three points of white in the darkness which then resolve into two large white eyes and the dazzling teeth of a large naked black man who raises his hands and drops to his knees with the word "*Jeeesus!*" It's really weird how our brains work because even in that most intense of moments I find myself thinking that this must be pretty much how he looks when attending the local church, except of course he would have his clothes on.

Clearly we had not struck gold, and I for one was very relieved. Calm as you like the Met D/I says "*Don't worry mate. It's only the police. Looks like we got the wrong place. No worries OK? Oh, and sorry about the door. Just send the bill to the Commissioner. He'll sort it,*" And with that we march out of his life with the only proof it wasn't all a dreadful nightmare being the door jamb split from floor to ceiling. Several of the other raids apparently met with similar negative results although arrests were made on a couple but I never did discover how significant they were.

iii

In view of the circumstances that had brought me back from Ashford my game plan was to keep my head down and work hard to re-establish the credibility I felt I'd lost by returning early. Pleased to still be working at headquarters where you could make contacts and create impressions by doing a great job I often mulled over what my next move might be to push myself onwards and hopefully upwards.

With my nice regular office hours and job that interested me, the school run organized and the kids happily settled; life at home took a distinctly positive turn for the better. Our personal relationship improved no-end and we were within reach of our respective families and friends again so everything appeared to be on a more even keel again.

Denise took an interest in the garden too and between us we soon had it sorted with new beds prepared for planting up in the spring. We were also getting to know the surrounding countryside a bit. Horsley lies just on the dip slope of the North Downs, that chalk ridge that runs from Farnham through to Canterbury. Now comprising part of The Surrey Hills it includes those well-known Surrey beauty spots Newlands Corner, Ranmore Common and Box Hill so beloved of the Victorian Londoners seeking a little rural escape from the pollution and noise of the capital. Just a short walk from home the Sheepleas Woods were a wonderful area of beech woods where we quite often walked with the children.

I got to know those of my neighbours who worked the Horsley section and their Sergeant John Forbes who lived in the police house next to the office. Pleasant enough as the rural policing life seemed to be it certainly was not something that figured in the slightest in my career strategy which was a bit unfortunate given the way things were about to turn out.

19 A COUNTRY COPPER

i

They told me it was a career development move. I didn't believe a word of it.

I had only been back from Ashford for about four months although it did feel longer given all that I'd managed to pack into the time but I was hoping that I'd be able to consolidate my training credentials before moving on again. However it apparently wasn't to be.

The Superintendent in charge of Personnel (as it used to be called) said *"We'd like you to take over as the Horsley Section sergeant"*
"But I don't want the job. Not in the least interested." I said
"It'll be a great career move Brian. Another useful experience when you're looking for the next rank." He countered
"Nothing to do with the fact that I'm handy. Already living there. Not going to cost a lot to move me" I retorted sarcastically and just vaguely aware that I was beginning to tread on slightly thin ice vis-à-vis the normal protocols of the rank structure. He chose not to notice.

"Not at all. You're the one we wanted for the job and we'd have moved you from the other side of the county if necessary."
I bit my lip only just managing to avoid an even sharper response but also feeling vaguely flattered despite not believing him.
"It's not public yet but John Forbes is being promoted so a time on the section hasn't done him any harm. Do a good job and it could be your stepping stone to the next rank too."

I said *"I don't get a choice in this then Sir"*
"No not really." He replied. *"It's all set up. We'll get Christmas out of the way and you can take over from Forbes in January."*

ii

So that's what happened. On the second week in January 1975 instead of driving to the office at HQ I walked the couple of hundred yards from my house to the little country police office at West Horsley.

Probably dating from the late fifties or sixties and situated on the edge of a small council estate of similar vintage, the Horsley office was a block comprising just two rooms and a cloakroom and joined on each side to a police house with interconnecting doors. The larger of the two rooms was the general and public enquiry office and the smaller second room was for the sergeant.

The section covered a fairly large area and included the main village of East Horsley with its railway station, quite a number of shops spread over two separate locations along the Ockham Road, parish church, surgery, two or three schools and a couple of pubs. Also within our area were the satellite villages of West Horsley, Effingham and Effingham Junction, each with a similar if smaller range of amenities. The surroundings were a large area of mixed farmland and woods.

At that time Horsley section came under Leatherhead which in turn was part of the Dorking Division. My immediate bosses were the Inspectors and Chief Inspector at Leatherhead who we only saw a couple of times a week at the most so I quickly discovered that the role I had dropped into was highly autonomous. Basically I was the boss as far as managing the policing in that area was concerned and I must say it was quite a good feeling.

Personnel for this small unit numbered no less than five constables, all of whom occupied police houses in the various locations described and which by today's standards was serious overmanning although it didn't feel like it at the time. In fact it was just about sufficient to provide the cover I had to maintain which was from 06.00 to 2400 or preferably 0200 if I could manage it. On the section, there was no need for the highly structured 'Earlies, Lates and Nights' type of rota and as absolutely nothing occurred at night it was clearly more cost effective to concentrate manning levels during the day and evening hours. Given all the above I quickly discovered that the happiest arrangement was for us as a team to decide amongst ourselves when we would work based largely, it has to be admitted, around our social diaries. Provided the section was covered and that no individual was habitually or unfairly creaming off the easy shifts then I was happy and more importantly, so were they.

My five PC's worked their home beat areas by bike or on foot more or less according to their inclination or needs on a particular day. They might also be rostered to cover the public office hours which were just an hour each morning and evening in which case those from the Effingham end of the section would have to bike in to West Horsley. There was also a car on the section which was mine for supervisory use when I was working and which I would allocate on as fair a basis as I could for use by the others when I wasn't on duty. The problem was that human nature being what it is they were all very adept at thinking of reasons they needed to use the car especially in cold or wet weather and frankly who could blame them. I didn't, as I'd done just the same as a PC myself.

Without in any sense demeaning my status as sergeant in charge, I was in no doubt that I was new at this particular game and knew little or nothing about rural policing. So in the same way as when I started newly promoted at Guildford, I was perfectly happy to feed off the knowledge and experience of my team, all of whom had been on the section longer than me. I always felt that it's a very foolish manager who ignores or rides rough-shod over the ideas or opinions of others based on their experience. After all, why reinvent the wheel or fix what's not broken? Actually as an organization the police did it all the time but then so does society.

A rural Section Sergeant

Policing a rural section is a very different experience to working a town such as Guildford for example. Town work is generally busy and police tend to operate a fire brigade type of service – rushing from one job to the next with scarcely a look back. In the villages life was more leisurely and it was very satisfying to be able to spend time with people who called for police assistance and in effect provide something approaching a kind of social service to the community.

A good example of this was in the case of sudden deaths when frequently a bereaved person had a need to talk about their departed family member and this was especially so if they were left alone without close family support. Most of us find it difficult dealing with the grief of others especially when it turns to tears and so the recently bereaved, divorced or otherwise distressed frequently find themselves alone when what they actually need is just to chat and reminisce and maybe weep a little too.

Talking about sudden deaths, I hadn't been on the section very long when I came across a very distasteful little practice that I soon put a stop to. Attending a sudden death where there are no suspicious circumstances the only thing really required is to offer any help the bereaved person might need such as contacting a close friend or relative to come along and provide a little support or perhaps to make the call to an undertaker and get that side of things in motion.

This is precisely what happened one evening when I was on duty with one of my PC's so we went along, took all necessary details and then did indeed make a call to the local undertaker. The bereaved person expressed no preference and agreed that the nearest available would be fine. End of story? Not quite.

A few days later the same PC that I'd been with came into the office and handed me a note. Five or ten pounds I think. I said *"What's that for?"* to which he replied *"It's the undertaker money."*

He then explained that for every callout the undertaker received from the police they paid a 'gift' to the officer concerned. I was horrified, took the money and the other half from the PC and went straight to the undertakers where I returned it and told them in no uncertain terms that it was to stop forthwith. The situation was the more idiotic given that they were the only funeral director in the village or for some distance so it was hardly a question of incentivizing the police to call them ahead of a competitor.

I made sure all my section officers knew where I stood on the subject and that it was to cease. The problem was that apart from being to my mind an abhorrent practice it dropped into a somewhat grey area legally. It was undoubtedly contrary to police discipline regulations which absolutely prohibit the acceptance of any gratuity on the basis that it might compromise an officer's impartiality. However, the law on bribery and corruption (as it was then) talked about the giving and receiving of any consideration in order *"to influence a person to do or reward them for doing anything contrary to the rules of honesty and integrity."* So it probably wasn't actually illegal in those terms but it certainly felt very wrong to me.

It was not an entirely new situation to me though. I had found myself in a similar predicament several years before when as a probationer I was on a two week attachment to traffic department. Without any discussion I was included in sharing the 'commission' paid to the traffic crew by a garage who had been called out to remove a vehicle after an accident. I hated it then but have to confess that I was too unsure of myself to make an issue of it but certainly decided then and there never to be part of that sort of thing again.

The problem with these things, apart from the plain distastefulness of it, is that there is no such thing as a free lunch and one always needs to ask why the giver is doing this. Out of the goodness of their heart? Clearly not. It is absolutely to ensure preferential treatment, as in being the first garage called and of course as a bit of insurance against the day when they need a lever of some sort over the police. It shouldn't come as a surprise, although it did a few years back when some police officers discovered to their acute embarrassment that a particular garage owner actually kept a record of the payments and to whom.

Rules may well be rules but there are undoubtedly occasions when it is better all round to gently bend a rule than rigidly adhere to it and risk giving offence to some good-hearted member of the public. A typical example of this is the arrival on the doorstep of the police station of the odd bottle or basket of fruit or biscuits etc. on Christmas Day. Given anonymously then there is obviously no problem but even when the donor is known surely it is infinitely better to gratefully accept such a gift in the spirit it is intended than to say *"Sorry but we are not allowed to accept gifts. You'll have to take it away."*

So bending the rule a little further, how about this scenario? The law around firearms of any sort is very strict. - No possession without a certificate. One day I had a message from a recently widowed woman at Effingham to call and see her about some guns she had found.

It transpired that following her husband's death some months previously she had started to sort through the attic and found a pair of shotguns which someone told her would have to be surrendered to the police which is what she wanted to do. However when I saw the guns I knew, even with my limited knowledge, that as a matched pair, they were worth quite a bit of money and here she was asking me to take them away for destruction.

I explained that I thought they were valuable and that it was probably a mistake to just hand them in and did she know anyone who used shotguns. Fortunately she did and so on her behalf I called him to come and take possession of the guns until they could be valued. The friend came immediately, removed the guns and I left.

About a month later I had a card through the post with a thank-you note explaining that the guns had been sold for almost two thousand pounds and would I please take my wife out to dinner using the two enclosed £20 notes. I could of course have simply returned the cash which I am certain would have upset her terribly. Alternatively I could have submitted the cash with a report that would probably have resulted in her being interviewed by the local Inspector to make sure everything was 'above board' after which I might even have been allowed to retain the gift. Well, talk about a sledgehammer to crack a nut! I kept the money. Took Denise out to dinner and then wrote telling her where we went and thanking her very much for her kindness. I used to call in from time to time for a cup of tea and was very pleased to see she was doing well in her new situation. She told me a lot about her husband and their life together and how much he enjoyed his shooting. He had to stop as he got older, put the guns away and just forgotten about them. She said the little windfall had made a useful addition to her fairly meagre pension and was very grateful for my advice so I felt it was a good result all round.

Another part of my work as the Section Sergeant was to go along to parish council meetings when invited in order to give the police perspective on local issues such as school crossing patrols, planning applications (much tact required), local crime stats which it has to be said were very low and unlawful parking.

The parking issue was a perennial, cropping up at least a couple of times a year and relating to the long term parking of vehicles on the local shopping parades. This was usually by people heading off to London by train which meant the vehicles were there all day long so it was hardly surprising that the local traders were up in arms.

With only a limited number of officers available it was impossible to maintain a continual police presence in that area and although traffic wardens could be brought out from Leatherhead they could only be spared for very few hours a week. So the cry went up *"Why can't we have yellow lines?"*

I explained that yellow lines were a possibility although they weren't going to appear over night as it required a certain amount of procedure to get a local traffic regulation order. Secondly I explained that even with yellow lines a police or traffic warden presence would be needed for enforcement so manpower and hours available were still an issue. And finally I said *"You need to be careful what you wish for because experience elsewhere has shown that it is often those that call the loudest for such controls that are the first to fall foul of them."*

"Nonsense!" they all cried. *"It's not us."* and I thought *"We'll see."*

About six months later the yellow lines arrived and the games began; literally. On both side of the road there was a service road in front of the shops with several free parking bays but with the remainder of the space restricted by yellow lines to allow some vehicular movement. Also, just behind one of the shopping parades was quite a sizeable free car park that was probably about seventy five yards from the shops but would they use it? No way. The majority would rather park illegally on the nice new yellow lines and take a chance. So whenever a police officer arrived on the parade harassed looking ladies would come hurrying out of shops, smile apologetically, clamber in their cars and drive off and all would be in order. If the officer happened to pop into one of the shops for a chat or a cuppa as if by magic the cars would arrive again only to evaporate as soon as he reappeared. It was a complete pantomime and nobody was taking it seriously so after a couple of weeks we decided that a little action was required. Several of us arrived at the same time and before the smiling ladies could escape we had tickets issued which soon turned the smiles to scowls.

It worked though for a while and it wasn't long before we heard that as predicted several of the local worthy ladies prosecuted were indeed the wives of the very councillors who had bleated loudest for the lines in the first place. Told you so!

The whole thing settled down after a while. We prosecuted any long term parkers who we felt were taking the mickey, the message quickly got back and takings in the station car park no doubt improved. We used to sting one or two of the local ladies from time to time as a reminder or whenever a shop keeper had a moan about his deliveries not getting in, but as for the parish council the matter never reappeared on the agenda.

iii

Quite a large proportion of the work on our country patch was enquiries on behalf of officers at other stations both in and outside of Surrey. These jobs could be interesting but more often were quite run of the mill. They included such things as visiting drivers to take witness statements following road accidents or other incidents, interviewing applicants for firearms certificates which included checking security arrangements for the weapons and sometimes having to go along and report a person for an alleged traffic infringement in another area. More often than not in these cases people professed that they did not recall any incident, their vehicle number having been taken by a witness as they jumped a light or whatever. Our role in these cases was simply to advise that a prosecution was pending and take any statement under caution they may wish to make. All pretty simple but not an interaction guaranteed to promote good police/public relations. The only saving grace was that we could feign a bit of sympathy at their 'misfortune' and blame it on someone else.

One such case stayed with me and led on to other things. I had to visit a woman who had failed to stop for a school crossing patrol in another part of Surrey. No actual danger to children or lollipop lady was alleged other than the simple offence of failing to stop.

Win was a sad looking stick-thin woman with a somewhat haunted look which was scarcely surprising given her history. Apparently two weeks prior to the offence she had come out of Brookwood psychiatric hospital having been admitted there for four months with severe depression following her husband's death the previous year. She clearly had no recollection whatever of the driving incident and was horrified at the allegation, full of remorse but also immensely relieved that no actual damage had been done. Win made a pot of tea and we sat together in her chintzy old-fashioned drawing room while she got the whole of the last year off her chest. As I said before, people need to talk but with the exception of one neighbour who sounded like she was more interested in what she could take from Win, it seemed she lived a very sad lonely existence. Geoffrey, her late husband who had clearly been the centre of her world had been quite a big wheel in the city so finance was not a particular issue but without children or near relatives she was isolated and in my view, well on the way back to Brookwood.

I explained that I had no option but to go through the motions of reporting her for the offence and although I didn't say as much to her I was determined to do what I could to get the matter quashed. I wrote up the interview making it clear that she was certainly not some maniac driver but simply distracted at the time by other circumstances and that as no harm was actually done there was no benefit to be gained by prosecuting her and maybe precipitating a relapse. Two weeks later she phoned me to say a letter had arrived with a caution and that no further action would be taken.

Win's house became another tea stop where I could pass the odd few minutes chatting over this and that and gradually helping her back into the real world. She even offered to babysit our children which worked very well on the couple of occasions we took advantage of the offer and helped her to feel useful again. Prior to losing her husband Win had been a very active long-term member of the WVS but sadly after her breakdown they declined her offer to return which was a real blow to her self-confidence and certainly not what she needed. I thought she deserved better.

An amusing episode associated with Win arose one evening after I'd dropped in on her for a quick coffee and then returned to the office to sign off. The telephone rang and it was Win in tears explaining that there was a bat in her bedroom. I jumped back in the car and returned to her road which as it was now just after ten o'clock caused a certain amount of curtain twitching in neighbouring houses. Win explained that she had gone to bed and a moment later felt something fly past her face, put the light on only to find a bat fluttering around her room.

She was in a bit of a state so I said I'd try to get rid of it and asked if she had a towel or something that I could either throw over it or use to direct it towards the window. So I went upstairs with this huge orange and yellow striped towel, put all the lights on and opened the windows. It was only in retrospect that we really laughed as we imagined how it must have looked to the window-peeping neighbours as I tried to shoo the bat towards the window. "Uniformed police sergeant practices nocturnal rain dance."

Win eventually decided to move back up to Cheshire where they had lived before Geoffrey's work bought them down south. We talked about the risks involved in going back and the difficulties associated with trying to pick up threads of a former life but as she said there was nothing left for her in Surrey anyway so why not. So she moved but it wasn't a great success. Other people and their lives had predictably moved on and with one exception no-one had time for her there either.

I kept in touch and even went up to visit two or three times, the last being after she had sold her house and gone in to a sheltered housing scheme. Win died in 2009.

iv

Unlike a number of my colleagues who thought the Special Constabulary was just a way of *"getting policing on the cheap"*, I had quite a lot of time for the Specials; that band of volunteers who give up their free time in support of the regular force. But I guess I would say that having been one myself during the time between leaving the Met and re-joining the Surrey force.

Most Special Constables with work and family constraints have no option but to restrict their volunteering to weekends and bank holidays which is why they are most often seen helping out with a bit of traffic direction at major events. However the two Specials that lived on the Horsley patch were different and were more than happy to turn out for an evening shift at any time of the year and crew up with a regular colleague on the section car. This was particularly useful during the darker winter months when running a solo car patrol was inherently more risky.

Sadly I don't remember both their names but Bob is the one who is particularly memorable for all sorts of reason. He was a distinguished looking bearded character; about fifty years of age, well spoken, well-educated and so interesting that even a long dark winter evening patrolling the back lanes seemed to pass in a flash.

Bob was actually Robert Alexander von Symes-Schutzmann a member of the Austrian aristocracy. He was and is still better remembered here in England as plain Bob Symes, engineer, inventor, model maker, railway enthusiast and TV presenter of such programmes at Tomorrow's World and Bob's Your Uncle.

Following the annexation of Austria by Nazi Germany in 1938 he left the country with his mother and sister. While they went on via Palestine to the US, Bob travelled to Alexandria where thanks to a letter of introduction from a friend of his father and his ability to speak French, German and Arabic he was signed on by the Royal Navy and saw service in the Mediterranean, eventually rising to the rank of Lieutenant Commander.

After the war he visited the BBC to seek out Monica Chapman a radio producer, in order to thank her for playing the requests he sent in.

The story goes that they went to a concert together and were married two months later eventually coming to live in Guildford and then Horsley.

Bob, Monica and their daughter Roberta became close friends and Denise and I spent several happy evenings in their charming Hansel and Gretel cottage in the woods. There was no mains electricity to the house so power was via a diesel generator. However Bob was an avid steam enthusiast and following a programme he produced at Kew Bridge Engines he was given a decrepit old steam boiler. He had this transported to his home where I helped him restore it and build it into a complete steam driven generator assembly so that at weekends he could fire it up and power the house by steam. We even put in a little train whistle so we could give the occasional blast to go with the large gauge model railway system that ran round his grounds.

I had the privilege of being invited by Bob to join him and his family at the Austrian Embassy in London. This was for his investiture when he was awarded The Knights Cross – First Class in recognition of his work in promoting Anglo-Austrian relations. We were treated to a magnificent banquet with more gold, silver and crystal than I'd ever seen. Then after the meal we moved into the drawing room for a most informal and relaxed reception where at one point I was sitting on a sofa with Bob and his family while the wife of the Austrian ambassador sat chatting on the floor beside me. Quite delightful.

Bob also invited me to go with him on a couple of outings. One was to a filming session in Carlisle and on another occasion I was able to go with him to the BBC studios to watch the whole process of creating the Tomorrow's World programme. Honestly, an hour before transmission time it was apparently such chaos that to my mind there was no way the programme would happen. But of course it did and according to Bob that was pretty much the normal scenario.

Although I didn't particularly share Bob's passion for railways, steam and things mechanical in general have always interested me so we had much in common and we spent many hours together in his workshop in the woods. Bob was a close and dear friend who became a confidant and very supportive in the difficult times later on. Bob died in 2015 and the world is poorer without him but he made ninety and as he would have said himself that wasn't a bad innings.

I was also fortunate enough to meet Sir Barnes Wallis who lived at Effingham. Famous for his invention of the Dam Busters' bouncing bomb, he was a fascinating man to talk to and I remember being in his study where a model of his 'Earthquake' bomb stood beside the desk. This was designed to be dropped from a great height and penetrate the ground at high speed then exploding to create subterranean shock waves to destroy major installations whilst minimizing civilian casualties. Later in the war it was used to disable the V2 factory, bury the V3 guns, sink the battleship *Tirpitz* and damage the U-boats' protective pens at St. Nazaire, as well as to attack many other targets which had been impossible to damage before.

He also worked on designs for hypersonic flight and his ideas around jet intake geometry inspired those eventually adopted for Concorde.

Despite the acclaim he received, Barnes Wallis struck me as a quiet unassuming man and his wife was equally charming and self-effacing. Shopping in the village, if anyone addressed her as lady Wallis she would immediately say *"No. Mrs Wallis please, or better still Mary."*

20 THE HORSLEY HOME FRONT

While my life at work was busy and interesting I found I also now had time for family life. Robert and Maria were growing up fast and becoming more interested and interesting every day. Denise and I made a point of doing as much with them as our limited 'pocket money' could cover but simple pleasures like walking and gardening don't cost a lot and do so much in cementing family ties.

However the initial 'bounce' we'd enjoyed following the move and settling in did not last for Denise and she quite soon complained of being bored and she said *"I want to be something in my own right. I'm fed up with just being known as the sergeant's wife."*

I could understand very well where she was coming from because apart from keeping our home there was little additional stimulus from just being there. So with the children at school and me working it was small wonder that boredom set it. I blamed myself to a degree for insisting that the children travel out of the village to the catholic school in Merrow as a reason for her not getting to know people. But it would have been simple enough for her to go and talk to the neighbours, join a local wives group or an exercise class. After all you can't expect the world to come knocking on your door. She could easily have taken a part time job but that apparently didn't appeal. Anyway, I had an idea to get a bit of interest into her life.

Denise had a very good singing voice and had performed with a band at one point in her teens so when I discovered that there was a theatre group in the village I suggested that she should go along and see if she could get involved. This proved to be a turning point in more ways than I could possibly have imagined.

The Nomad Theatre group was putting on a variety show and more than happy to welcome anyone on board who had a bit of talent. Denise certainly had the talent and finished up making quite a name for herself. I'd never heard her sing properly and was so impressed. She really was very good indeed and naturally this improved her confidence and introduced her to a whole new group of friends that seemed to give her a real lift.

Through the Nomads Denise also got to know Alan one of the theatre group and through him his wife Helen and so as was the way then it wasn't long before we were around each-others houses for dinner and drinks etc. Like Denise, Helen was suffering from a bit of boredom and lack of direction and they both decided to look for part-time work. Their first and as it turned out very brief experience in that direction was in the café at the nearby Royal Horticultural Gardens at Wisley. I think it was less than a week when Denise announced that there was no way she was going to carry on dish-washing and that was the end of that. I never did know if Helen carried on or not. However, work or no work Denise seemed happier and home life seemed once again on a fairly even keel at least as far as outward appearances were concerned.

Indoors though, things weren't so great between us. I loved her so much but felt powerless to solve what was clearly a developing situation. The only thing I felt able to do was just try to be the perfect husband; caring, practical, helpful, considerate, affectionate: all the things in fact that I'd observed in my father and imagined would work perfectly for me.

Whilst the theatre group had enhanced our local network considerably we were also still in touch with my friends Dave and Dick. Dave was settled in a long term relationship with a lovely girl called Lesley and we saw them quite often. They even joined us on a family holiday one year down at a rented cottage in Devon. I'd mentioned to them that the situation between Denise and I was a bit difficult and so presumably they were more attentive to how things were indoors. I remember one day when we were all sitting in the lounge after dinner and something was needed from the kitchen. As Denise got up to go I said *"I'll do that."* She said she was fine and as she left the room Lesley said to me. *"They're the words most often on your lips. You do too much for her."* Denise came back at that point so Lesley couldn't say any more. She did explain to me later though that what she meant was that my well-intentioned kindness could be part of the problem in that I was not allowing her to be independent.

I thought long and hard about that conversation and hope I changed a bit. It was hard though because my whole social conditioning was based on the male role learnt from my father in the 40's and 50's but we were by then in the era of the 1970's emancipated woman.

Being surrounded by countryside, Horsley was the ideal location in which to have a dog. I can't remember whose idea it was but of course the kids were over the moon at the prospect as indeed I was. We set off to the RSPCA kennels at Chobham and after a false start with one dog that proved completely unsuitable we settled on Barney a mongrel of indeterminate parentage but lovely for all that. He was medium sized and probably had a bit of Labrador with possibly some German Shepherd or Doberman so whilst he was soft enough to pet he also had a strong and quite territorial nature. Barney settled in well with the family and soon longer walks in the Sheepleas Woods and other surrounding areas became the norm of family life.

Friend Dick by that time had one failed marriage behind him and having been made redundant from his rag trade employer was working for himself as a small builder. He'd begun by helping out with his brother's business but soon realised he could probably do better working for himself. Starting small with garden walls and porches he had graduated to erecting houses for Guildway the Guildford based timber frame specialist and had quite a good little business going. I asked him one day where he learnt his building skills and really laughed when he said *"Readers Digest DIY Manual."* At the time of that conversation I was visiting one of his sites and I asked how he worked out his quantities to which he replied *"By counting every brick because I can't bear to see unused materials just buried on site as you do in some places."*

He had also married a second time and although they wanted children, despite their best efforts none had appeared. As Richard had also been unsuccessful in the baby-making stakes with his first wife he had started to wonder whether it was he who had a fertility problem but not taken it as far as getting tested. I don't suppose any man likes to be told he's firing blanks.

Suddenly to the surprise of everyone who knew them Richard's wife Vicki fell pregnant and although the words were never spoken there was a definite suspicion that Vicki may have been seeking company elsewhere. Anyway she had a son that Richard accepted as his own and life went on.

Then he had a real bit of bad luck. He went out one evening to buy a bottle of wine and fell on his driveway cutting his hand severely which meant he was unable to work in any practical way. As he couldn't drive at first he was also for a while unable to get on site to supervise the workers or to follow up new orders and in the space of a very few weeks the business was gone.

Not long after this his second marriage fell apart and rather in desperation he went off to Australia in search of pastures new. During the course of those travelling months he met and fell for Cristina a stunning blonde Scandinavian girl. They decided Australia was the place for them and came back to England to organize things staying for the duration with his sister who happened to be living in Horsley.

Dick had everything he owned from the house plus his trusty Landrover sent by ship and they followed a few weeks later and that was the last I saw of him for a year or more, although I did get the odd letter describing some interesting adventures.

On arrival they decided to drive the length of the east coast heading for Cairns and the Barrier Reef. Apparently at one point they had the Landrover stuck in a bog so while Dick attempted to lighten the load by tossing stuff including the fridge off the roof, Cristina ran around the nearby bush cutting timber to shove under the vehicle to stop it sinking further. They eventually made it up to the Cairns area and decided to settle at Mission Beach. Here they set up a beach caravan called 'Mad Dick's Choock and Chips' knocking out fried chicken and chips for the surfers.

Money came rolling in so they bought a little piece of rain forest and Dick build a stunning Polynesian style house with flyaway roof set up on stilts. All was very well for a while until the Australian Air Force came and built an airfield beside them. No appeal. No compensation. Just noise. Not long after this Cristina left. Dick eventually managed to get some money for it and came back to England where he stayed with his sister again while he re-thought his future.

21 MORE HORSLEY

i

The most serious incident during my time in charge at Horsley was in November 1975 when Mrs Maud Cock an elderly widow was bludgeoned to death in her home at Effingham Junction.

Evidence at the scene was scarce and partially due to the limitations of forensic science at that time no strong leads to a suspect emerged although it was not helped by the subsequent loss of a piece of evidence in the form of a sticking plaster found at the scene. In later years with the development of DNA profiling this might have been significant. There aren't too many unsolved murders in Surrey but sadly, despite extensive and protracted enquiries this was destined to be one of them. I always felt that we as the local officers should have known more to contribute to the investigation. When things happen on your watch so to speak it's hard not to feel some responsibility.

Some of the crimes that crop up can on occasions adopt a sense of the bizarre as in the case of the disappearing potatoes. There were two greengrocers in East Horsley who had deliveries of potatoes twice a week which came by lorry very early in the morning from a firm at Bookham. In fact they usually came well before the staff arrived and so were left on the doorstep in a half hundredweight sack. Not the sort of thing to be that easily pinched you might imagine. Until they were.

The shopkeepers first reported the loss to the delivery firm thinking that perhaps the driver had just passed them by but when it was clear this was not the case we were asked to investigate. Unfortunately the thefts, if that's what they were, appeared sporadic but the only obvious approach was to mount an observation. I came out early with one of my guys and sat up in the car semi-concealed but within view of the doorstep and the first two times nothing happened. We saw the potatoes delivered and then about twenty minutes later the bread was dropped off by the local baker's van but still no thief.

The third day we were there the spud lorry came along as usual and then it happened. As we watched, the bakery van pulled up, dropped off a couple of trays of bread and then quick as a flash the bag of spuds went in the van. We couldn't believe our eyes because the van driver was known to us as co-owner of the bakers in the village. Anyway we started the car and discreetly followed the van to the next shop where the same thing happened at which point we stopped it and asked to look inside where as expected we found the two sacks of potatoes. The guy broke down completely and admitted what he'd done in addition to the several previous occasions and so was arrested for theft. However his greatest anxiety was that he should finish his bread round so as not to let down his own customers. Well that was a bit of an odd call but it wasn't as if we didn't know who or where he was so I agreed and we followed him around to several more shops and then back to his premises where he was properly arrested. When questioned he explained that potato prices had gone a bit high recently and he had given in to temptation and used the stolen spuds in his Cornish pasties. He probably sold them later to the greengrocers.

There was another very interesting family that I got to know on our patch having gone to the house in the first instance on some routine enquiry. Murray Rainey was a racing driver and brilliant mechanical engineer. He was also very short; what back then we might have called a midget or dwarf but in today's politically correct world are more likely to describe as a little person. Given my enthusiasm for cars and motor sport I couldn't really have bumped into a more interesting local resident.

At home in his native Australia Murray developed a winning combination of Cooper chassis and Manx Norton motorcycle engine into a successful Formula 3 and hill-climb car. He quickly established himself as one of the fastest Formula 3 drivers, frequently beating cars in the bigger classes with which they often raced, and twice becoming Australian Hillclimb Champion. He was also passionate about classic Alfa Romeo sports cars of which he had two; one so precious that he kept it in a huge hermetically sealed and insulated box beside his garage.

A skilled engineer, Murray had a very comprehensive workshop and could even cast new aluminium components for his historic collection in his own forge and then finish them to high tolerances on his array of machinery; and all this behind the hedges of an innocuous residential house in a quiet Surrey village.

Murray racing one of his beautifully restored Alfas

If I remember correctly his wife was Joan, a lovely lady of regular stature and their daughter Joy was also a little person. Joy followed in her father's footsteps and carved an impressive record for herself in motor sport and endurance driving as well as being a motoring journalist. I was lucky enough to meet some great people as a Surrey copper and it was set to continue.

I got to make a few faux pas too. Once again in the course of some routine enquiry I had to go to a house where the door was answered by a particularly attractive woman dressed in a beautiful and revealingly cut negligée which to be honest made it quite difficult to concentrate on the matter at hand. Anyway, like the gentleman I am I managed to maintain eye contact, did what I had to and left but then a few days later I had to see her again but this time at her place of work which was a local golf club.

I asked for her at reception and in a few minutes she appeared but this time she came in off the sun-deck wearing a stunning swimming costume. Once again a real challenge in the eye control department. Not quite the end of the story though.

About a week later I was shopping in Bookham and was waiting in a queue outside a shop when a voice behind me said *"Not talking to me today then?"* Turning round I immediately recognized the same woman and in front of the whole queue said *"Sorry Barbara. I didn't recognize you with your clothes on."* I could have bitten my tongue off but was too embarrassed to say more. When I got home I phoned her to apologise for the crass remark but her husband answered so I explained to him and he just fell about laughing. I begged him to pass on my apologies but he said he was sure she would see the funny side of it too. I spoke to her later and am pleased to say she did.

1977 was the Queen's silver jubilee and the Horsley Parish Council were planning a parade that would include a marching band, a British Legion contingent as well as local Scout and Guide groups and any other patriotic flag-wavers who wanted to join in. The plan was that they should march the two miles or so from East to West Horsley. Unfortunately the Inspector at Leatherhead got wind of the plan and for some bizarre reason decided that the local sergeant should lead it. I was horrified and grizzled like mad to him about it but he went on about needing a police presence and I was the perfect candidate being the force figurehead in the area. So that's how it went. And I have never been as embarrassed as I felt for the forty-five minutes or so that I marched the two miles along the centre of the road leading the decidedly motley participants in honour of our Sovereign Lady - bless her. I hope she'd have been impressed.

I lead the 1977 Jubilee Parade from East to West Horsley

As time went on Denise became more involved with the theatre group which seemed to do a lot for her self-confidence although it did mean that she spent quite a lot of time out for evening rehearsals but I felt that was all to the good as far as she was concerned.

I can't remember quite how it happened now but we got an additional PC on the section by the name of Tim Smythe and he moved into a local police house with his wife Anna. She was a confident, attractive and outgoing woman who somehow didn't quite fit with Tim's more retiring personality.

They settled in and, rather unwisely with the benefit of hindsight, I invited Tim to bring Anna round for drinks or a meal one evening. This was with the intention of making them feel welcome but also with the idea of helping to extend Denise's social circle. Unfortunately it couldn't have backfired more spectacularly although it wasn't apparent at first.

The girls got on well and started going to yoga (or some other exercise) classes and after the sessions they used to come back to our house for a coffee, still in their leotards. I don't recall whether I asked the question about what they'd been doing or whether Anna just decided of her own volition to show me. Anyway the next thing is she was down on the floor sprawling and stretching about in front of me still in the skimpy outfit that left very little to the imagination. I hope I didn't give too much away but it was quite an arousing sight.

Anna worked for an American bank who each year gave a summer party for their staff and that year, 1976 I think; it was being held at the Burford Bridge Hotel at Dorking and Anna and Tim invited us as their guests. It was a fantastic day with a super lunch, free bar all day and a barbecue disco in the evening. The swimming pool was available and being a warm day was very popular. There were showers near the pool which were communal and only intended to rinse off the pool water before going to change but I was in the shower when a pair of arms came round me from behind and it was immediately obvious that close up against my back was a curvaceous female body. Husky words whispered in my ear *"Are you having fun Brian?"* and then she was gone.

I don't know what it is about a predatory woman (and I've heard this from other sources) but they seem to sense if a man is unfulfilled in his relationship, although I guess it applies equally well to men of the same type. Anyway it seems I had become a target in her eyes. Whether it was because I was a challenge being the senior officer of the area or whether she simply fancied me, I've no idea and indeed was oblivious of it at the time.

So oblivious in fact, that like the proverbial lamb to the slaughter, I went and offered to give her driving lessons as she had her driving test coming up. A few days later we went off in their car and trundled around the lanes for half an hour or so and then she stopped in lay-by for a break and I started to talk about her driving and points she need to concentrate on. The next thing is she's all over me, kissing me and I must confess for just a few moments I was kissing her back and then common sense stepped in. *"Anna stop it."* I said. *"We can't do this and we both know that so let's just stop before it goes any further."*

She said *"You want me though don't you. I can sense it."* I said *"That's got nothing to do with it. I'm married, I love my wife and I'm Tim's sergeant so this can't happen. End of story. I'm sorry."*

The driving lesson finished in silence and was not repeated and that I thought was the end of it. No so.

A bit later, it may have been weeks or even a couple of months; Denise had arranged to go to the Channel Islands with her mother for a friend's wedding. One evening I was at home, the children were in bed and I was getting rid of some of the ironing in front of the TV when there was a knock at the door. It was Anna. Well, polite as ever; instead of keeping her on the doorstep I asked her in and offered her a coffee which she drank as I carried on ironing and made small talk. Then she started on about how she ached for me to love her and couldn't stop thinking about me and how now was the perfect opportunity for us to go to bed and have some fun.

What I thought was" *Oh my God. Yes please that would be amazing and there's nothing I'd like to do more than make love to you for a fortnight"* but what I said was

"Anna this has to stop. It is absolutely not that I don't find you attractive because I do. Another place, another time, another life and it would be a very different answer. If you've worked out that my marriage could be happier at the moment then you're not wrong. But I am married; I love Denise and the children and despite any difficulties I want my marriage to work so please don't make it any more difficult for me. So can we just stay the friends we are and pretend this conversation never happened?"

Anna could spend money and did so in fine style eventually running them into difficulties. As a result the force welfare department had to become involved with things like attachment of earning orders etc. in order to deal with debts. Tim had always been interested in fraud investigation and eventually transferred to the Met; they split up and Anna went back to the States. Gone but not to be forgotten!

iii

He was a big man and his name was Jim and he was dead in the bathroom when I arrived. Jammed tight in the corner behind the door and almost under the basin. Basil Grant the senior village GP had been and certified him dead although I'm not too sure how he managed to get in because it was a struggle for me. The doctor had been called at about eight in the morning and had left by the time I arrived but had called the report in to the office when he got back to his surgery. He said it was almost certainly a major heart attack but as he hadn't seen him recently there would have to be a PM but better not say too much about that to his wife.

Jim Perkins was eighty-three and his wife Emma was seventy-eight. She was a little woman, barely five feet in comparison to his six feet one and she was remarkably composed sitting in an old leather chair in the back room that served as a kind of kitchen/sitting room.

"I knew he was dead as soon as I heard him fall." she said.. *"It was just so heavy and then total silence."*

Apparently he had felt a bit poorly first thing. They'd had breakfast and as she handed him a cup of tea he'd said *"Thank you Emmie for being so kind to me."* which were his last words before he went into the bathroom to shave.

She made me some tea as I took the necessary details and then said *"When will they do the post mortem? There'll have to be one won't there?"* I said yes there would and it would take a day or two to arrange but being Friday with the weekend coming too it would probably not be until mid-week that the exact cause of death would be known.

She then said *"I must let the pension people know."* and I explained that there was no rush for a few days and asked if she had any family or friends that I could call for her to come along and keep her company and she said *"There isn't anyone I would want to come at the moment. I can manage everything."* Thinking that the most important thing at that moment was to have the body removed I said *"Would you like me to call the undertaker?"* and she said *"Yes that would be helpful. There's one in the village isn't there?"*

I couldn't get over how controlled she was and hated the thought that as soon as I left she would probably break down with no-one to support her. But there's only so much the village bobby can do so I set to and phoned the undertaker and spent the next hour taking a few more details and talking about this and that until they arrived. To spare her the sight of him being man-handled out of the bathroom I took her into the lounge which was an enormous surprise. Given that the house was just a small and rather run down bungalow this room was like a baronial hall. Not huge but a decent size with a high ceiling, oak panelled walls and an impressive carved oak fireplace with wrought iron dog-grate and at one end large windows and a French door opened onto the terrace and a magnificent view towards the Sheepleas woods.

"What an amazing room and what a surprise."

"Yes." she said. *"Peter made it."* I said *"Peter?"* *"Peter was my first husband."* she replied. *"We built the house ourselves. Just the two of us in 1927. He even made the bricks."*

I was fascinated and thought I had to hear more of the story but then was not the time. I told her I would come back the following week once I had the cause of death information which she would need to register the death.

22 EMMA

i

As promised I went back to see Mrs Perkins the following week from which point my life was about to change more than I could possibly imagine. I don't know what it was about this diminutive elderly woman but there had been some sort of almost instant fascination. Whether it was her reserve, control and dignity in adversity or the couple of little items she told me about the house building I don't know but I really felt I wanted to know her better. And so my normal practice of casual call-backs to some of my lonely locals had another name added to the list for future action.

The main reason for my return on that first occasion was to provide the cause of death information that she would need to register Jim's death in Guildford. The PM had as predicted, confirmed death due to a heart attack with no attendant circumstances and was consistent with his age and general state of health.

By the time I got back there she was well organized and with an ancient Underwood typewriter had written letters to relevant authorities, building societies and so on that only awaited the death certificates to be sent off. She knew the procedure and had already arranged an appointment with the registrar in Guildford to get Jim's death registered and pick up the required number of certificates. And still not a sign of tears, only love and gratitude for the twenty-four years they'd had together.

A week or so later I called in again for a chat and a cup of tea and found she had moved things on even further; having received a probate application form which she needed to take to solicitors in Guildford but she was struggling a bit as she had twisted her ankle and walking was painful. It was not so serious but was going to make a trip to town on the bus uncomfortable so I offered to drive her which she happily accepted.

It was summer when Jim died and the large garden they had both tended constantly soon began to get away from her. She was indefatigable at her work in the vegetable plot and almost every time I popped in she would be out there in pretty much any weather. However the lawns and hedges were just beyond her, not physically but just in terms of the time so I offered to run the mower over the grass occasionally

For me it was a joy because the location was so idyllic. A wide open west-facing plot with big skies and distant views over the adjoining woodland and then beyond towards Guildford. The managed garden around the house was probably about half an acre. There was a productive vegetable plot and the remainder was mostly down to grass with a belt of tall pines at the front above the pretty sunken lane that ran down to the main A25 Guildford Road. Behind the house and garden they also owned a lovely wildflower meadow which they cut by hand once a year and stacked the grass to make a huge supply of beautiful clean compost that kept the rest of the garden in good heart.

Probably because things at home weren't so great at the time a couple of hours walking up and down behind the mower allowed me some head space to either think or not think according to how I felt.

My visits continued in this way for some time with just the occasional mowing session and as the months passed I learnt a lot more about Mrs Perkins, her two late husbands and her life since she was born in 1897. A true Victorian.

ii

With two older brothers and a sister; Emma or Emmie as she was called by all the family (and me eventually), was born in Surbiton just across the river from Hampton Court. Rather like my own situation she was brought up as a catholic because her father was very devout although her mother professed no strong beliefs and apparently Emma didn't stick with the faith any longer than she had to either.

It was quite a strict upbringing both at home and at school but Emma was a diligent child and did well at her lessons. She had to leave school at only fourteen years of age, just a couple of years before the First World War broke out. Her father apprenticed her to the accountancy office of a draper's shop in Surbiton where she soon became a valued member of staff albeit unpaid for several years whilst still apprenticed. In fact it cost her father a premium to have her taken on there in the first place.

Emma the youngest of the Edwardian Family and aged nineteen in 1916

With the outbreak of war the pretty and petite teenager soon found herself the subject of attention from the many soldiers always around and although she enjoyed dancing she soon found that many were looking for much more which repelled her when as she said she *"perceived the beast within."*

In 1916, then aged nineteen, Emma met a man she recognized as different from the others and who she was immediately attracted to for his calm and educated character, his intellect, musical appreciation and kind, considerate manner. His name was Cyril Edward Watts, known to all as Peter and who was to become the love of her life. It was however to be a long and tortuous road to eventual happiness.

Eleven years older than Emma, Peter was an electrical engineer and although conscripted to the military he was employed in his capacity as an engineer to ensure the London Electricity supply and so did not see service at the front.

In terms of their friendship the main stumbling block was that Peter was married and although separated from his wife he was not divorced (not surprising for the time). He had been married in 1912 to a French woman who, as soon as war broke out had abandoned him and returned to France. Thereafter the only communication between them had apparently been via her solicitor demanding maintenance payment.

Regardless of these circumstances, Emma's father would not countenance the relationship to continue and forbade her to meet him; an instruction she obeyed for eighteen months although unknown to her father but apparently with the collusion of her mother they continued to correspond.

This heart-breaking separation caused Emma to have a nervous breakdown and so in desperation to aid her recovery her father relented but even so on the very clear understanding that all the while Peter's wife was alive and he was still married there could be nothing more than friendship.

The war ended and the friendship deepened. Emma told me there never was any more despite their urgent desires. I remember how she smiled wistfully as she told me *"He was always the perfect gentleman and so anxious not to compromise my reputation even though by then I loved him so much I didn't care. I'd have made love to him in the park."*

Whether they were always as chaste as Emma suggested I've no idea but in 1925 fate took a hand when her father died and along with him all objections to the fulfilment of their relationship.

With their friendship resumed Emma's health improved and she found a new job in London with Burroughs the adding machine company who were later to become major players in the brave new world of computers eventually merging with the Sperry Corporation to become Unisys. From her office in Regent Street her role back in the early days was to manage the locations and rental payments of the company's machines most of which were leased rather than sold to users around the world.

Meanwhile, Peter's wife had made it clear there was no relationship left and she wouldn't be returning to England but refused to consider divorce although there was no shortage of communications asking for money.

In desperation Peter even arranged to provide her with evidence to sue for divorce on the grounds of adultery. He booked a room at a hotel and paid a woman to accompany him there and to be seen with him then presented the whole package to his wife's solicitor but all to no avail. She may not have wanted him herself but no-one else was going to have him either.

Emma aged thirty-one in 1928

Faced with this intransigence Peter and Emma decided it would not keep them apart. They decided, much against the norms of the day, that they would live together and set about looking for a home which brought them to East Horsley. Trips out into the country had familiarized them with the area, parts of which were becoming popular with better-off Londoners for building weekend retreats and their enquiries eventually led them to a plot for sale in Hillside. There was neither water nor electricity to the site and the view was that because of the hill there would never be water to the top end of the lane. Peter however was undaunted and according to Emma had said *"This is God's own country and it's where I want us to live and it is where we will live. I have no doubt."*

Hillside around 1930

Her brothers and sister were married by this time and it seems Emma felt an obligation to support her mother and as she explained it to me when she told Peter he agreed that wherever they went Mother would come too.

The land was purchased in 1926 but it was not going to be an easy task to make it into a home, not least because following the war building materials for private projects were expensive and in short supply. However, undaunted, Peter laid his plans to achieve the seemingly impossible with the first challenge being the water supply which in his mind he had already solved. He decided it would have to be the only natural source available – rain.

Accepting that there would be a household of three, he calculated the reasonable daily water needs for three adults and researched the average annual rainfall for the area. A simple calculation meant they needed a house with a one thousand square foot roof area and non-absorbent tiles that would immediately shed water into a catchment system.

Drawings were produced and duly approved by the Guildford Council but Peter still had not worked out where he would actually source the building materials until he realized that excavating foundations would result in many cubic yards of spoil which happened to be solid chalk. Although there are examples of chalk block buildings when it is known as 'clunch' the spoil would not be in block form which was a problem. However Peter thought that crushed chalk might very well be used as an aggregate with cement to mould into large building blocks. He then also realized that the excavation of a water cistern would also yield useful chalk rubble and so the decision was made.

Unable to afford professional builders Emma and Peter determined they would actually do the whole job themselves which is exactly what happened even though it took the next three and a half years of evenings and weekends.

Peter dug the foundations by hand with pick and shovel whilst Emma barrowed the spoil away to the block making site. Here she pummelled it into large granules to produce what would eventually become their building blocks. The water reservoir was going to be an even greater challenge for Peter because it would have to be about ten feet deep. This meant going down in stages but once he was down to about his own height below ground level chucking the spoil up and out of the hole became impossible so an intermediate platform was build which meant that every single shovel of spoil had to be double handled to simply get it out of the ground.

In their research into block making they went to the Ideal Home Exhibition in 1927 and purchased a block mould but in use it turned out to be cumbersome so with his considerable practical ability Peter designed and built something better. Basically the process of block making involved placing an inch or so of strong mortar into the mould and them tamping in the cement and chalk concrete on top. It had to be a stiff mix to avoid the blocks slumping when removed from the mould and left to cure. The result was a nine by nine inch cement-faced block about a foot long which could then be built up into the walls. Carefully pointed the cement faces provided a durable and weatherproof exterior wall.

The floor plan was for a medium-sized bungalow with two double bedrooms at one end, a large central sitting room with a single bedroom, bathroom and kitchen/living room at the other.

Building in progress

Peter then set about building the roof using pure calculations to determine rafter lengths and the necessary internal struts. Given that the man had never laid hand on a saw or shovel in his life his ability to rapidly master the skills involved was outstanding and all the while Emma was there at his side to pass him whatever he needed as the structure took shape.

Peter's practical ability was so good that he made literally everything they needed including as mentioned previously the wood panelling for the sitting room and the impressive carved oak fireplace. Even metal work proved no obstacle to him as he fashioned a set of fire tools to complement the iron dog-grate.

The water supply included a sand filter based on the system copied from the local water works at Surbiton. With a final storage capacity of some eleven thousand gallons the system was ideal. Water was pumped to a header tank in the roof by hand pump initially and later by electricity. Even the mysteries of private drainage were not alien to Peter and he created a septic tank system that was still working perfectly fifty years later.

The finished house with changed roofline and taller chimneys

In the early days cooking was done on two or three little Beatrice paraffin stoves on a worktop beside the sink in the kitchen and Emma was still using them when I arrived on the scene. When electricity first arrived in the lane they purchased a two ring Belling hot plate but Peter did no more than actually build an electric oven from scratch. He even wound by hand a pair of transformers to step the current down to twelve volts to ensure Emma's safety.

Once the house was complete they moved in along with Emma's mother, an Irish Terrier puppy called Jack and very bravely at that time set up home as Cyril Edward Watts and Miss Emma Cozens

By this time Peter was working for London Transport as electrical engineer in charge of their installation which by then included the developing Underground railway and the Trolleybus system. Emma was still working for Burroughs.

In 1937 they received word that Peter's wife had died in France leaving him free to marry which they did immediately and life continued blissfully at 'Westwood', so named for its wide woodland and sunset views. The garden flourished with flowers and vegetables in abundance. Sacks of potatoes, turnips and onions were stored and saw them through the whole year

Peter's practical inclination and knowledge was such that he was able to make almost anything they needed, which even included a rotary grass cutter that they used to cut the field. This, to my mind potentially lethal machine, consisted of an electric motor mounted over an axle between a pair of motorcycle wheels with a large rotating blade attached that must have been two and a half feet in diameter at least. It was still there when I came on the scene although I never used it, preferring my trusty (and far safer) Honda brought up from home for the purpose when required.

Peter was even clever enough to mount the blade at a slight angle so that the cut grass was thrown out to one side for easier collection. In use it must have been quite a hairy operation requiring two people working together. One to push the cutter and keep it level to avoid the blade jagging into the ground and the other to look after the hundred or so yards of cable that was plugged into the mains. No blade guards or electric circuit breakers back then. It was certainly a bit of a beast but it did the job for years.

When the war came in 1939 Peter's role with London Transport was so important it was designated a reserved occupation so he didn't have to fight but spent many nights away from home helping to keep the city mobile. They had some London children billeted on them for a couple of years and when the bombs came they all had to get into the little air-raid shelter Peter had dug out of the bank in the side of the drive. He built two sets of tiny bunk beds and with their paraffin heaters and sheltered by the steep banks they were as snug and safe as possible short of a direct hit which was pretty much unheard of out in the country.

During the war Emma became aware that she had an abdominal swelling making her think at first she might be pregnant but this proved not to be the case. It was eventually determined to be a fibroid growth but being non-life-threatening no action was taken at the time as all medical resources were diverted to more urgent needs. When the war ended she was seen again by which time it was almost the size of a melon and its removal necessitated a hysterectomy thereby ending any hopes of a future family although that would have been unlikely then due to her age.

In 1949 Peter was diagnosed with bladder cancer and had an operation that went seriously wrong. Apparently the surgeon managed to sever an artery and micro-surgery not being then what it is today he suffered a slow and painful demise over two weeks with Emma visiting daily. His last words were *"Thank you Emmie my darling for all the time you've put in."*

Peter had been everything to Emma and she took his death very hard, so much so that she was unable to continue working at Burroughs. Jack the dog had died a month before Peter's cancer was discovered and been replaced with another called Pat who was inseparable from Emma and it was long woodland walks with the dog around the paths she and Peter had walked so often that she believed saved her sanity.

James Perkins was the postman at Horsley whose round included Emma's house. Widowed himself for some five years, he shared her interest in gardening and often used to stop for a cup of tea with the mother and daughter and compare gardening notes. On one occasion when he called, Emma was in the Sheepleas with the dog so leaving the Royal Mail bag and bike propped against a wall he went off into the woods to find her. They were married in 1951.

From Jim's perspective, Peter must have been a very hard act to follow although Emma told me she was always careful not to make too much of the fact. Not that Jim wasn't ably practical, but he was just different to Peter who had been the innovator. Jim however was the great mender and fortunately for him Peter's legacy was a workshop in which he could always find the right tool or material to effect a repair.

Emma and Jim had twenty four happy years together until his death in 1975 when I became the third man in her life although I didn't see it that way for some time. (Not in any romantic sense I hasten to add)

Emma and Jim around 1968

iii

One day towards the end of '76 I called in at Westwood to say hello and maybe have a quick cuppa. I hadn't been in touch for a couple of weeks because work in the garden had more or less come to an end for the year and I'd been doing other things at home although I had checked in once by phone to see if she needed any shopping. Since Jim's death one of Emma's neighbours had started doing a regular shop for her but I usually gave her a call before we did ours in case she needed the odd item.

There was no reply at the house but I could see the dog indoors and started to feel a bit concerned as the house was locked and I knew the only time she ever went out was with the dog. There was no sign of her in the garden and then a neighbour called to me from the house next door.

It turned out that Emma was in hospital having fallen in the woods and broken her arm whilst walking the dog. That was two days previously and the dog was being fed and walked by the neighbour.

I went to the hospital to find her with a severely fractured right arm, all strapped up and feeling very sorry for herself, frustrated mainly I think, because she was not in control of things and that to Emma was the worst possible situation.

The whole incident was down to the dog which was so accustomed to being taken into the woods by Jim twice a day that it wouldn't do its business in the garden. But somehow or other in all the months I had known her this information had never come out and she had apparently been trudging off to the woods twice a day for the dog to make itself comfortable. She always kept it on the lead because it was a bit of a roamer but on this occasion it had seen another dog, pulled her off balance and against a concrete post beside the path.

Not realizing how serious the injury was she had told nobody for twenty four hours until a neighbour had come round with a newspaper for her by which time she was more or less in a state of collapse and was whisked off to hospital by ambulance. According to the hospital the delay in coming to hospital had resulted in internal bleeding and associated swelling and until that subsided it was not possible to make a decision about further treatment. In the meantime they were looking to discharge her and I turned out to be just what the hospital wanted, namely someone to take an interest and responsibility for her.

The agreement was that she would come home and stay with us for a couple of days but almost as soon as we got home she insisted in going back to Westwood and looking after herself. It was a ridiculous idea but she wasn't to be swayed so that's what happened. I saw her the next day and took some food and made her tea which she couldn't do for herself and she insisted she was managing which I could see she wasn't really.

When I went again the following day the swelling had started to subside and the strapping was hanging quite loosely around her arm. When she tried to raise the limb it hung at a grotesque angle and it was possible to see the end of a broken bone jutting up beneath the skin. I was appalled and called out the GP who took one look and sent her straight back to hospital with a very strong follow-up phone call to the orthopaedic surgeon attached to A&E to ensure he saw her himself.

I think the bottom line was that due to her age and poorly state when first admitted, she was more or less written off because the surgeon even said *"We should have done a better job than this."* The following day Emma had an operation to insert a long pin down through the bone from her shoulder to elbow and she was sent home in plaster after a couple of days with a follow-up appointment three weeks later. To cut a long story short the arm did eventually mend although it was decided to leave the pin in situ for added strength.

I continued to support her with visits both on and off duty mainly to take the dog out for his toilet walk which was a ridiculous state of affairs. Fate took a hand here three weeks later when we noticed the dog seemed a bit off colour and I took him to the vet who diagnosed advanced kidney

failure. The options were to medicate, which the vet suggested might give him another couple of months, or put him to sleep there and then. I called Emma who sadly opted for the latter but asked me to bring the dog back and bury him in the garden. She showed me a precise spot marked with steel pegs where she explained *"The others are under here."* I said *"Others?"*
"Yes." she said. *"At least three, maybe four."* I dug down a couple of feet and sure enough under the remains of a sheet of plastic was a dog skeleton. I added the last one.

With the dog gone a lot of the pressure was off both Emma and me although I was still keeping in touch. My visits were mostly now at weekends or rest days when I would give her half a day's help around the place, either in the garden or dealing with the odd maintenance item. I also used to cook up a saucepan of soup or a casserole that we could share for lunch and that would do her for another day or two.

During the summer of 1977 I was helping Emma with some weeding in the veg plot and the following is my best recollection of a conversation that changed my life.

She said *"You really love it here don't you?"* I said *"Yes Emmie. It's beautiful and wonderfully calm"* After a few moments silence she said *"You can have it if you like. When I'm gone."* Not quite certain I had heard right I said *"What do you mean?"*

She said *"Listen. I have no-one else to leave it too. I have loved this place for itself and for the two wonderful men who have shared it with me and I want to spend the rest of my life here if I can. The accident with the dog made me see how vulnerable I am but with your help it might be possible. You have been very kind to me and I think we are quite close now. I also think you could be content here too which would make me very happy."*

I said. *Emmie, that is a most generous offer which obviously I would love to accept. But you need to know I can't give any guarantees that I can carry on supporting you at this level. I might be moved to the other side of the county next month. We don't know what the future holds and you might have to sell up to pay for care when you are older.*

"I understand all that Brian." she said. *"I know what I am offering is a bargain and if we agree then we will both have to do our best to keep our sides. We can't expect any more than that. I trust you will do your best and I hope you trust me. If I name you as my heir then whatever happens you will have either the house or what's left of any money. All I want from you is a promise to help me as much as you can and also that you will not ship me off to hospital unless it is absolutely necessary because I would rather die here than anywhere else."*

And that was the basis on which we agreed to continue our friendship. It was quite a fine balancing act allocating time between my own domestic responsibilities and giving what help I could to Emma to keep Westwood functioning all round.

If any single personality trait characterized Emma it was her fierce independence and her often repeated mantra *"Paddle your own canoe."* So I imagine it must have been an enormously difficult decision to make the above proposition. That said; it soon became very clear that she had given it considerable thought and indeed correctly anticipated my agreement because within the next couple of visits it was apparent that she had been doing a lot of preparatory work.

Despite her comments about not shipping her off to hospital, she explained that she understood at her age she could die or be taken suddenly ill and she wanted to be sure that I knew everything I needed to about her affairs and family history. So on days when the weather didn't favour work outside she set about bringing me up to speed with everything.

There were already packs of letters in ancient paper wrappers marked *"Brian to read – important."* Or *"Family stuff – Brian keep these"*. She had everything immaculately sorted and marked up; which she wanted to show me and then keep and other things she wanted me to see or read before she destroyed them. These included some lovely letters between her and Peter and from Peter to her father that would have been such treasured items for me, especially now as I try to bring her more to life on these pages. She said she wanted me to understand but beyond that they were to be private and she destroyed them.

As both her needs and physical ability were much less than previously we gradually reduced the amount of land under cultivation and put most of the veg plot under grass. She agreed to buy a petrol hedge cutter which made that job faster and less arduous and I managed to get a local farmer that I knew to come in and take the hay off the field once a year.

Actually my attempts to make things easier backfired on me somewhat with the regard to the grass. Having decided that the veg plot would have to go I went to the same farmer and scrounged enough grass seed to do the job which I liberally sowed confident in the knowledge that I'd dug it over for the last time. What I didn't know was that unlike lawn grass meadow grass is bred to be extremely prolific in order to provide good pasture. The wretched stuff grew like there was no tomorrow and where I might have cut the main lawn once I had to mow the old veg plot two or three times.

Well you live and learn.

If all this is sounding a bit intense there is an amusing story to conclude with. One of the neighbours used to bring round a copy of the Telegraph every day that Emma read avidly and then expected me to be able to discuss with her the latest national and international news which was a challenge to say the least.

One day after lunch on a Saturday we were just chatting when she suddenly said *"What do lesbians actually do with each other?"*

You could have knocked me over with the proverbial feather but I'll leave you to imagine how I dealt with it.

iv

Apart from my policing duties at Horsley I had developed a little spare time interest of my own although to be honest, what with my own family life, keeping our own garden under control and helping Emma out at Westwood there was little enough real spare time.

Through Denise's involvement with the theatre group we had got to know a couple called Peter and Debbie. Debs was a very good actor and active theatre member and her husband Peter ran a second hand car dealership adjoining the Horsley Towers garage and petrol station. Our joint interest in cars connected us and after a while I started buying the odd part-exchange from him at trade prices. I couldn't afford much money so they tended to be 'bangers' but I knew that even a rough old car, given a good clean and polish could usually be re-sold at a profit.

I did do this a few times but my downfall was that I took my eye off the commercial ball and was tempted to buy his traders that interested me rather than those that might quickly turn a profit. If I bought something I liked I tended to use it myself and keep it too long instead of turning it over quickly at a modest but useful mark-up. One of these was a white Rover 2000 which I loved and kept for a couple of years I think. It was motoring on the cheap though which back then was important.

On the theatre front we had met a number of interesting people and although I had nothing to do with the actual productions there were various social events like the Christmas parties and then the odd dinner round with other couples which were very enjoyable.

At a personal level however, our relationship seemed to take an inexplicable turn for the worse around the middle of 1978. Denise became very depressed and started to withdraw from family activity so things like walking the dog that we often did as a family were now left for me and the children to enjoy together She would not talk about what was an obvious but unidentified problem between us and as she was no longer inclined to any form of physical relationship with me I began to wonder if she might be involved with someone else.

The pantomime that was planned for 1978 was to be Cinderella and Denise had been cast in the lead role with our friend Alan as Buttons so there was considerable anticipation around the build up to this event in addition to lines to be learnt and rehearsals to be attended. I had high hopes that this might prove to be something of a positive turning point in Denise's mood and our relationship. How wrong I was.

v

At the beginning of August, Brian Roberts the Chief Inspector from Leatherhead came to visit the section and I had to see him for my annual appraisal when naturally he asked me how I was doing out on the section and had I given any more thought to my future career plans.

I said that promotion to Inspector was my next target and that I hoped, given the fact that my predecessor had been promoted off the section; the same route might be open to me. He thought that seeking a move back to HQ might be a more proactive tactic rather than just waiting it out in 'the sticks'. My heart sank somewhat at this because despite the fact that the job of rural sergeant had never been part of my plan I was actually enjoying it and especially the autonomy that went with the role. There was also always the issue of supporting Emma floating around in my mind but I knew that when the chips were down the career and family prosperity would have to take priority.

I told him that I felt I'd rather ticked the HQ box with my time in training and was surprised when he said *"Why don't you think about having a look at Public Relations?"* and I said *"Why. Is there a vacancy? "I don't know."* he said. *"It was just a thought."*

"What was that all about?" I wondered. I didn't really have much idea about the Public Relations Office at HQ so I made a few calls and dug out a copy of the previous year's force Annual Report which pretty much gave chapter and verse about the functions of all the specialist departments in

the force. From what I read it seemed just the job to put me at the centre of things.

Right at the heart of major incidents, in the know about the latest events and plans, writing press releases, mounting exhibitions, doing media interviews and guiding groups of visitors around Headquarters. I must say it sounded a great job and decided to have a word with Denise. I explained that it would probably mean another house move but as she said, it would make a change to be closer to Guildford with more things to do and still close enough to continue her association with the theatre.

The following day I put in a report expressing an interest in the Public relations Office should a vacancy arise. A week later I got the job. It would seem that Brian Roberts knew more than he'd let on.

23 PUBLIC RELATIONS

August 1978 and we moved to a very nice large semi on the headquarters estate on the outskirts of Guildford. The house had originally been built for senior officers based at HQ and was in a very quiet and private close, just a few minutes' walk from my new office. With acres of grounds and playing fields available for us to enjoy especially at weekends, it really was the ideal place to bring up the family. In addition, a mini-bus from HQ was available to take the children down into the town for school.

For me it was a new and very different type of police-work and a job that just a few years previously had not existed in any of the county forces. Owing to its size and unique situation the Met did have a press liaison branch although liaison was not always the result.

For years the established attitude within the police service with regard to the press and media in general was *"Tell the buggers nothing or as little as possible."* The problem was though, that in the early seventies with local radio and TV companies proliferating, the demand for material to fill the numerous news bulletins had become far more intense. This coupled with a public being continually indoctrinated by the media with the idea that they had a right to know everything, meant it was becoming increasingly difficult to stonewall media demands for information. Also, in the absence of official comment an increasingly courageous and intrusive media was just as likely to print inaccurate guesswork or even fabricate a non-attributable story.

Surrey's Chief Constable Peter Matthews in company with other Chief Officers such as James Anderton of Greater Manchester, Ken Oxford of Merseyside and John Alderson of Devon and Cornwall, was among those that decided total media exclusion was an unwinnable game and actually counter-productive. Rather, they argued, it was preferable to establish a structured set of rules and systems to provide a liaison process with the media and even over time to develop a working rapport. That way it was suggested, there was even a possibility to get the media 'on-side' to assist when publicity was actually required and to respect embargo requests when deemed operationally imperative.

To this end the Surrey Constabulary Press and Public Relations branch was set up which, by the time I arrived in August 1978, comprised Inspector Bernie Buck in charge with me and Sergeant Mick Morley assisting. We also had a civilian admin assistant. Mick had been a colleague at Leatherhead so there was an immediate comfort factor there for me.

We occupied a huge and airy ground floor office in the then relatively new Operations wing. With a great array of display and exhibition photos, mannequins wearing historic uniforms and a collection of international police headgear the room was frequently the destination for the Chief and visiting dignitaries for the obligatory photoshoot.

Whereas most people will remember that Chief Constables Alderson, Anderton and Oxford quite often made the media themselves during the ensuing years by dipping their toes, some would say inappropriately, into political waters; Peter Matthews did not. As a result he kept himself and the Surrey force out of the national limelight to a large extent although locally it was a very different story.

Away from the tricky issue of satisfying a demanding media, Matthews had a very clear understanding that the term 'police force' should be regarded as a misnomer in the modern world. Whether he truly believed it or not I can't say but he preferred to promote the term Police Service where the relationship with the public should be one of policing by consent. As a result he viewed the promotion of the force's public image as our primary role, more so even than jumping in response to every journalist's question.

To this end our brief in the office was to do our best to promote or generate positive human interest stories regarding the force or individual officers in every one of the dozen or so local papers in the force area every week. It was a pretty tough call which we managed quite a lot of the time.

The stories didn't have to be earth-shattering or dramatic. Simple things like an individual officer giving his time to run a youth group or finding a lost pet were quite adequate but it did mean we had to work hard at ferreting out the information then write up a press release with a photograph if at all possible. As they say *"A picture is worth a thousand words."* So true.

To support our efforts at HQ, local press liaison officers were appointed on each division whose brief was similar to ours. They were expected to develop working relationships with local media representative like reporters and editors and be available to respond to enquiries about essentially local matters. At the same time they were expected to bear in mind our need at a force level to have information about significant crimes or other events. This was not a full time job and so they usually also held responsibility for school liaison or road safety at a divisional level.

The problem with any sort of PR effort, whether it is promoting the image of Surrey Police or selling a tin of beans, is that after all the work and success one achieves it only takes a sliver of metal in the beans or a silly copper being rude to someone to undo all the good work. It is a curious thing about the public that the collective memory for bad news is much longer than for the good stuff and the same holds true about the extent to which the bad news story seems to sell more column-inches than the good one.

That said, we did have some great successes and one of the best I recall involved Pc Len West in the village of Peaslake. One way to get a good picture story is to combine your smiling policeman with a child or an animal or both together is even better. Add a good happy storyline and you have a potential winner as far as a newspaper editor is concerned. The bald fact however is that no matter how good your picture and/or story is, it can easily be pushed aside by other events so timing is everything. We quite often held stories until we identified a slow news day when it was more likely to be used.

I had in mind to use Pc Bob Biddles who I'd worked with at Horsley and who I knew had a good relationship with the village school but unfortunately he was away on leave. Then someone said that they thought the Peaslake officer was very involved with his village school. I asked around the village if anyone had seen the local bobby and the general view seemed to be that if he wasn't patrolling the village he was likely to be at the school so I headed off there.

The sight that met my eyes was pure gold dust.

PC Len West was out in the middle of the playing field surrounded by primary school children. In full uniform with his tunic undone and with enormous balls of mud on his police boots, he was refereeing a football match with his police whistle. It turned out that he also taught the children woodwork and that together with his wife they ran a little gardening class at the school.

Not having a camera on hand I had to set it up again and approached a news agency we worked closely with who sent photographer Roger Allen along a few days later. In the event the pictures and associated story made a centre page spread in the Daily Mail. Some cynical colleagues were inclined to say. *"So What."*. The answer to that at one level is *"Fair comment if that's what you think."* Everyone is entitled to their view and a lot still found it hard to stomach the relatively new situation of the police and press cosying up together.

The above is a copy of the story carried by a local paper.

What for the most part critics failed to comprehend was the way the world was moving on and that it had even then become an immensely image conscious society. Had we wanted to take a centre page spread in a national daily to say that Surrey police officers care about their community and their kids it would have cost thousands whereas with a little imagination and cultivation of contacts we had achieved the same for nothing.

One job none of us particularly enjoyed was the daily paper cutting task. We had to go through all the local and national newspapers each day and put together a briefing pack for the Chief and other senior officers. This provided valuable feedback about the success or otherwise of our own efforts but also kept the force in touch with major issues of interest as well as anything else being said locally about the force. It was a repetitious job that I didn't like but I have never been as up to date with current affairs as I was then.

After a while in the office Bernie was replaced with a new Inspector in charge. Bob Ball was a real live wire and a completely different character to Bernie Buck who was the perfect gentleman. Charming and always perfectly groomed, I only ever heard him raise his voice once to a particularly pushy and obnoxious journalist who frankly needed the put-down.

Bob on the other hand was an ideas person who was certainly not looking for a quiet life and was almost always prepared to run with ideas we came up with to help push the image of the force. Bob's view was that we could do better than just responding to enquiries but if we were sharp enough we could manage the media to our own ends. It certainly made life more interesting.

I came in one morning to find a piece on the overnight sheet about a tramp with infectious TB who had discharged himself from hospital and set off on the road coughing his lungs up and spreading infection all around.

When Bob arrived I said *"How d'you fancy setting the world alight?"*
"Yea. Great." he said. *"What have you got?"*

By carefully bearing in mind things like news bulletin timings and their areas of interest we managed to get the story carried by all the relevant TV and radio stations including appeals for the public to report sightings.. As a direct result of our activity, connections and rapport we had built with news editors and so on we had the man traced and back in medical treatment by mid-afternoon. It was an excellent example of using our media relations in the real world of police work – public protection.

To be fair though there was the odd time when we were caught on the back foot and had to be quite smart not to let it show.

A Superintendent at Guildford had made a remark to a local journalist about the problems some of his PC's faced in affording bikes to patrol their beats. He imagined there must be loads of unloved and unused cycles languishing in garden sheds which some of the local bobbies could make good use of. He wasn't actually appealing for the public to donate old bikes to the cash-strapped police force but that was how the journalist chose to interpret the situation.

Around that time police pay was a bit of a current issue with the Edmund-Davies Review about to report so the journalist thought she might make a little commission by running the story to the nationals or even TV.

The first we heard about it was a call from the BBC asking to come and interview the Superintendent who was appealing for the public to donate their old bikes to his officers. Obviously this had the potential to make the force look pretty silly but to have stonewalled would have made it look as though we were seriously embarrassed or had something to hide. We therefore had no option but to go with it, running quite fast to catch up in order to ensure that we still had a handle on events.

A film crew from the Tonight programme turned up and an interview was arranged which we had decided in advance the officer concerned should treat in a light-hearted way making the point that it was by no means an appeal for donations. He was nevertheless to make the point that some of his young officers on low pay and with families to support would be more than happy to hear of second-hand bikes they could purchase rather than having to buy expensive new ones.

One of the journalists wanted to know what type of bikes police officers used and had the idea of getting the Superintendent to carry out an 'identification parade' of bikes to point out machines.

Crazy though it was; as I said before, closing down on them was not going to help so we agreed. In the end the broadcast piece contained a very good interview where the points we wanted were included plus a short film. This had the camera focused on the officer's 'size nines' walking up and down this row of old bikes (dug out of the lost and stolen store) to the theme tune of Z Cars or one of the other popular TV police programmes of the time.

Not exactly the most dignified result but when the piece ended and cut back to the studio the smiling presenter thanked the force for being 'good sports' so as they say *"Out of the jaws of defeat -."* we managed to snatch a victory of sorts.

At a more serious level the office staff were also key players in managing media interest in major crimes and incidents and at one time I remember we were managing the press on two murder enquiries at the same time. With two of us out of the office, life for those still manning the phones was extremely testing at times and really did need some control on occasions not to lose it with some of the more pushy callers. By being on site at an incident and working alongside the investigating team the press liaison officer could very usefully provide an alternative focus for the reporters and their crews, allowing investigators to get on with the work unhindered.

As I quickly discovered, personal relationships with media individuals were absolutely key to keeping the liaison working well. To this end we often donned our civvie suits and went out to meet and have the odd drink with our contacts. The most regular of these was with Don Leigh and Dennis Cassidy of Southern News Service. These two guys and their two or three photographers were totally trusted and as a result often got an inside briefing from us on breaking stories in exchange for help and ideas in promoting the sought-after human interest stories to the national media.

Another important relationship was with members of the National Crime Reporters Association and in order to keep them on-side there was an annual drinks and buffet reception at HQ with an address from the Chief and a question and answer session. These were the most experienced and highly respected journalists of the national media with responsibility for reporting crime and kindred matters. It can't be emphasized enough how important the trust in this two-way relationship was for both sides. From their perspective they knew that if they kept trust they could rely on direct and accurate information from the heart of an incident whilst we knew that if they were asked with good enough reason to keep the lid on a particular piece of information, then it would be done. Equally both sides also knew that if that trust were once broken it would be end of information flow from our end and media support from theirs.

These carefully nurtured relationship could also bring unexpected and arguably rather unprofessional bonuses. I was the press liaison person on a murder enquiry on one occasion when a member of the Crime Reporters Association invited me and the Detective Chief Inspector to have a drink at his home which happened to be nearby. It was obvious that this was no more than an attempt to relax us enough to get a bit of the inside story on the case. Nevertheless we went along to a very smart large house on the outskirts of town where the sun shone as we sat by the pool enjoying drinks and nibbles served by the reporter's extremely attractive bikini-clad wife. *'Not a bad way to earn a crust!* I thought and in the end he didn't get very much more than the rest of the press pack.

Even with our friends at Southern News things could go awry and ruin a great idea. One such occasion was to do with a squirrel. Some of the staff at HQ had a ground floor office where over time they had managed to persuade a squirrel to come to the window and take food from their hands. Thinking it would make a great picture to have a uniformed officer feed the squirrel I arranged with Don and Dennis for one of their guys to come up and take the shot which is where fate took a hand. Driving into headquarters which was overrun with squirrels, one ran straight under the wheels of his car. You've guessed it of course. Of all the blessed squirrels on the estate the dead one was the one he was coming to photograph.

Other activities handled from our office included the publicity for the annual 'Child Safe' road safety campaign part of which was the production of a T shirt printed with the Child Safe logo. In order to generate more publicity we needed celebrities who would come along and wear the T shirt for the predictable publicity photo. We never ceased to be impressed at the goodwill with which busy local celebs agreed to help out. We had Cliff Richard and DJ Keith Chegwyn on two successive years.

My two children Robert and Maria and Roger Weedon's two girls with DJ Keith Chegwyn

We also used some of our pretty young woman officers to model the T shirts and I even got in on the act with a bright yellow one on under my open tunic. The bonus for my kids was that we needed some children in the pictures so they got to meet some famous people to brag about at school.

The things you do for the job!

With my daughter Maria wearing the 1982 campaign T shirts

Probably the best coup in this area was getting Joan Collins involved. If a T shirt is one of your props it is probably best fitted over a beautiful body so we contacted another one of our local 'friends'. Photographers International was the company operated by the late and great Terry Fincher the well-known international news and war photographer. Terry came up with the idea of asking Joan Collins as he knew her and she also lived nearby in one of the Surrey villages. Further to that she had a daughter who had been involved in a road traffic accident so she had a personal interest in promoting our cause. I finished up with Terry in Joan's pretty garden complete with the Cinzano umbrella but sadly no Leonard Rossiter. Once again with Terry's connections, his excellent photography and Joan Collin's generosity we made the national dailies to tell the world about Surrey Constabulary's concern for road safety.

Another one was the 'Stranger Danger' campaign and here we managed to co-opt the late Ed Stewart to work with Basil Brush in the production of a film to be shown in schools. My own children Robert and Maria were also enlisted as the two potential 'victims' with the bad guy played by Dc Dave Mason from Crime Bureau. My kids received a nice little presentation from the Chief for their contribution which I thought was a nice touch from him. Life for them was almost as interesting as it was for me.

I couldn't resist including this picture of The Chief with Basil Brush. He really liked the shot but would not let us publish it at the time as I think he felt it undermined the dignity of his office a bit. Well he's no longer around to object but feel sure if he's looking down from somewhere he will be laughing again.

There was the odd occasion where things backfired somewhat and we had to keep our heads down.

Someone in Traffic department had the very good idea that instead of always stopping motorists to tick them off it might make a change to stop people who drove well, congratulate them and give away an embossed Road Safety pen. I can't actually remember what the campaign was called but it worked well and attracted some good coverage by making the point that being stopped by a traffic cop doesn't necessarily have to be bad news if you are a good driver.

By absolute chance one patrol spotted an example of good or courteous driving and stopped the driver who turned out to be none other than motor cycling ace Barry Sheen. We got in on the act at this point and persuaded the Chief to make the presentation at Barry's home in Charlwood and they were pictured in his garage against a backdrop of numerous racing leathers and motor cycles.

Bernie Buck was still in the office at this time so chancing his luck he suggested the Chief might like to join Barry on one of the bikes. Clearly of the view that getting him out of HQ to a garage in the middle of nowhere was quite enough, he said in very un-Chief Constable language *"You can go piss up your kilt Bernie."*

Once again by utilizing someone else's high profile we managed to promote our road safety efforts. However, we heard a couple of weeks or so later that Barry Sheen had been prosecuted for exceeding the speed limit. We kept very quiet and by some miracle the local court reporter missed it so no egg on our faces that time.

Quite a few people in the force have over the years been critical of the way Peter Matthews always seemed to have his photo in the local papers. Many viewed it as nothing more than his personal self-promotion and nicknamed him 'The Kodak Kid'. Whilst that may well have been partly true it was also a fact that we were extremely fortunate to have a Chief Constable who was prepared to put himself up front to help inform and promote the force to the public who were paying our wages.

I was walking back to my house one evening as the Chief was driving out and he stopped to say hello and ask how I was enjoying my job in PRO. One thing led to another as we chatted and he said *"I know what they say about the Kodak Kid and all that but I tell you this. Where I go Surrey Constabulary goes too."* The following is a good example.

As part of the 1981 School Liaison programme the force had produced the 'Spot-it Book' This was a bit like the 'I Spy' books for children except that the things they had to spot were to do with policing and included among other things police insignia of rank. As one of these was the Chief Constable's laurel wreath which was not exactly a daily presence on Surrey's streets, the Chief agreed that he would do a walk-about in Guildford High Street one Saturday morning. The school liaison officers put the word out to the schools and we of course had our very good friends from Southern News send a photographer.

The result was a real show-stopper with the Chief Constable of Surrey walking down a busy shopping street in full uniform surrounded by crowds of children like the Pied Piper. This happy scene made several national dailies whilst other pages showed police and rioters knocking hell out of each other in Toxteth. I guess you could take your own message out of that. Either Surrey Police were doing something right or we were living in cloud-cuckoo land. Interesting discussion

Although we quite often had to work some long hours there were compensations. From time to time a news crew would come to the county to report some incident or other and one of us would be deputed to go along as facilitator. Apart from arranging access to locations or people the reporters wanted to interview, we also advised the crews the best location for a decent pub lunch to which we were also invited. – Result! Because back then ITN in particular had a very good lunch allowance.

Requests for demonstrations and displays also came our way so we were often involved in arranging everything from police dog displays at village fairs to traffic patrol cars to visit schools or a Police tent at the Surrey County Show. The main annual event was the force open day at HQ when the public could come in and watch arena displays, climb all over our cars and motor bikes, make a fuss of the dogs and get guided tours around the HQ building and Control Room.

Although I have always enjoyed writing going right back to my school days, it was probably my time in the press office where I got my first real buzz from seeing my own words in print. The office produced a stream of press releases to the local media on a whole range of subjects ranging from pure PR through road safety to crime statistics and it was the charming Ann Dent, news editor at the Surrey Advertiser who gave the advice I have tried to live by ever since. *"You have to tell the whole story in the first sentence and if you can do that in one line so much the better. That gets a reader's attention. After that you can come in with the background and detail."*

Between us in the office we must have been getting it right most of the time because our press releases were often published unchanged.

Towards the end of my time in the press office I also got involved with County Sound (now Eagle Radio), the about-to-be-launched local radio station for Surrey based in Guildford. We negotiated a daily five minute police input that went out live called Police Beat and we decided that a mini studio was needed in the office. I did our first broadcast in 1983 shortly after the station was launched.

24 A SAD TIME

i

Denise never did warm to the house at Mount Browne despite its generous size, ideal situation and her undeniable attempts to take a positive view about it initially. It certainly wasn't exactly at the heart of things but then neither was the house at Horsley. But at least on the Headquarters estate we were barely a mile from Guildford's busy High Street and all its amenities. It wasn't as if she didn't drive either so access to her beloved theatre, her parents and other friends was no problem.

If I'm honest I'd known for some time that her unhappiness was much more about me and our relationship than about where we happened to be living. Nor can I deny that my ambition resulting in the various changes of house and my repeated absences on training courses had caused some stress between us. However our problems were now more deep-seated. I was sure so much of this could have been resolved if only I could have persuaded her to talk things through but she never would. It later became clear why not.

As time passed Denise became progressively more withdrawn and uncommunicative at home and despite my concern and attempts to get her to open up to me about what was troubling her she seemed set on a downward path which broke my heart to see. The only interest in her life was the theatre where she spent several evenings a week ostensibly at rehearsals although they often appeared to go on a good deal later than seemed reasonable and it was often after midnight when she returned.

At this time my friend Dick was still living in Horsley with his sister and her family and one day early in '79 he came to see me. He clearly had something on his mind and eventually blurted out that gossip was rife in the village about Denise and a man she was thought to be having an affair with. Dick said he had hesitated to say anything but in the end hadn't wanted to see me being made a fool of any longer. The man concerned was apparently our friend Alan that she had been cast with in the pantomime and they were regularly seen together in the pub and were apparently much more than friends.

I was totally devastated by this information because, although I had begun to wonder whether she might have become involved with someone else, this news was the confirmation I had never really believed would happen. It was hard to escape the irony of the situation as it had been me that introduced her to the theatre group in the first place and now this man who we had welcomed into our home along with his wife had apparently stolen mine.

I thought about this for a while and decided I couldn't let it go. When challenged Denise refused to either deny or admit it but simply refused to discuss it at all. I know many marriages have their ups and downs and couples do sometimes manage to get over periods of difficulty, even infidelity. I hoped this might be the case with us provided we could talk it out but clearly that was not to be.

Without getting into too much detail it soon became clear that our relationship was beyond repair and we decided to divorce. I contested the custody of the children as Denise had no idea where or how she might look after them whereas I did rather hold all the cards. I had a secure job, a very comfortable and safe rent-free home and a guarantee from the Chief Constable that I could remain in the same house with regular 'office hours' for as long as I needed to. I was far more involved with the children's activities than Denise, they were settled in school and I was bringing them up in the catholic faith. Faced with the almost impossible question of which parent they would prefer to live with both Robert and Maria said they wanted to stay with me at Mount Browne and carry on in the same school. My contention was that security and maintenance of their status quo was the priority. A court welfare report supported me and in December 1980 I was awarded custody of the children along with my final divorce decree. A thirteen year marriage was sadly over.

What almost certainly also disappeared at that point was the tag that I had been carrying marking me out as having 'senior rank' potential. This would presumably to be replaced by a 'domestic issues' label, and I knew that until I could put myself up for twenty-four hour shift work again I was unlikely to see the next promotion.

Although this sad time has been summarized in a few lines it was a very difficult time for all concerned that lasted for almost two years. There were few outbursts and for the most part, mainly for the sake of the children we co-existed as affable strangers sharing a house but no relationship. I tried several times over that period to talk about reconciliation but to no avail. There is nothing that kills off love so effectively as repeated rejection and in time I knew that the love I'd felt for her was effectively dead – replaced by resentment at the lies and betrayal.

On a day to day level the emotional stress of being at home with Denise was almost unbearable and I found going out to work a welcome relief. I remember that as I walked the couple of hundred yards to the office it felt as though a monstrous weight was being lifted off my head. Fortunately the job was always busy and interesting but going back to the house after work of course the weight returned. The children were my saving grace during off duty time. Not only did I spend hours doing stuff for them in a practical sense like cooking, washing and homework etc. but made a point of getting out quite a lot to the cinema, bowling, or trips to various places. Sadly Denise had little appetite for involvement with their activities which even with the difficulties between us was one area where I felt she could have tried harder.

Guy Fawkes firework trip to Stoke Park

Basically we led separate lives under the same roof with Denise spending almost every evening out of the house and returning late to sleep on the sofa each night. On evenings she was at home we either watched TV in silence or I went out to friends.

As far as I was concerned we were still married and until things were finalized there was no way I was going to give anyone the chance to criticize my integrity regarding our relationship. There were two reasons for this. One was that I happened to think that married meant married to the exclusion of others. This was what I had promised and despite a general loosening of morals all around us I still believe the same thing. Without fidelity in a relationship there is nothing. If things go wrong I think people should be brave enough to be honest with each other and not retreat into a web of lies and deception which is what I was faced with.

The second and somewhat more practical reason was that as far as my job was concerned I needed to be whiter than white. We had a Chief Constable who was a puritan Scot with views to match and I had seen before how he could all too easily pass a moral judgement on colleagues who had in his opinion stepped out of line. This happened to a friend who separated from his wife and despite his honesty with the job was rewarded with a posting about as far away from his new partner as was possible.

It was during the two years we lived in this way that along with my love my faith also died. I loved Denise more than I can say and I guess in some sort of naive way I hoped that because of that she should love me back. So I prayed like I'd never prayed before that somehow it would all change and there would be reconciliation and a 'happy ever after'. I continued to go through the hoops with the children, taking them to church and saying prayers but my own once fervent and deeply held faith in God was no more.

ii

Around the same time we had moved to the headquarters house a further complication arose involving my father and adding further to my considerable preoccupation with domestic issues. He had suffered a stroke a couple of years previously which although relatively minor had meant he was unable to continue in his area manager role with the supermarket.

He made a reasonable recovery and the company took him back in a shop-based role at the Epsom Branch. They were extremely good to him, presumably in recognition of his many loyal years with the company.

Unfortunately after a year or so it had become obvious that the stroke seemed to have accelerated the aging process and he decided of his own accord to retire and also stopped driving.

It all blew up again in late 1980 when we heard that Eileen had arranged for Dad to be admitted to a psycho-geriatric ward at West Park hospital where she used to work. I suspected that without her hospital connections it is highly doubtful that this could have happened and my sister and I were of the view that she had effectively dumped him as an inconvenience.

Looked at rationally and with the benefit of hindsight I guess it was easy enough to understand. Dad was effectively becoming senile, a bit unsteady and slightly incontinent. Eileen was a very house-proud woman and given that she had spent all her working life looking after demented and mentally disturbed patients, Dad and his issues were about the last thing she needed in her clean and tidy home. Without the background of many loving years together she just didn't have the commitment to take on the additional responsibility whereas I am sure that had Mum still been alive it would have been so different.

However, with him now hospitalized he became yet another issue in my life and finding time to visit him was added to my already difficult 'to do' list. I visited Dad as often as I could and used to take him out in the car for a pub lunch somewhere. Returning to the ward was always difficult though as he invariably wept when the time came for me to leave and I hated leaving him like that.

iii

My friendship with Emma was still a factor in my life but she was fully aware of my domestic situation and so made very few additional demands. In order to give myself a break and to get out of the house at weekends I usually arranged to go to help her for half a day each Saturday or Sunday depending on what Denise was doing.

Getting out into the garden and doing some physical work was a great stress reduction activity. In addition, Emma by this time had almost come to fill the role of a mother figure in my life and was always willing to listen and offer wise counsel whenever I needed to talk which at that time was often. I lost count of the number of times she patiently bore my tears of despair as I described the disintegration of my marriage and the loss of the only woman I had ever loved.

25 A SORT OF FREEDOM

i

Although desperately sad at one level, the custody decision and the arrival of the divorce Decree Absolute in December 1980 was the best possible Christmas present I could have wished for. Denise moved out into single accommodation and we agreed without need for court intervention that she could have ready and frequent access to the children. In practice this meant that she had them every other weekend which suited everyone well enough.

As a Christmas present to myself and by way of celebrating my new status I bought a new hi-fi system. It was a good quality bit of kit at the top end of the Sharp range of stacking systems that were the in thing at the time. It certainly had all the bells and whistles including rows of green LED's that bounced about with the volume, base, treble and balance levels.

It was quite mesmerizing and together with a couple of big speakers it sounded just the business. I had quite a varied collection of music from classical through country to pop and as I anticipated spending quite a bit of time at home doing my single parent thing it seemed a great idea.

Despite my already full involvement with the children's lives, I found that being a lone parent for twelve days a fortnight was certainly pretty demanding. It also made it quite difficult to meet the occasional evening commitments where I had to work at headquarters showing parties of visitors around the building. The children at this time were ten and twelve and just a bit too young to leave in the house. Fortunately I had a ready source of baby-sitters in the police cadets based at HQ who were more than willing to come and spend an evening in front of my TV or new music system and earn a little pocket money as well. Most of them were girls to whom Maria related very well whilst Rob being the elder was quite happy doing his own thing playing with the Sinclair ZX81 computer which seemed to fascinate him at the time.

At this early stage of my single parenting I was not getting out much even when the children went off to see Denise. On these free weekends once I'd given the house a once-over and got up to date with all the jobs I was often at a bit of a loose end so during the days I put in more time with Emma at Horsley keeping on top of the garden and a variety of other jobs that needed doing around the place. In the evenings, more often than not I'd chill out at home with a bit of music, TV or a book.

One weekend though I agreed to house-sit for Bob Symes while he and Monica were away for a couple of nights. It was a lovely little cottage right out in the woods and although to some it might have seemed a bit spooky, I loved it. Monica had made a particular point that I shouldn't let the cat out at night as they feared it might fall prey to a fox which was all too likely so I took that on board and off they went leaving me in charge.

About half eight in the evening I took the fancy for a pint, hopped in the car and went off to the Duke of Wellington in Horsley, had my pint which turned into two after I met someone I knew so it was close to eleven when I got back to the cottage and let myself in and turned off the alarm.

I'd just started to get ready for bed when I realized the central heating was still on high which meant I had to step outside the door to the boiler room to turn it down. As I went out the cat tried to dive out between my legs so I grabbed the handle and slammed the door shut. I will probably always remember the sound of that CLICK! and the awful realization that I was outside but the door key was not. You probably don't want to know what I actually said to no-one in particular but it was loud and extremely uncouth. It didn't help a lot so then I had to start thinking. Peering through the letter box I could see the keys taunting me from where they were hanging in the alarm panel inside the under-stairs cupboard barely seven or eight feet away but it might as well have been a mile. At least I had light under the porch so I looked around for something that might reach them. No clothes prop or similar device, nothing. Away from the house the darkness was complete so although I stumbled about a bit to see what I could find I was more in danger of falling over something than solving my problem.

As I had started to get ready for bed I was minus jacket and shirt and dressed only in trouser but fortunately still had my shoes on and even more fortunately I discovered that my car keys were in the trouser pocket. Somehow I had to think of a way to reach those keys but I really was fishing in the dark. And then it hit me. *"A fishing rod. That's what I need."* And then I remembered Pip.

Pip Kerridge was a neighbour on the HQ estate and was one of the keenest fishermen I knew so I jumped in the car and headed back to my place at Guildford. I found a cup hook in the larder which I unscrewed and then went to knock up my neighbour. Pip Kerridge was known for many things, chief of which was probably his rich vocabulary and not suffering fools gladly, so I knew what to expect when I tapped on his front door at about half past midnight. Nothing. I tapped a little harder and a light came on in the bedroom and then Pip appeared at the front door. He was more amused than cross although you wouldn't have known that by the strength of his language. *"You want a f***ing fishing rod. In the middle of the f***ing night you want a f***ing fishing rod. Are you off your f***ing head?"*

He laughed like mad when he heard the story and seeing the idea he managed to find me an old rod. I took it back home, lashed the cup hook to the end and set off back to Bob's house. Half one in the morning sees me squatting outside his front door and fishing through the letter box for the keys. By some unbelievable luck I managed to hook them out of the alarm panel and draw them back through the letterbox. I was in at last although it was a long time before I got off to sleep. I did tell Bob about it some years later much to his entertainment.

I have always been a fairly red-blooded sort of guy so not surprisingly the physical rejection by my wife and the many months of self-imposed celibacy was quite a difficult issue for me. Now that I felt the brakes were off I yearned for some female affection. The problem was that my confidence in that area had pretty much disappeared; well to be blunt the world had moved on and I no longer knew the rules of the game.

My press liaison role meant that I had on occasions to visit the offices of a local newspaper in the far east of the county and if I could manage to arrange a babysitter I took the chance to call in and spend the evening with a friend whose counsel I came to value.

This was Lesley, the former partner of my friend Dave from the garage days. They were together for a long time but had eventually gone their separate ways and Lesley was then living alone in East Grinstead.

Living alone maybe but she was very much 'out there' and regaled me with accounts of her and her girlfriends going out *'on the pull'* as she put it to the local DSS clubs. Definitely nothing to do with social services, this was the 'Divorced, Separated and Single' scene. (so perhaps arguably it was a social service.) Held at local hotels or other dancing venues these were disco events where people who fitted the categories could meet and socialize and whatever else you like to imagine. Basically I guess they were the fore-runner of today's on-line dating scene.

She was tremendously encouraging and thought that I'd go down a bomb out there in the singles world of the 80's. *"Mature, good-looking and worldly-wise, newly single. You'll have no problems."* she said. *"Keep going."* I laughed. *"I'm almost convinced"*

One evening when I went to dinner with Lesley she was saying she hadn't been out much herself recently and after a glass or two of wine we got to talking out our frustrations which were basically sexual. It was interesting how the conversation developed to the point where we actually considered whether we might go to bed together 'just for the fun of it'.

I thought *"Just for fun? You mean sex can be just for fun and doesn't have to be serious, intense and accompanied by earnest protestations of undying love?"*

Given my rather outdated experience from the sixties and my religious background, this was a bit of a revelation. However, as my religious convictions by then were a distant memory, my main reaction to everything Lesley was saying was *"Why the hell not?"*

To be honest I think we were both very nearly up for some 'just for fun' but eventually concluded it would have felt almost incestuous, like making love to my sister or her brother. I can't say the idea was unattractive though. We laughed and had another drink. It was interesting though as it began the process of opening my eyes and mind to the idea of sex as fun. Throughout my teenage years even the slightest intimacy was an achievement and for many people of my generation and upbringing even sex within marriage was something men did and women allowed them to do. Or quite often not do.

Fortified by Lesley's encouragement, a couple of weeks later I took myself off to the DSS venue at Farncombe near Guildford. The last time I'd done anything like this was way back in the 60's when I used to go with mates to the Orchid Ballroom and Streatham Locarno. It felt so strange after all that time to be out socially by myself with the explicit intention of meeting someone and enjoying a social evening of dance and conversation. Well if that's what I hoped for I was in for a big surprise.

The venue was buzzing when I arrived and wandered into the dimly lit disco. I had heard these events dismissively referred to as 'meat markets' and to be honest, at one level that was not too far from the truth. It took a bit of getting used to before I made out the dance floor lit almost solely by pulsating disco lights and occupied mainly by a throng of women in a variety of outfits ranging from micro minis to skin-tight pants and almost everything in between, or in some cases not a lot in between. Down one side of the room the only slightly better illuminated bar glittered with polished surfaces and mirror tiles while the long bar counter itself seemed to be supporting a line of men trying to look cool and nonchalant as they leant back on the bar surveying the dance floor. There was in fact no barrier between the two areas although it looked almost as there might be but still the evening was young. Surely it had to get better.

I got myself a short for a bit of Dutch Courage and joined the row of observers even attempting a bit of casual conversation with one of them to virtually nil response. I continued to observe.

Music I find is infectious and for me the disco beat in particular, so it wasn't long (well two more drinks longer actually) before my foot was tapping and I really wanted to dance so I began to scrutinize the dancing talent more closely or as far as the lighting allowed. I spotted a very pretty dark-haired girl who wasn't actually dancing but was chatting to a friend beside the floor. Short with softly curling hair below her shoulders she looked from behind remarkably like Denise. Quite spookily so in fact.

"Well. In for a penny." I thought and asked her to dance. A couple of fast numbers allowed us to jig about a bit but not talk a lot but at least it broke the ice well. A slow ballad allowed a bit more contact and conversation when I discovered that she lived near Dunsfold, was divorced and was singly parenting three daughters. In the course of a couple of drinks and another dance or two I discovered her name was Cathy and that she'd love to know me better over a cup of coffee at her place after the dance.

To be honest I still didn't realise exactly where this was going because in my experience it wasn't women that made the running so I thought *"That's nice of her."*

An hour or so later I followed her car back to her rented cottage in the middle of nowhere south of Godalming. Her children were all in bed so she quietly made some coffee and we sat down in the living room which is where she rather took the lead. Well, absolutely if I'm honest. With the exception of American Anna at Horsley when I was not in a position to respond, my experience with sexually experienced women was virtually nil so here I was in pretty new territory but I have to admit enjoying every second. Half an hour later she took me to bed and treated me to a several hours of interesting and active sex including a few things I'd never experienced before. This to me was the Kama Sutra brought to life, and the best part about it was it was fun. We laughed, panted, gasped and giggled our way to an exhausted sleep. I had discovered that sex didn't have to be intense and serious. It really could be fun.

I stirred with the morning light and contemplated the previous eight hours. Given how relaxed she had been about taking me to her bed I did momentarily wonder who had been there the night before and then decided *"What the hell."*

Cathy woke and I told her I thought I should go before the children were up and that she could perhaps introduce me to them another day. So I slipped out of the house before six and drove home with a very contented smile and ready for the day.

We continued our interesting and (for me) highly educational affair for a couple of months until I received a phone call one day in the office from a sergeant at Godalming. He said he had heard I might be seeing a certain divorcee in Dunsfold and perhaps I should know about her ex-husband. It seemed that whenever he learnt that Cathy had a new man in her life he had the habit of getting drunk and coming through the door with a felling axe. *"Just a word to the wise mate."* he said. Cathy and I drifted apart after that. Shame really but a bit too risky.

What the experience had done however was to reignite my libido and boost my confidence. I felt wonderful and I looked forward excitedly to the alternate weekends when the children were away with their mother. If I'm honest I went a bit mad at this point and had several brief liaisons following the discos at Godalming and other venues.

One day when we had been out to lunch with some of our press associates at The Seahorse pub in Shalford I caught the eye of a very attractive girl working behind the bar. As we left I asked if she would like to have a drink with me sometime. She agreed and a couple of days later after a drink at a local pub we returned to my weekend bachelor pad at the headquarters estate.

Whilst at Horsley I had taken up home wine and beer making; an interest I continued after the move to Guildford. As a result I always had a ready supply of various home-made wines which sat maturing in demi-johns in the under-stairs cupboard. Not that much of it ever got as far as being bottled as the majority was consumed by me and a string of attractive visitors.

It would be crass to start listing my Mount Browne house-guests but I imagine you get the picture. A child and a cookie jar would be a good analogy for my life around that time. However, quite soon I began to weary of the shallowness of the DSS pick-up scene but quite by chance hit upon another way to develop a social life 'with benefits'.

I had first heard about Gingerbread from a single mum I was chatting to one evening. Today it is a UK charity providing expert advice, practical support and campaigns for single parents but in its earlier days seemed to be more about providing a social scene in addition to support activities. In Surrey it had also resulted in a number of unofficial local off-shoots the sole purpose of which was social. I got in touch with the Woking group and discovered that in addition to walking trips or bowling sessions, it was usual for one of the members to host a weekend house-party. Everyone was supposed to bring a 'party-food' contribution and something to drink and generally socialize and naturally enough from time to time we would hear that this or that person had found their soulmate. Great result if that's what you were looking for.

A new long-term relationship was certainly not on my wish-list at the time as I just wanted to socialize, relax and have some fun. The house parties were great though and worked very well for me to develop a social scene. The good thing about this group was that we were all pretty much in the same boat and with a lot of shared experiences so there was little difficulty finding common interests or topics for conversation. It was also understood if unspoken that the majority were probably open to something more than conversation with the right person.

This openness made for some very relaxed and fun gatherings and even on those days when I went home alone I always felt I'd had an enjoyable evening. This in itself was a great antidote to the pressures of day to day life as a working single parent.

Sharon was tall, blonde and extremely attractive and was the hostess at one of these gatherings. I was immediately attracted to her and as on other occasions one thing led to another and I stayed over. However on this occasion there was more to it and our friendship continued and developed over several months and she was the first girlfriend that I decided to introduce to my children. She was a hairdresser and very much into clothes and make-up so my daughter Maria took to her straight away. She had two children of her own who were younger than mine by several years. I got on with them OK but could well have done without on the basis of *"Been there, done that, thanks very much."* But clearly I never voiced my feelings in those terms.

I suppose I fell in love again with Sharon but when the chips were down, in the longer term it would have meant bringing our two families together and sadly that was something I just couldn't bring myself to even consider. I was afraid of getting hurt again and shy, not just of commitment but even more of doing the young children thing all over again. I knew I could never make it work, reluctantly told her so and we parted very sadly. Honesty above all has to be the rule.

ii

During this rather silly but exciting period I was living a somewhat Jekyll and Hyde existence, being the dutiful and attentive working parent most of the time whilst breaking out every other weekend when the children went to visit their mother. Looking back now it all seems a bit surreal.

One of the things I did with the kids was a trip up the Thames from Staines to Oxford. John Hoey, my former neighbour at Horsley had built a river cruiser which he kindly allowed me to borrow for a week but seemed totally unfazed by the fact that I had absolutely no boat handling experience. Initially I was just going to go with Robert, Maria and the dog but then thought it would be good to have some adult company too.

My friend John Bowyer who I'd known since my teenage years in Ashtead was actually in the same position as me having been divorced and also having custody of his two girls Lisa and Tracy. It was an interesting little group that set off. Two dads, Four kids and Barney the dog.

We learnt our boat handling by trial and (mostly) error as the only instruction John thought necessary was to explain the forward and reverse throttle lever. We had one brief practice at mooring the boat to steel stakes hammered into the bank but the most important thing (we later discovered) was not mentioned. Locks!

There are a lot of locks on the Thames and manoeuvring through them can be a challenge especially the first few times. It's not so bad if the lock is open and you can just go straight in but if it's closed then one has to moor and wait – if there is space! If not then it's even more difficult as you have to try and hold the boat on station in the stream and as there is usually a weir nearby it is almost impossible not to find yourself drifting sideways towards it. The only solution then is to power up and describe a circle in order to get back in position.

I'd been a bit worried about taking Barney and imagined him either falling in off the narrow side-walks on the boat or even leaping into the water in pursuit of wildlife. As it happened he was very surefooted and seemed to really enjoy the whole thing, standing up on the bow like a ship's figurehead with his ears blowing in the breeze.

He let himself down however at the second lock we had to negotiate by leaping ashore and peeing on the lock-keepers lovingly tended flower borders.

Thereafter, as we approached a lock we had to put him below in the cabin. Well, talk about Pavlovian conditioning; after only a day of this practice, as soon as Barney heard the engine revs drop he went down to the cabin of his own accord.

John and I navigated by pubs, arranging our overnight stops where we could moor and walk to a nearby hostelry in the evening, ideally with a garden where the two dads could quaff a pint or two while the kids had their soft drink and crisps. Local shops were also a must so we could stock up on provisions for the next couple of days.

Maria and Tracy found a CB radio set on board and it wasn't long before they were chatting to everyone from passing lorry drivers to enthusiastic radio 'hams' and even a couple of house-bound elderly ladies whose only social contact was via their CB's

It was a super week and we were very lucky with the weather which was a bonus. We managed to get into the suburbs of Oxford before we had to turn and head back downstream again and would you believe on the day we got back, as we were mooring Barney did actually fall off into the river.

I continued to do a lot with the children including a couple of holidays down in Devon where we stayed with my cousin and his family near Dartmoor. He had four sons roughly the same age as my two so it all worked very well.

Me, Robert and Maria with my cousin Gerry
and his four boys in Devon.

I usually managed to fit in trips to the cinema, museums, swimming, Guy Fawkes night, school parents' evenings and any other activities I could think of to develop, entertain and educate them. The social club at Mount Browne used to put on a Christmas outing for the children which was usually to a London pantomime or film in addition to the children's party in the headquarters bar. Regular discos were also held there much to Maria's excitement although Rob preferred to stay at home which was fine as he was a sensible thirteen year old by this time.

It was around this time that I first met Marilyn. I had seen her around the headquarters building where she worked as a communications officer in the Control Room taking emergency calls and managing incidents around the county via the force radio scheme. I was in the bar one lunch time when I saw her chatting with Gwen Kidder the HQ telephonist who introduced us. Marilyn was a keen independent traveller and was about to head off on a trip to Australia and was talking to Gwen about not having a camera so I said she could borrow mine. She never did but must have got hold of one because on her return she contacted me to ask if I'd be interested to see the pictures.

From the start it was her independence and determination that I admired hugely but she was also attractive, lively and intelligent although she could also be a bit fiery on occasion. A friendship began and became more as time passed so that by the early part of '83 she was spending a lot of time with me at the Mount Browne house but not actually living there. We felt it was a bit too much 'under the HQ eye' to do that without in some way making it official.

Ever since Denise and I had to sell our little home in Horley I had harboured the ambition to once again get back onto the property ladder although this had been impossible all the while the children were growing up. The Edmund Davies police pay award in 1979 substantially improved the situation across the board but getting back into a home of our own would still have needed a decent deposit which we didn't have. In any event by that time I had so little confidence in my marriage that there was no way I would have embarked on joint home ownership with Denise. What a good thing I didn't.

Despite the arrangement with Emma regarding her house I still felt that I should try to be independent of that situation and in early 1983 an opportunity arose. Due to a general move among police officers towards house ownership since the pay award a number of police houses had become surplus to requirements. And in the same way as the Government's

Right to Buy Scheme worked for council tenants, serving officers were allowed to bid for the surplus police houses. In the end I got top bid on two and decided on a 1960's semi at Merrow on the outskirts of Guildford.

There was a local building society at Guildford where the branch manager was a former police officer and offered preferential terms for force members. He got me the hundred percent mortgage I needed and we moved in April 1983. I even did my own conveyancing which turned out to be much simpler than solicitors would have us believe.

It couldn't have been better really as it was an easy commute for me to work and close to St Peter's Catholic Comprehensive school for the children. It was actually the same school I had attended in the late fifties although back then it had been a private grammar school. I may no longer have had the faith but I still believed in the values instilled by a religious based education. So, a good result all round.

26 RECRUITMENT

i

Towards the end of 1981 there was much talk about the length of time people should be allowed to remain in specialist posts. This was against the background of political pressure to maximize the number of officers on the streets and where possible to replace desk-bound police officers with civilian personnel.

Argument veered to and fro around the relative pros and cons of extended specialization. Against was the suggestion that police officers away from operational work could become de-skilled in what was called 'core policing ability'.

This, it was argued could necessitate expensive re-training or even mean some would never be able to become operationally useful again due to age or loss of confidence. It could also mean that by allowing individuals to occupy such posts for lengthy periods other colleagues were denied the opportunity to learn and develop new specialist skills which was regarded as an important factor in supporting individual morale and career development.

Alternatively the counter argument was that longer periods allowed those concerned to build up often critically valuable knowledge and abilities. These could be lost to the force by returning the individuals to the more routine range of operational street duties where the specialist skill sets would be less useful. It could also mean that following the departure of a skilled specialist there would a drop in the performance of the relevant department while a new incumbent picked up speed.

It was a very tricky and emotive issue especially for those actually occupying such posts which included all of us in the press office which it has to be admitted was a pretty plum job. For me it was doubly difficult as due to my family situation I was not able to put myself forward for normal shift duties and the force had gone on record with an undertaking that I could have my 'office hours' for as long as I needed them.

It was in June '82 when our Chief Superintendent called me in for a chat. He explained that having been in PRO for almost five years it really was time for me to have a move. In his view a return to divisional duties was the preferred option, both in terms of my career development and to satisfy the pressure for rotation of specialist personnel. He said he understood my situation and asked if I had any assistance with looking after the children and in particular leaving them overnight.

I had been anticipating this conversation and as Marilyn and I were not actually living together I had my answer ready. I explained that whilst Robert and Maria were fourteen and twelve respectively and could be left for a few hours during an evening if necessary it was not quite yet appropriate to leave them alone in the house overnight. He had also anticipated this reply and smiling said *"I guessed that would be the situation so we have another plan for you. The Chief Constable would like you to take over as the Force Recruiting Officer."* Well I definitely had not seen that one coming but when he explained the role, challenging though it was, I grabbed it with both hands.

He explained that premature wastage of new recruits during their two year probationary period had been causing concerns as it was in the region of twenty three percent. This was a problem for various reasons, one being the considerable cost involved in their recruitment and training. Secondly as wastage through retirement continued at a more or less steady rate it meant that the professional skill level of the force as a whole was diminishing as the percentage of officers with only limited experience gradually increased.

Apparently a working party had been looking at the problem and come to the (I thought, unsurprising) conclusion that the fault was in the recruitment process. I didn't say anything but imagined cynically that it had probably taken several out of touch senior officers much deliberation to come to a conclusion that was not exactly rocket science.

What was apparently needed was for someone to take a completely fresh look at our recruitment process and come up as soon as possible with some recommendations to improve the situation. This person was to be me. *"Blimey."* I thought. *"Talk about making or breaking my reputation."* I was hugely flattered of course but also very daunted by the responsibility.

I took over as the Surrey Constabulary Recruiting Officer in June 1982 and set about reading the working party report which in essence had concluded that we were not looking closely enough at applicants. Apparently we needed a more sophisticated and robust process that would firstly examine potential officers across a range of characteristics that might indicate whether they were temperamentally or intellectually right for the job.

Such closer examination should also indicate whether recruits would survive the initial training followed by the probationary period and then the transition to the full range of operational duties. (This as far as I can recall was the essence of the conclusions which I thought somewhat woolly and used a lot of words to say not much.) What the report didn't define was what the desirable characteristics were.

There were two clear parts to this new job. One was running the existing selection process on a day to day basis whilst at the same time trying to create something more effective to replace it with. First though was to get familiar with the system as it existed.

Aspiring police constables had to be British subjects, of good character, 5'10" in height (it was later reduced), be physically fit with good eyesight, be literate and numerate as determined by the entry examination. If these criteria were met candidates were called to headquarters for an interview. This was usually carried out by the Chief and if the interview went well they were in. Beyond that point the rule seemed to be *"The Chief selected them now you lot train them."*

Looking at this system, the first thing that came to my mind was how much of a one way process it was. There was no attempt whatever to inform the potential recruit about what life as a police officer would be like so that was one element I decided needed to be addressed in any new process.

Secondly, a ten minute interview based pretty much around the interviewer's gut feeling seemed to me a rather poor indicator of likely future performance. I felt that what we needed was first a list of criteria that would define suitability and then a process that would test candidates against them.

Looking at this today when the process of recruitment and selection has developed into the hugely sophisticated speciality we call 'human resource management' it seems hard to believe that it really was that basic. I thought *"We can surely do better than this for the force and the applicants."*

A bit of research led me to the idea of extended interview processes or what are now usually called assessment centre selections and I discovered that the military and Marks and Spencer and the Special Course had been using them for some time so I arranged to go and have a chat with them.

This is probably a good point at which to make a long story short so it is sufficient to say that I arrived at a point where I had a list of essential and desirable competencies on which to base our own assessment process which I envisaged could usefully fill a couple of days. Given that the police entrance test was going to cover basic numeracy and literacy I came up with a programme designed to test things like confidence, problem solving, ability to think on the feet, team work, verbal and written communication and so on.

Social skills and attitudes around things like gender and racial prejudices were very important but hard to test formally in a short time so I came up with the idea of using serving constables in the process on a one to one basis with each applicant. The arrangement was that an experienced and appropriately trained PC would be introduced to each candidate halfway through the first day after they had completed the physical assessment which was just a series of gym tests and a short run.

Their brief was two-fold; the first being to effectively befriend the candidate and inform them as fully as possible about their own life as a working police officer. How they did this was entirely up to the individual and some married officers even took married candidates home to meet their families whilst others spent the evening together in the HQ bar where inhibitions soon disappeared and any less desirable attitudes and traits could more easily surface.

The following day the constable assessors sat in on the presentations and other exercises and kept their own records for later discussion. They were fully involved in the process and the second element of their brief was to consider *"How would this person fit in working with you?"*

I devised one other little test that I thought was worthwhile but some people didn't like because they felt it was a bit underhand. It was a form of peer assessment which was quite anonymous and produced some interesting result. Each candidate was given a paper on which to write six names in response to these questions.

Who among your fellow candidates would you:

1. least like to work with?
2. most like to work with?
3. least like to socialise with?
4. most like to socialise with?
5. least like as your leader?
6. most like as your leader?

As an exercise in group dynamics it was very revealing and the best part of it was that mainly it confirmed our own impressions of the candidates so was also a worthwhile validation tool. Interestingly, the most popular individuals socially were not so often seen as good to work with or accept as a leader. The most interesting way of interpreting the results was to draw it up as a diagram with 'love' and 'hate' arrows pointing to the names. It was very dramatic.

To ensure fairness and transparency, full records were kept of all the scores and comments and for me this would have been enough. However we still had to tip our hats to the former system so the final hurdle was a relatively brief interview by an ACC (Assistant Chief) and a divisional Chief Superintendent. During my time in the job the ACC was Chris Atkins who I had first met way back in '69 at the Horley air crash and who I have always held in high regard.

Initially the arrangement was that I presented each candidate to the board and then left the room. I hated this, as having put all the effort in to get them that far, the icing on the cake was to see how they performed. When I spoke to Chris Atkins he was more than happy for me to stay and even better, he allowed me to share my views having sat at the back of the room throughout.

Following the introduction of this process the improvement was immediate with almost no drop-outs in the first year. However the proof of the pudding would take a bit longer.

Other aspects of the job included attending a national police recruitment exhibition in London as well as any number of talks on police careers to schools and army resettlement courses.

The police rank structure is a broad based pyramid with loads of indians, quite a few senior indians but relatively few big chiefs. For example at the time I am talking about the total complement of the Surrey force was around sixteen hundred officers of which some thirteen hundred were constables. The number of other ranks depended largely on the number of divisions in the force which varied over the time I served in Surrey between three and nine and back again (probably more than once and another good example of an organization inventing and re-inventing the wheel). So the number of Chief Superintendent posts varied periodically as required to have one per division plus another three for HQ departments and a proportionate number of sergeants, inspectors, chief inspectors and superintendents.

With PC Les Hubbard at a school career convention.

As the force recruiting officer I was rather back in the PR role at times as I endeavoured to promote the job as a career with good prospects for advancement. This was absolutely true but truer still was the fact that competition for senior ranks was always going to be fierce although I contended that like cream on milk good people will rise to the top. All this however was without the complication of the Graduate Entry Scheme which I also had to administer.

I don't recall the full details but, a bit like the Special Course, this was another programme foisted on the service by Home Office in an effort to get some bright kiddies into the job and promote them rapidly to more senior ranks.

Basic entry requirements were the same but graduate candidates were exempted from taking the entry exam. This was on the assumption that they could write, spell and add up which didn't always prove to be the case. While a degree in a subject like law, psychology or sociology was seen as beneficial to a police career the view promulgated from on high was that the nature of the degree was more or less irrelevant but indicated a level of intelligence and ability to study and learn.

Well that may be true up to a point but once we started the two day assessment process we soon found the flaws. Time and again our bright graduates turned out to be seriously short on common sense, confidence and leadership potential. Curiously one of the best I recall was a girl with a degree in drama who ran rings around the others because she was basically brighter and more imaginative.

Even with the new system to operate I was still essentially a one-man band with just dear old Hilda – known as 'H' as my typist and admin support. Around the same time as we got the two day process going the new training school opened at HQ and my department was moved into slightly more spacious offices. And as the new system needed more paperwork I also managed to poach another admin assistant from HQ Registry by the name of Rowena who became a friend I am still in touch with today.

Due to the economic situation at the time when unemployment was relatively high we were fishing in a very large pond of people who fancied their chances in the police service; quite often I guessed out of desperation for employment rather than an urgent vocational desire to be a police officer. I was mindful here of my own entry into the service which was also to an extent born of desperation to secure my family so I had to try hard to read between the lines to find a motivation I could live with.

At times we were receiving dozens if not scores of applications a day which I had to read as soon as possible to avoid keeping people waiting for a result and so the pile of application forms on my living room floor in the evenings just seemed to grow and grow.

This was the first paper sift and rightly or wrongly I made it quite a severe test. So if it seemed to me that someone had been slapdash over their completion of the form, their writing or spelling let them down, their job history raised too many questions or they sounded more like a couch potato than a person who was prepared to get up and do stuff then I chopped them at that stage.

We also had many very young applicants who were difficult to deal with especially if they were otherwise well qualified. However, the police service demands ideally a level of life experience and maturity rarely found in someone at the minimum entry age of nineteen.

Some youngsters who had been well advised at school had already joined the police cadets so arguably by the time they were nineteen they did at least have a working knowledge of the force and gained some maturity along the way. Generally speaking serving cadets did find their way through to the assessment centre but by no means all made it out the other side.

Other applicants I deemed too young or immature were advised to go off for a while to gain some life experience and joining the Special Constabulary was an idea I often suggested. Not only would it provide a valuable insight for the individual into aspects of the police role but it would also prove to me a level of commitment when they re-applied. Other things that impressed were completion of the Duke of Edinburgh Award scheme, voluntary work and independent travel, all of which indicated a level of maturity, determination and self-sufficiency to my mind ideal in a job like the police service.

I was immensely proud to be the force recruiting officer, mindful that I was representing the force at the various outside events and also of the responsibility I bore in bringing on board the right people. Over the years I have gained enormous satisfaction from seeing a good many of my own recruits rise through the ranks in Surrey as well as a few who transferred to other forces and even achieving Chief Officer rank as in the case of Adrian Leppard who eventually retired in 2015 whilst serving as Commissioner of the City of London Police.

The individual or small team scenario seems to suit me although it can be a bit high risk in career terms but then if it's not a challenge, it's not worthwhile. Anyway the work I did seems to have paid off and although the process has been further developed to a point I guess I would hardly recognize now I hope my contribution was a worthwhile first step.

It wasn't all as intense as perhaps I've made it sound, in fact there were plenty of laughs along the way especially after we moved to the new training wing where we were very much part of a larger group with all the pranks and social banter that went with that situation. One that comes to mind was in relation to a girl we had in the office as a temp for a while. She was a tall attractive blonde and I think her name was Ann.

Chief Constable Brian Hayes joined Surrey in 1982 and his enthusiasm for sport and running in particular infected many of us at HQ to the extent that lunch times saw a mass exodus of runners heading off into the surrounding countryside. I went off one day along with a couple of other guys as well as Ann who was also into keeping fit. We headed for St Martha's Hill which is on the other side of the River Wey and a round distance of about five miles.

It was a hot day and on the return leg we got to the foot bridge over the river at St Catherines and on a rash impulse decided as a group to jump off the bridge into the river to cool off. That was fine as far as it went but when Ann emerged from the water it was the classic wet T shirt image. She was wearing no bra and the briefest of panties so once soaking wet not a lot was left to the imagination. She was more or less Ok with that and saw the funny side especially as she knew us all but when we left the river to go up to cross the main road we came upon a team of road workers who had arrived since we came down on the out run. The only way Ann could cover her embarrassment was to get one of us to run very close behind her while she followed as close as possible to the guy in front which was extremely pleasant for the two concerned, neither of which was me unfortunately.

ii

The new house at Merrow was great, especially knowing that it was mine, or as much as any mortgaged home could be. Probably built in the early 70's, it was a semi and one of six that had been tucked in between the private Boxgrove Park and the council owned Bushy Hill estates. It was similar to the one we'd had in Ashtead with three bedrooms plus a spacious lounge, dining room and kitchen.

There was a single attached garage and a good sized rear garden with a magnificent oak tree at the end. Although it was tidy not a lot had been done to the garden so it was pretty much a blank canvas on which I hoped to put my own mark. Our immediate neighbours were police colleagues Ian Robertson and Alan Hobbs with their respective families. I'd worked with Ian on CID at Guildford a few years previously so it was very nice to renew acquaintances.

The good thing was that there were no rules around how I lived in it as there were with the various police houses. So I knew I could paint, decorate or change it any way I wanted which may only have been a small thing but gave a great sense of independence. On the down side, as it was a move I had chosen to make there was no removal allowance so once again curtains and carpets etc. had been pulled up and cannibalized to fit the new place.

Another plus to being an owner occupier was that police regulations decreed that we had either rent free accommodation provided or were paid a rent allowance which for owner occupiers made a valuable contribution towards paying any mortgage. The allowance was based on rateable value so for those lucky enough to have only a small mortgage to pay, it covered that with some to spare. Unfortunately not so in my case but it made a very healthy contribution.

The other major benefit to the rent allowance rules was that it was tax free. In practice tax was deducted at the time but then each financial year came back as what was known as the compensatory grant which, would you believe, thanks to the peculiarities of the tax system was also taxed and then returned the next year. The net result of this was that after several years of this 'rolling-up' system the compensatory grant accumulated to the point where it was a very welcome chunk of money arriving in the spring just in time to boost the annual holiday fund.

My friendship with Marilyn had been on-going and after I'd been in the house a few months we decided she should move in. This was always going to be tricky because Robert and Maria were accustomed to having me more or less to themselves. Anyway, apart from the odd hiccup and with a bit of effort all round it seemed to work OK although I'm guessing that the others' perspective on this might be a bit different.

We had the usual ups and downs as the kids got into their mid-teens including the mood swings and boundary testing that goes on around that age and it was a huge challenge for Marilyn coming on board at that potentially difficult time. She handled it wonderfully well but it was far from stress free. For me an added dimension was that I was always on the lookout for any signs that the divorce experience had caused emotional damage over and above the obvious upset. Denise and I had both worked very hard at keeping life for Rob and Maria on as even a keel as possible and whatever our differences were, they weren't aired in front of the children.

As they grew and matured it was only natural that they sought more freedom and as far as Maria was concerned the clothes she wanted to wear was an area that often became contentious. Frankly it wasn't a situation helped by visits to Denise who seemed only too happy to let her dress in a way that to my view was inappropriate for her age.

The problem was that after years in the police I had seen enough over-dressed and under-age girls flaunting themselves and then coming to grief. Despite this I had always tried to take a fairly calm and balanced view about this aspect of their growing up whilst also being mindful of the inherent dangers of allowing teenage daughters to wear the sort of clothes they thought appropriate. So I was very protective of my own pretty 'fifteen – going on twenty-one year old' daughter who seemed more or less blind to the risks and deaf to my concerns.

However, despite all my own personal angst around these things there were many moments along the way which whilst not so funny at the time, were in retrospect. One of these moments was in relation to my rapidly developing and extremely pretty daughter who was as much if not more interested in the boys than they were in her.

Maria had a friend whose parents owned a weekend caravan out in the country down at Lurgashall in West Sussex and she and the friend came up with a plan to go and spend a weekend there. They were probably about fifteen at this time so we felt they were old enough to enjoy a little adventure. I mean how naïve can you be? But I suppose if you've grown up with Swallows and Amazons this looked like a fairly safe way to let them feel their feet.

Her friend's parents dropped them down there and the plan was that they would stay just a couple of nights. They had all the food and other stuff they needed and I guess we imagined they would just sit in the van and do 'girl-talk' or maybe have a walk in the fields. As I said, how naïve.

They had gone off on the Friday evening and I think it was either on the Saturday evening or Sunday midday that Marilyn and I thought we might take a run out that way to say hello to them. They weren't in the caravan so the only other ideas we could think was that they had gone for a country walk over the fields or along to Lurgashall village.

A nature walk was hardly Maria's thing so we set off back to the village. There is hardly a village as such just a very pretty cricket green with a few little period cottages around the edge and the pub. And I guess in that moment we knew exactly where they were.

Inside, the pub was busy and there in the thick of it playing darts and surrounded by quite a few local youths were the girls. Flies and honeypots would be an apt description of the scene. They were both dressed to the nines, and Maria was in a short and very tight red dress over fish-net stocking and was tottering around (quite expertly actually) on these tall stiletto heels. I can't recall Clair's outfit but pretty much the same sort of thing as far as I remember. Our arrival didn't exactly make us top pf the popularity poll and I was pleased to see at least half of the 'flies' buzz off back to the bar. Not wanting to embarrass them we didn't make a big thing of it at the time but I was quite pleased we decided to visit.

I tried later to once again make the point that her outfit was not exactly appropriate to either her age or an evening with a bunch of drunken lads in the middle of nowhere not to mention being in the pub at all at that age. She still thought I was boring but I will always remember how the actress Susan George came to grief in the film Straw Dogs and that really does show my age.

It was probably around the same time that I had to chase a young Romeo off our garage roof where he had climbed to either spy on or get to chat with Maria in her bedroom. I had to smile a bit though as I remembered my own youth when I managed to lock myself out after a midnight sortie to meet up with some girls who had invited a friend and me to visit them in their summer house. So perhaps not a lot changes except in my case I was discovered by a passing policeman as I tried to break into my own bedroom window which meant having to wake my parents to vouch for me.

It was such a joy to have Marilyn with me all the time instead of just coming and going, being around some days and not others. Her obvious warmth and affection worked their magic on me and the mistrust and fear of a further relationship which had been holding me back emotionally began to dissipate. I felt able again to give more of myself and to believe that it didn't have to all go wrong again which is what I had been feeling.

From a practical point of view Marilyn's arrival on my domestic scene was a real godsend because with work and lone parenting I had rather let my financial affairs slip into disarray. Because Denise had been awarded legal aid for her representation at the custody hearing my own solicitor advised that I too should engage counsel to put my case. However I did not qualify for legal aid and had to fund my own costs. So, I had my custody award but also a thousand pound debt which I was finding hard to manage.

Getting me organized moneywise seemed second nature to Marilyn which was brilliant. And I must admit that as she was a great deal better at it than me I tended to let her take over somewhat in that department.

I think it was in 1984 that we managed a foreign holiday for the first time. Marilyn had a friend whose family owned a villa in Spain so we went there as a family for a week. Maria loved it because the villa had a pool and the sun shone the whole time which suited her temperament perfectly.

Rob was less excited, didn't want to try the local food and was desperate to find somewhere he could go and play video games which of course there wasn't. Still, we survived and although I probably didn't realise it my love affair with Spain had begun.

It would be boring to recount daily life indoors with its various ups and downs but as the dust settled our relationship felt strong enough for me to put myself up once again for promotion to Inspector and this time I could say that the ages of the children were no longer a problem and I could if required, perform normal operational duties.

The feedback from on-high regarding my performance in the recruiting role was very favourable especially as the early years wastage rate was still holding its own at a very much lower level than before we brought in the new system. On balance I felt that all other things being equal I should now have a reasonable chance of moving up the ladder a bit further.

27 PROMOTION

i

Just a little more than two years after I took over the Recruiting job I got my reward as the Chief said when he saw me *"for a job well done."* In August 1985 I was promoted to a post as uniform Inspector at Godalming.

I hand over the Recruiting files to Sergeant Mick Day

If I'm honest I was very nervous, maybe even terrified of going back to operational duties because to quote the argument on the subject, I was conscious that after some seven years on HQ specialist duties I was very much de-skilled in core policing abilities.

I don't know why but promotion or a move to a new station almost always means that you start work on a night shift which was just what happened when I went to Godalming.

It was my very first night and I was sitting-in on the section briefing, listening to the sergeant allocating beat and car patrols when the call came in that there was a big punch-up in one of the local pubs. I have to confess it was just about the last thing in the world I needed at that moment because I didn't really know what to do but was incredibly conscious that it was me everyone was looking to for a command decision.

"*OK. Let's go and have a look at it.*" I said, trying to sound fairly relaxed.

Someone else said. "*It'll be pikies in that pub. No need to rush. Let 'em fight it out first.*" I couldn't have agreed more but as most of the guys were already heading for their cars and pleased at the prospect of a bit of action I said to the sergeant "*I don't even know where it is so I'll come with you.*" And off we went.

Even now I can't recall the name of the pub but judging from the noise the fight was still going a bit when we arrived and some of the guys' initial enthusiasm seemed to have evaporated.

I can't tell you how my knees were knocking but I thought "*Better do something I guess.*" so I said "*Come on then. Let's sort them out.*" and marched in the door, fortunately with about eight blokes behind me.

There were five actually fighting so I shouted "*OK What's all this then?*" which had absolutely no effect. I then took a deep breath and shouted louder. "*You're all fucking nicked.*"

That stopped them dead and then just for a moment I wasn't sure whether they were going to start on us but they thought better of it and started trying to make little of the whole thing. So I said

"*You're all arrested on suspicion of assault and affray and you can make your excuses up down at the nick. Take them in Sergeant.*"

And that was it really. We didn't charge them with affray which would have been too heavy duty and to be honest now I don't remember how it went. A public order offence would probably have been in order but as no one would make a complaint assaults against the person weren't an option either. The most important thing was that we attended and stopped the trouble and from my own perspective I got off to quite a credible start.

Overall my time at Godalming was pretty run-of-the mill with no particular high or low spots worthy of comment. And to be honest I probably didn't score too highly with my section as the charismatic crime-fighting team leader I might have wished to be.

Some guys get their buzz from leading a team into action whether it is into a scrum of striking miners or simply to sort out a bit of trouble on the High Street but I regret to say that's not me. You have to know and be honest with yourself and after a few months as a patrol Inspector I knew that the type of specialist role I'd just come from was far more my forte.

This was probably the proof, if anyone had been looking, that too long on non-operational roles does indeed result in loss of confidence and core policing skills. Anyway, I had been at Godalming about nine months when fate took a hand and attempted to rescue me.

ii

On the home front, things were settling down quite nicely with only the usual minor domestic issues around where the kids went, who with, what time they came in, why they treated the house like a hotel, etc. etc.

As teenage girls tend to mature rather earlier than boys it was hardly surprising that Maria had been the one to kick over the traces and test the boundaries first. However that is not to say that Rob's teenage years were uneventful although he started slightly later.

I think the first memorable event was one evening when Marilyn, Maria and I went out to a HQ disco leaving Rob behind playing Dungeons and Dragons with his friend Steven. We arrived back around midnight to find two very poorly, as in drunk, fifteen-year-olds. They had decided to sample some of my home-brew beer and found it very much to their taste although deceptively strong. Steven had got to the point of being very sick in the garden and Rob was on the verge.

I shall never forget poor Rob as we put him to bed with a plastic bowl on the floor beside him and being impressed by his overriding concern for his friend as he repeated over and over *"Please look after Steven, Please look after Steven."*

Then there was the time we awoke to an overpowering stench of cow-manure which on investigation turned out to be coming from the airing cupboard. Once again alcohol was the cause.

Apparently Rob had been to a party, had too much to drink and been offered a lift home by someone. Dozing in the car he woke to realize he was heading north up the A3 which was totally the wrong direction so he got the friend to drop him off but then had to find his way home.

Knowing only roughly where he was he decided to walk across country where he stumbled into copious quantities of cow shit and water filled ditches. Frankly, he was lucky not to have fared far more seriously as in that state he could easily have drowned.

Arriving home in the small hours he just dumped all his clothes in the laundry basket which lived in the bottom of the airing cupboard and went to bed. The warmth of the nearby hot tank very soon had the cow poo fermenting nicely and smelling strongly enough to wake us. Needless to say he slept on.

"What's brought this on now?" I asked, looking up at Rob and trying to keep a note of exasperation from my voice but probably not succeeding.

Most parents will be familiar with that "What now?" feeling. Those moments when you wonder if the next part of the offspring package is about to be delivered and hoping desperately that it might turn out to be the brain.

My 17-year-old son was standing holding two plastic bags containing what looked like grey pebbles and gravel and had just announced that he was giving up meat.

"We all need to give it up," he said . *"Producing meat protein is a long way round and it costs too much. We could easily get all the protein we need from vegetable sources like this Soya"*

He stood there looking earnest. Actually with long straight hair well past his shoulder he looked pretty gormless to me, rather like Neil in 'The Young Ones' TV series.

The trouble was, that with my 'short back and sides' and 'smart appearance' mentality born from years in the police, I had a bit of a problem dealing with the teenage need to look like something the cat dragged in.

At least the worst of the 'hair thing' had past now; namely his decision not only to grow his hair but not to wash it. The theory went like this. *Frequent washing removes all the natural oils and dries the hair out. If you leave it long enough without washing the natural oils build up repelling dirt and keeping it lustrous, and naturally clean'.*

"Oh Yea." There was no way he would see it any other way and I'd have to give it to him for determination. He even stuck it out when we replaced his pillowcase with a black plastic bin bag. So we just shut up and one day without saying anything he started washing his hair again. We didn't say anything either. It seemed a bit unkind.

So now I was thinking *"Oh no! – Here we go again"*

I said, *"It doesn't look very appetising. What do you do with it?"*

A sort of messianic glow came over him. *"It's fantastic stuff."* He said. *"You can do all sorts of things. These are the meat substitutes and you use them like mince or chunks of beef. You can make curries, casseroles, shepherd's pie, anything. They can even make it into milk so in time we won't need all the dairy herds either"*

I said. *"That would be a shame. I like cows and anyway what will happen to the farmers?"*

He was on a roll now. *"They'll just change over to growing more vegetable crops to feed people directly. Instead of using cows to process acres of grass they can grow all the grain and other things we need to feed the world's exploding population"*
"Did you know," he went on *"that the digestion processes of cattle is a major factor in changing our climate?*

"You what!" I said. *"It's right. They produce methane in vast quantities and it's been discovered that it's a greenhouse gas."*

A sense of the ridiculous began to come over me and I started to laugh.
 "What! Cow farts are going to destroy the planet?

He looked hurt. *"Listen. It's serious and it's really possible to change things if we all do our bit"*
"OK." I said. *"You do your bit and I'll think about it.*

Of course the greenhouse gas – global warming theories hold tremendous sway now so it seems that Rob was pretty much in the vanguard at the time although like the hair and a few of his other ideas it didn't last too long.

With scientific evidence to back up the theory, it probably would be beneficial if we got our protein directly rather than via meat eating but the whole subject still makes me smile. I suppose it's that schoolboy sense of the ridiculous and the whole of the 'fart' thing.

I can't help imagining life in the average office if at a stroke everyone went 'high fibre'. My God! It's bad enough when the odd person has a night out on the beer or a curry supper. If everyone turned 'veggie' they'd have to invent new high efficiency ventilation systems which would use even more energy so we'd all be back to square one. It's pure Monty Python.

However, that's not the end of the Soya saga.

I've always liked cooking and one of the things I really enjoy doing is curry. I especially like preparing the spices and doing the whole thing from scratch – none of your ready-made sauce for me.

It was probably a couple of months after the Soya phase had run its course that I found myself home alone one evening and having to knock up some supper for myself. Now, whilst I like cooking curry and we both enjoy eating it, Marilyn hates the cooking smells that tend to linger so as she was away overnight I decided it was the perfect time for a curry supper. Until, that is, I found that she'd apparently eaten the chicken I was planning to use.

I was about to give up the idea and hit the cereals - always a good stand-by; when I remembered Rob's Soya chunks, and sure enough they were still there in the back of the cupboard. "*Great!*" I thought.

I soon had a good basic curry sauce on the go and lobbed in a handful of the Soya and gave it a stir. I had no idea at all how long it would take to cook but assumed that like packet soups and those awful 'pot-noodles' it would just need a while to absorb some moisture and turn into nice tender meaty chunks. Wrong!

After twenty minutes simmering with periodic stirring the Soya chunks were still hard although he sauce was getting too thick. More water, more stirring and another twenty minutes and still the damn things had hardly softened at all. *"No wonder this never caught on"* I thought *" but it's a great way to lose weight"*.

Half an hour later I'd had enough. I was starving and the Soya was just beginning to soften so I decided I'd better eat before I went off the idea altogether.

Well, it was certainly a curry to remember. The sauce was absolutely wonderful as all the flavour had developed beautifully but the meat- sorry, Soya, was terrible. It was still hardly cooked. Gooey and incredibly chewy would be the best description. I did persevere with a couple of chunks before giving up. *"Well, at least the sauce and the rice went down well enough"*

I'd gone to bed by the time Marilyn came in but at breakfast she said *"Sorry I didn't have time to leave you anything out for supper. Did you manage to sort something out for yourself?"*

I said, *"Yes I made a curry but I can't say I think much of Rob's Soya"*

"We haven't got any Soya. I got rid of it ages ago" *"Yes we have"* I said and pulled the remains from the cupboard. *"I found it in here but it was awful."*

Her mouth fell open and then she collapsed into hysterical laughter.

"What" I said.

"That's not Soya" she choked, scarcely able to speak for laughing.

"Yes it's those chunky things he had" I said

She was more or less incoherent by now *"It's not"* she spluttered

I was between cross and anxious. *"What is it then?"* I demanded

Still hardly able to contain herself she said *"Dog biscuits"*

I said, *"You're joking!"*

"No Honestly. Caroline gave them to us for Barney. Her dog can't eat them because they're too hard."

Fortunately my sense of humour returned. *"Oh Woof!"* I said as I reached for the marmalade.

iii

Promotion, inheritance, children, careers etc. apart; the really big milestone for me during this time was when Marilyn and I were married on 31st May 1986. It had taken a long time for me to come round to the idea as having been so hurt previously my main reaction was *'Been there, done it, not again thank you."* However it was clearly very important to Marilyn that I display the commitment and now, writing these words thirty one years down the line, I know it was the best thing I ever did in my life.

28 COMPUTER TRAINING

i

My former Public Relations colleague Bob Ball had become the Superintendent in charge of what was called the Force Project Team charged with bringing the force into the rapidly developing computer age.

The team needed a training officer and Bob had asked the Chief if he could have me for the job as he knew we could work together and I had the right experience from my time as an instructor. Unfortunately the Chief was of the view that I needed to be outside a bit longer so another Inspector got the job. However, fate came to my aid again when for domestic reasons he had to leave the project and rather than embark on a selection process, when Bob asked again the Chief agreed and in early 1987 I found my-self back at HQ.

At that particular time the main project was the introduction of a new computer aided dispatch system for the force. Basically this was a system that brought computer assistance to the recording of incidents and the deployment of various resources in response.

Hitherto all calls for police assistance whether to local stations or via 999 calls to the HQ Control Room were manually logged using a paper record. Cars or beat officers were deployed by radio and had to call in their locations, activities or needs for further assistance, all of which was also hand-written on the paper log sheets. This was the role that Marilyn had been employed in for many years so I had the inside track to some extent when it came to trying to understand the job which was critical for me if I was going to design the training.

This was the first major computerization project the force had undertaken and the projected cost was many thousands of pounds and far more than the force had ever spent on a single project. There were a few political issues at play as well because most other forces were also engaged in similar modernization programmes. Indeed some were a good bit further ahead than Surrey and there was a certain amount of kudos involved not just for the force but by association, the Chief Constable of the force with the latest and best kit.

Several computer companies had designed systems which they were naturally keen to sell to the latest force seeking to get involved. The systems were evolving rapidly in their level of sophistication and each Chief Constable was keen to have the latest version with all the clever bells and whistles.

This situation was recognized by Home Office who were partly funding these projects via the central government grants and eventually they said enough was enough as there was a serious risk of reinventing the wheel with each new force project getting under way.

The Home Office directive was that there were enough systems out there by that time for forces to select one that best suited their purpose and customize it to their individual requirements rather than have yet another system designed and built from scratch.

At this stage I had not the foggiest idea what computer aided incident handling looked like in use so I took myself off to the South Yorkshire force who had recently gone live with a system from the same computer company we were involved with. The south Yorkshire colleagues allowed me to sample part of their training course which gave me an insight into what the system could do and how we might go about the training ourselves.

My initial report to Bob said that the first thing I needed was a small team of three or four to assist me and I suggested a sergeant who could be my number two plus two or three pc's. The next thing we needed to address was a location where we could carry out the training and as far as I could see at that time the most obvious and only available location was the basement classroom currently designated for communications training.

This would need to be refitted with computer terminals connected to a server running a copy of the live system for training purposes. We then had to work out how many individuals would need to be trained. Fortunately this was not going to be a force-wide programme so it seemed the numbers would be reasonably manageable. All personnel currently working in the HQ Operations Centre would need to be included and as the local control rooms would also have access, that meant all divisional communications and front office staff would have to be included as well.

Once the training team was assembled they all had to go off to the South Yorkshire Force who had kindly agreed that we could avail ourselves of their training which was being run at the force's Rotherham HQ. When I went up I was given some very comfortable quarters in the force training school (as well as a very boozy evening in the bar by the Divisional Superintendent). My three PC's did equally well but my sergeant, the charming Steve Wood had a rather different experience.

Just before he went I was advised that unfortunately on that week there would be no rooms available for us so I set about finding him a local B&B and my goodness, did he give me stick on his return.

Steve liked things to be about right both at work and in his private life too by which I mean he was accustomed to good accommodation and good food. It turned out that his digs were less than ideal. Situated close to the church his slumber was regularly disturbed by the chiming of the clock, the owner had a bulldog that wandered around the breakfast room farting and as if that wasn't enough he had to put coins in a meter to get hot water for a bath. He took a long time to let me forget that one.

It was not until we had actually begun the training that we discovered this was not just about teaching people how to use a new system but it was also something of a 'hearts and mind' job to convince many of them that the new system would actually be better for them. Very few people like change, particularly if it makes them feel insecure, and as most of the trainees were only one finger typists at best, their sense of insecurity was understandable.

Whilst Steve and the other three guys completed the training plan I was mostly concerned with getting estimates for the new training room conversion and then subsequently managing the project so we had a venue ready to begin the training as soon as the system was available to use.

In practice the project was a bit of a three cornered arrangement with the boffins from the supplying company, the team who were running the project and liaising with the company over the design and functionality of the system and me as the training officer. Clearly we all had our own priorities but I did find that neither of the other two parties quite understood the need for the trainers to be kept fully involved in order to ensure that our training plan reflected the latest version of the software. As a result I had to work hard to keep abreast of frequent system changes.

In addition to all the above there was a requirement for a users' manual for the system that would initially form the step by step guide book to back up the training as well as a day to day reference manual where users could look up how to do some of the less common functions offered by the system. I undertook to do this by myself, firstly because I thought the style needed to be consistent throughout and secondly because it's the sort of thing I like doing.

One of the features offered by the system was an extensive database that could be accessed from any terminal in the force and I thought could provide a fantastic reference tool for very rapid retrieval of information.

A feature of the HQ Operations room was the existence of a cabinet of operation orders which were full instructions for dealing with any kind of emergency you might think of from, fuel spillages to air crashes to prison escapes to serious flooding ad infinitum. Not only did these files provide a set of instructions to be followed but also included all the necessary contact information for calling in specialist support from other services. A fantastic resource certainly but with the limitation that as there was only one such file it could only be viewed by one person at a time which would normally be the Control Room Inspector who would usually take command.

In addition to the above there were in most operator's desks and in pretty much every police station a 'Useful Phone Numbers' book which was an amazing resource of information and contacts built up from experience over years by hundreds of conscientious station officers. They were a complete 'hotchpotch' in terms of layout, indexing and content but fundamentally I thought that once sorted, checked and collated they were too valuable a resource to be disregarded.

We set about the task by getting all the information collected and eventually loaded thousands of pages onto the database from which it could be very rapidly retrieved by a number of search criteria and from any terminal in the county. Updates could also be done online so when a user found outdated information it was easy to edit.

FANTASTIC! It certainly was and worked brilliantly but I had so underestimated the way that people want to hang on to the old ways rather than embrace the new.

One of my team was visiting Egham police station and said to the station officer *"How are you getting on with the new database system?"*

"Absolutely brilliant. We love it. It's all up there at our fingertips." he said pointing to an eight foot shelf along the back wall, and there in dozens of lever arch files was the entire database printed out on thousands of A4 pages. He was so proud and we were still such a long way from the much dreamed-of paperless office. I'm sure the copier people were delighted though.

My team at this time included the incredibly reliable and charming Steve Wood, my number two; Ian Came-Johnson, Ian Parrott and Mervyn Young. There was some rotation over the time I was there and it would be wrong not to mention Pc's Geoff Alder, Derek Harding and Jane Bellingham all of whom made a great contribution to the force's transition into the world of IT.

ii

Although the above has been described relatively quickly it actually occupied the best part of two years from inception until the system went live. Meanwhile away from the office, life went on.

Robert and Maria finished school and by about the age of seventeen Maria had moved out to live with a boyfriend and apart from a number of hiatus moments over the years when relationships have collapsed and she's come back to regroup she has lived a very successful independent life. She has held down two or three good jobs in which a she has done very well, largely I guess due to her cheerful, gregarious personality and 'can do' attitude. She is a bright girl, well into current office technology and social media and has used this aptitude to make herself a valued member of staff wherever she's worked.

After his A levels Rob went out to work and then went up to university a couple of years later as a mature student to study environmental biology and psychology, got his degree and has been fully employed in a science based capacity and in his own accommodation ever since.

It was also in 1987 that the next step in our love affair with Spain happened. Marilyn was reading the local paper one day and said *"How do you fancy hosting a foreign student for a month in the summer?"* Whilst it certainly wasn't the first thing on my mind at that time, as Maria had moved out we had room and I thought it might be interesting so said *"Yes. Why not."*

We had no idea which country our house guest would be from but in the summer holiday we met Alex, a charming and intelligent thirteen year old from Barcelona. Naturally a bit shy at first, his limited English was only matched by our own fairly poor 'holiday' Spanish and the vocabulary for ordering a drink and paella doesn't get you far in a conversation. However he was so nice and eager to learn that between us we enjoyed a lot of misunderstood communication whilst bit by bit we learnt more about him and his family. Alex's father is a doctor/professor in a large teaching hospital and his mother we thought was a medical administrator.

He lived with his family and younger brother in a city apartment but there seemed to be other homes they went to as well. He spoke about *"a far village"* and *"a near village"* where another house was being built *"at the beach"*. It would be some time before we got to the bottom of that but in the meantime Alex went off to his English classes every morning whilst in the evenings and weekends we treated him as we would our own kids when younger. We went off for visits to various places of interest, walks with the dog and trips to the coast and anywhere else we thought he might enjoy.

All in all, Alex's time with us was a most enjoyable experience and it would seem it was for him too judging by the very appreciative letter of thanks we got from his parents albeit in rather odd English.

It seemed they were anxious all the while he was away as they had heard of host families who made very little effort to really welcome foreign children and were clearly just doing it for the money. They were so grateful that we were left in no doubt that whenever we wanted to visit Spain we should regard their home as our home too. Over the ensuing years we became very close to this and several other Spanish families whose children we also had to stay with us. A rewarding experience I cannot recommend too highly.

iii

During this whole time I had continued to support Emma at her Horsley home which to be frank was starting to crumble a bit although she would never accept that anything Peter had built or made could have a problem and consequently she would rather muddle by than spend a few pounds to get something properly fixed.

To be fair, on the couple of occasions she agreed, getting someone in turned out to be a great deal easier said than done because the place was so unique. The average guy that attended only ever had one response – chuck out the old and fit something new. This went terribly wrong when we had someone in to fix the TV aerial. He started whacking masonry nails into the chimney and brought a complete cement face off a couple off Peter's chalk blocks. He walked off the job as he'd never seen anything like it before and I finished up on the roof trying to render up the blocks before the weather could get into it which would have brought the whole lot down in no time.

One day Emma called me at home to say there was something wrong with the telephone. She explained that when she turned the oven on the telephone rang. I realized immediately that there must be a massive earth leakage from the cooker that was feeding back through the telephone earth connection. I told her not to touch anything until I arrived.

Under the cooker were a couple of transformer coils that Peter had wound himself with copper wire which back in those days was insulated with silk fabric. I could see that this was degrading but Emma was adamant that it couldn't possibly be a problem with anything he had done until I showed her and she reluctantly had to accept it. Closer examination of the hotplate also revealed extensive corrosion and so I told her that too was dangerous.

It would have been so easy to buy a little Baby Belling mini oven and hotplate but she was reluctant to throw the old things away even though they could no longer be used. I'd made sure of that by disconnecting them both. This left her with a couple of little paraffin Beatrice stoves that she used for all her coking which in truth wasn't actually a great deal. We didn't know at that time but Emma would not be in the house much longer.

I was so grateful to Marilyn during this period for her patience and acceptance of the relationship I had with Emma because she understood that having made a commitment it was not something I could just walk away from. She also understood that it probably wouldn't have to be for very long. I couldn't help feeling a bit irritated with Emma though because she was quite jealous of my new relationship with Marilyn and on a couple of occasions we had words when I tried to explain how my loyalties were being stretched and then she would come back with remarks like *"Well do you want this place or not? I can always sell it or get someone else to help me you know."*

My response was to call her bluff and say *"You know I've always done the best I can for you and will continue to do so. But it's your house Emmie so you must do what you think best."*

I guess it was taking a bit of a chance but she always came round and the dust settled again. To be honest I had by this time started to ponder a bit on how I would want to deal with the house once Emma was no longer around. I thought that if I'd been alone I would probably have just moved in and muddled by, doing what was necessary over time to upgrade the place; but as there would be two of us I knew there was no way we could live at such a basic level.

I became quite an expert on the subject of self-build versus restoration and concluded that for today's world, innovative though it was in 1927, Westwood would have to be rebuilt. But the time had not yet come, so I tried to put these issues out of my mind because, for all I knew the place might yet have to be sold to pay for care in Emma's final years.

Around the middle of '87 Emma called me to say she thought she may have had a stroke but on no account was I to call the doctor. I left the office and went straight to Westwood. Albeit fairly minor, I thought she was probably right as her speech was a bit indistinct and she complained of being numb down her right hand side. I pleaded with her to let me call the doctor but she wouldn't have it and reminded me of the promise I'd made never to do so. She insisted that if I would help her to the bathroom she would then sit in the chair all night and use the little electric fire to keep warm and asked if I could come back the following day which of course I was planning to do anyway.

I went into the office first thing in the morning until Marilyn phoned to say Emma had called to say she had burnt herself. I shot off to the house again.

I'll never forgive myself for letting her persuade me not to call the doctor the previous day because what I found was almost horrific. Presumably because of the loss of feeling in her leg she hadn't noticed the heat of the electric fire which had scorched then melted her stocking into a severe and gruesome looking burn on her lower leg which she apparently couldn't even feel. With no further discussion I immediately called the doctor who had her whipped into hospital and that was the last day Emma spent at Westwood although she never stopped talking about going back home.

Following a stay in hospital for the burn to be treated she went to Milford Hospital for a period of rehabilitation and then a home visit with occupational therapists to see if she could manage to live there again. As the stroke had affected her right hand side which was also the arm she had broken previously it was immediately clear she couldn't even lift a kettle. And when the OT's saw the state of the place and the way in which she was proposing to live they said there was no way she could manage safely and she would need to go into residential care.

We found a place for her at a nice home near Haslemere and a new period of my life began. This included two visits a week to see Emma and a couple of days a month to keep the house and garden in some semblance of order. She still imagined that one day she might return home and so whenever I cut the grass and hedges I would take a few photos along to show her the place was still being looked after.

As her executor Emma also granted me Power of Attorney to deal with her affairs which included managing her investments. This was back in the days when a few thousand pounds could provide a reasonable income, which added to her pension and attendance allowance pretty well covered her fees for the home.

We did get a bit of a shock in October of '87 when the Black Monday crash wiped almost twenty percent off her worth. We talked about it and she was determined that even if all the cash went she wanted the house to remain her principal asset so that *"You can enjoy it as I have."*

Visiting Emma at the Haslemere nursing home with Marilyn
and our dog Benjy who she loved to see.

It was also around this time that Marilyn decided she had worked for the police for long enough because with her working shifts and me on normal office hours we were both spending too much time apart. The problem was that she didn't really know what to do so she sought some careers advice. After a lot of questions and discussion about what kind of things she was looking for in a job, one of the things suggested was a career in housing.

She found her first position with Waverley Borough Council as a housing advisory assistant but with local authority staffing levels the way they were it wasn't long before she was picking up a much wider range of housing experience including homelessness. She then made what she hoped would be a beneficial career development move to the private sector in estate management where she stayed for nearly two years before taking up a position at Mole Valley District Council. She very successfully established herself there, where following a brief period assisting the Homelessness section she advanced to the position of deputy manager for all the council's sheltered housing schemes.

Sadly in October 1991 Marilyn's mother died quite suddenly, the shock of which precipitated what was in effect an emotional breakdown and resulted in her leaving work.

29 MORE COMPUTER TRAINING

It soon became apparent that computerisation, like Topsy, was set to grow and grow, and that there would be no sitting back once the first major system was implemented because there were more jobs right behind it.

One of the things that had been niggling away in the back of my mind all through the new dispatch system training was the fact that we had stolen the communications training classroom and as a result no comms training had been done for two years. In an organisation so dependent on accurate, clear and concise communications it seemed a sin to me that it had (with fair reason) been so neglected. It was obvious if I listened to radio communication in particular, that the conventions so important to ensure clarity were starting to be replaced by a chatty almost conversational style that I felt had no place in that context. It was also important that operators remember others could well be eavesdropping police broadcasts and so a degree of circumspection was necessary at all times.

I put together a report recommending that its priority be reviewed and that since the opening of the new training school, the much under-used lecture theatre in the old building could be refitted for Communications, Major Incident and PNC training. The Police National Computer had been given a major overhaul and PNC2 as it was called was going to be available down to a local level with an attendant training requirement so it seemed our short to medium term employment was secure.

My proposals were agreed and I got stuck into project managing the total restructuring of the old lecture theatre and in due course we had a brand new classroom where we could do PNC training and then get a new programme of training set up for both new and existing control room staff.

While this was all going on I decided that my team might as well also be up to speed with the look and functionality of the PNC2 so arranged for us all to go up to Durham where the national PNC training facility was located.

One team member, PC Derek Harding was over the moon about going to Durham. He was a church bell ringer so on practice nights at the cathedral he could go off and ring their bells which was apparently some sort of seventh heaven. I thought *"Each to his own."* although I now have a far better understanding since Marilyn took it up as a hobby. Still leaves me a bit cold though.

However, staffing the new communications training was another issue altogether as my small team weren't going to be available to take it on due to the start of yet another major computerisation project – a crime information and recording system. I suggested we appoint a new and separate communications training team selected from experienced operations room staff. They weren't experienced trainers but they knew the job and training skills could be taught and so I found myself responsible for two small teams busily taking Surrey towards the 21st century.

The training task for the proposed new crime system was on a very different scale to anything we had done so far as it was going to involve training virtually every operational police officer in the force in addition to quite large number of civilian support staff in places like Crime Bureau, Fingerprints, Scenes of Crime and a few others besides. In round figures it was going to be approaching thirteen hundred. Furthermore, just from what I had seen and heard at that very early stage it promised to be a far more sophisticated system than the previous one but I had very little to go on from other forces' experience in this area.

In London the Met were also in the process of implementing their CRIS (Crime Recording and Information System) project so I went and had a chat with their training officer. He was honest enough to tell me that they had already gone seriously wrong and grossly underestimated the training element. If it wasn't so serious the story would have been laughable.

Apparently it had been the classic case of people with no training experience failing to even consider it from the start. As a result the project timescales had been more or less established before any trainers had even been consulted. The story was that there had been a meeting in which the senior officer running the job had been asked what the demand would be in terms of abstractions from duty for those undergoing training. Not apparently having even thought about it he asked *"How many to be trained? How long have we got?"* Quick division sum *"Four days."* (I think) It might even have been two days, but whichever, it was completely inadequate given the complexity of the system.

As a result the trainers were almost literally tearing their hair out trying to work out a way of dealing with this fait accompli. I believe in the end they had to go for a more phased implementation than they would have wanted. Their honest view was that at least a week of traditional style training should be the absolute minimum. Ideally longer. Anyway, forewarned was forearmed and I returned to Surrey ready to stand my corner and shout loudly to ensure the training issue was addressed from the start which it more or less was.

Chatting it through with Steve Wood and the others we concluded that bringing people in to the HQ training classroom from the far reaches of the county for a week or more at a time was not going to work as the costs of travel or accommodation in HQ would prove unacceptable. And as the HQ training space was so small the timescales would have been impossible. So somehow we had to come up with a form of decentralized training model which was a concept totally new to us at that time.

I think it was also around this time that Bob Ball decided to move on from the Surrey Force and his place was taken by Superintendent Ian (Fred) Page. I had never worked with him but we soon came to understand each other and he was a great ally in ensuring the training aspect of the project was always considered a priority. He also agreed that the idea of decentralizing the training activity had merit but at that time we couldn't quite see how it would work out. My feeling was that decentralization was only part of the answer and that somehow we had to start thinking outside the box.

The way these programs progress is basically along two fronts with the force explaining to the supplier what the functional requirements are and then the boffins coming back with the software to make it happen. The users then test it and either sign it off or send it back with change requests.

Obviously this is hugely over-simplified and it needs to be remembered that with highly complex systems the scope for mis-communication is enormous and the continual introduction of new *"It would be good if it could also do this."* ideas further complicates the issues and extends timescales.

For the trainers it was vitally important to be fully au-fait with all of this in order to keep a handle on what the scale of the training was likely to be. Fortunately, unlike in the Met, we were kept well involved even if at times we had to push ourselves forward and shout a bit to achieve it.

We eventually came to the conclusion that the traditional style of training which had always been along the lines of *"Hear what I say, watch what I do, then do what I tell you."* was not going to work with the numbers involved. We too were under huge pressure to keep training abstractions as low as possible. So, what was the alternative?

I felt convinced that if the computers were so clever surely we could come up with some form of computer-based training that could be done on local terminals. I envisaged a kind of flexi-time process that would avoid travelling to a central location and allow absences for training to be managed locally. There would clearly have to be a fair amount of discipline applied on stations to ensure that enough personnel were adequately trained by the 'go live' date.

Every local station would have to allocate a training room where people could go to get on-line for undisturbed sessions and my team would have to provide the local support. This was all very well in theory and the perceived benefits were well received but we still had to work out how to actually make it happen.

There was quite a bit of resistance at first based on the cost of providing the required training terminals until it was realized that they would have to be purchased anyway for eventual distribution around the many offices. The way I imagined it, subsequent to the initial training programme, was that all terminals would have access to the training system so users could log on and do a bit of refresher training whenever they needed.

Once we trainers had a reasonable feel for the system's very complex functionality we felt that we could begin to write a training syllabus which was initially going to be in the form of a work book that would lead students through the programme. Then we had the brain wave. Why not build the actual instruction manual into the system itself?

Nowadays this is far from rocket science as we are all very familiar with the help systems built into the computers we used every day at work and at home but back then it was a relatively new concept.

So in the event that is precisely what happened. Two duplicate systems were built into the whole with one being available for training and the other for live use once we got to the 'go live' date. An additional benefit to this was that the two were kept completely in step so that any changes arising from experience or further development would always be reflected in the training programme. We then set about writing the training which like so much that we see on-line today, comprised 'pop-up' boxes of instruction that led learners through the numerous functions and also provided help on request when needed.

Here again the 'hearts and minds' issue mentioned earlier surfaced again but even more so than with the dispatch and PNC systems.

Dealing with crime is at the very heart of the police mentality so the introduction of something so very different into this area of police work produced a great deal of resistance born of insecurity. Long established and experienced officers, experts in their fields but who had never touched a keyboard were coming out with remarks like *"I joined the job to catch villains not be a bloody button pusher."*

Understanding the psychology is important but an overly gentle or sympathetic approach is not often the answer especially in services like the police (at least as it was then) because nobody wants to be seen as being unable to take the pressure. In practice the much needed support has to be very subtle and the whole process is something of a tightrope walk.

30 SELF BUILDERS

i

With Emma's passing in January 1992 I had to add executor to the roles of husband, father, gardener, DIYer, police manager and computer trainer. I'd never been involved in such a thing before although in anticipation of the time coming I had read a lot around the role and responsibilities of dealing with an estate. As I was not only executor but sole beneficiary I was anxious that everything should be dealt with absolutely correctly to avoid any suggestion of impropriety.

At the time Emma made her will I was concerned with its legal validity for obvious reasons. One reason was a certain amount of self-interest but also because she insisted on using the very basic home-drawn will she and her previous two husbands had used. However my research confirmed her assertions that provided it was properly witnessed and followed a certain form of words all should be fine. That was now about to be tested.

Listing Emma's assets involved getting a valuation of the property itself, her investments and fairly meagre chattels. She had been a very frugal person and after ninety-five years, I felt a bit sad that apart from her house and the remains of her savings there was virtually nothing of significant value with the exception of two rings.

We had considered simply selling Westwood as a development plot which would have made good money but in conscience I found it hard to contemplate knowing how much Emma had wanted me to live there. There was also the fact that a sale would have attracted a capital gain tax liability so we had decided that we would at least have to live there for a period in order to avoid that. In my heart however, I was pretty well clear that Westwood would be our new 'forever' home.

I used a local estate agent I knew to give me a probate valuation who's first observation on arrival was along the lines of *"Well this is your pension isn't it."* I don't think until that moment I had realized the scale of the gift Emma had left me.

Anyway the will went through probate without a hitch and I found myself the new owner of a run-down bungalow on an acre and a half of prime land in one of Surrey's most desirable locations plus what was left of Emma's savings after several years of residential home fees.

Although I had tried hard to resist doing so, it had been impossible not to day-dream about the home we might create there and by the time I am describing I had rough plans drawn for our dream home which we then had properly drafted and costed. I had always felt that the site deserved a good house both from the point of view of our own lifestyle but also to maximize its resale potential if and when that time should come.

In order to fund the building project we would have to sell our house at Guildford and more in jest than anything I'd said to Marilyn that perhaps we could try selling it privately to save agent's fees. *"I'll put a sign up in the garden."* I said but then just didn't get round to it. Eventually after a certain amount of badgering from you know who, I did put the sign up and the very same day we had a note through the door expressing interest and in next to no time the house was sold, all our stuff went into store and we moved in temporarily with Marilyn's father at Capel.

I must say we felt ever so rich with all the building money in the bank but we were also conscious that it really was the only money we had and realistically we might even have to borrow a bit more to create the dream home that was beginning to emerge on the drawing board.

The plans were for an L shaped chalet-bungalow with three or four bedrooms, en suite bath and shower rooms, a study and extensive kitchen-breakfast room all arranged around a spacious south-west facing terrace. Not exactly modest it's true, but better still the design included the then rather advanced technology of underfloor heating, heat-recovery ventilation and even a centralised vacuum cleaning system.

My grandiose plans started to crumble when the architect came to me one day and explained that the design I'd come up with would have to include a lot of steel and would need a large crane to install it.

The extra costs involved in opening up the access and paying for the crane would push the build way over budget and what did we want to do about it.

Tear it up and start again seemed to be the only answer so we did and to cut a long story short we agreed to buy a factory made timber framed home from Potton Homes in Bedfordshire. Their Heritage range featured loads of exposed timber beams which ticked our boxes and as each house could be individually customized we were still able to include the fancy technical features too.

Ideally I would have wanted to manage the building project myself but reality eventually dawned and I realized that trying to do so and hold down a full-time job at the same time was not going to work. Potton had a list of their approved builders and we eventually signed up with John Pollen from Staines. This was a really nice family firm who we soon developed a great relationship with so then all we had to do was wait until the house came out of the factory.

ii

While all this was going on we were still living with Marilyn's father which was OK. But we had a dog and the presence of three extra bodies in his space was not ideal so we decided that to resolve the situation and to enable us to keep a close eye on the build we would get a mobile home for the site.

Obviously we didn't want to spend a lot and eventually located one in East Sussex which we agreed to buy for a couple of thousand pounds including delivery. Almost as soon as we had agreed the deal a friend contacted Marilyn to ask if we were still looking for a caravan because her grandmother aged ninety-nine had at last reluctantly agreed to move in with them leaving her caravan available for disposal.

We asked how much she wanted for it but she didn't have a clue and asked how much we might pay so we said *"How does five hundred sound?"* She was delighted and agreed the sale so we then had to contact the dealer who was surprisingly understanding. He agreed we could hardly turn it down but was happier when we agreed to buy a tiny towing van for us to use as a site office and gave him the contract for collecting and delivering them both.

A week or so later he delivered both vans to the garden at Horsley and asked if we would be interested in selling them to him when they had served our purpose. He offered us £2000 payable there and then which all considered didn't seem a bad deal; pretty amazing in fact. We connected the van to the existing septic tank and moved on site in April 1993.

iii

One day Marilyn asked if she could take a thousand pounds of the building money for a business idea she had. She explained that she had in mind to start a mobile clothes business selling into residential homes. Apparently, whilst managing the Mole Valley homes she had seen traders coming in to sell their wares to the residents and one day she had heard one of the ladies say *"Well I may be old but I wouldn't wear that."*

It seems there was a tendency when designing clothes intended for older customers to rely on very basic and somewhat old-fashioned style with a lot of zips and Velcro. In essence establishing an *"old equals simple and boring"* stereotype. So Marilyn thought *"No. Why should you wear it?"* and felt sure she could do something better.

She told me she wanted to go and buy some stock in the East End (even though at that point she didn't know precisely where the East End was) and offer to do some sales in the homes where she already had a connection because she knew the wardens.

She went off and bought a couple of collapsible hanging rails and a collection of separates like skirts, tops and jumpers and set about arranging a programme of sale days around the local sheltered housing schemes. Well, the idea took off like a rocket and in no time she had a full diary for months ahead, increased her product range and even began to extend the client list to homes in Sussex and South London.

At first she was running this venture out of the back of our estate car and every corner of Dad's house was stuffed with stock. However, once we moved to the caravan that was no longer possible so we put up a timber shed in the garden at Westwood to serve as a stock room. This wasn't exactly ideal either but it was the best option we had at the time.

Marilyn certainly seemed to have a good eye for styles that appealed to the residents. By careful selection she was able to offer good quality products at attractive prices and because we had such limited overheads we could still make a handsome mark-up. Everyone it seemed was happy.

The only slight downside was that the customers tended to the treat her visits like a rummage sale so that we had to spend each evening with knitwear laid out all over the floor in order to carefully fold and re-bag the items for the same thing to happen again the next day.

iv

Alongside Marilyn's commercial empire building I had been thinking about the demolition of the old house and wanted to salvage what useful materials I could before the shell was finally destroyed. There was a lot of woodworm in it that was mainly confined to the plywood in the ceilings and wall panelling, but the roof timbers, floor and ceiling joists were in remarkably good condition and I couldn't bear the thought of all that timber being lost to the flames. I also wanted to save the roof tiles which were a French pantile that someone had told me could be worth good money.

So while we waited delivery of the new building, every hour that I wasn't at Mount Browne was spent with Marilyn's help carefully stripping the roof tiles and stacking them up for later use or sale. Any good timbers too were carefully removed and de-nailed and then put to one side for some future use although I had no idea at that point what that might be.

Saving some of the tiles and timber.

The factory notified us in May that delivery of the building was imminent and John Pollen and his team moved in with their machinery to complete the demolition and prepare the site for construction to begin.

We see big machinery around us all the time with scarcely a second thought but they really are awesome in operation when seen close up and personal. And personal it was for me as I watched with tears in my eyes while the old house that had taken Peter and Emma so much labour and love to create over almost three years was reduced to rubble in as many hours.

The old Westwood bungalow succumbs to horsepower.

31 A NEW JOB

i

A short time before the Crime System was finally up and running our Superintendent Fred Page went off on a temporary transfer to a Home Office project dealing with automated fingerprint recognition. A newly developed computerised process was being trialled in a neighbouring force that would hopefully transform the laborious manual comparison of crime scene marks. There had been a number of problems with the project and Fred was tasked with doing a review of the implementation. A couple of weeks later he arranged to borrow me to have a look at the training programme and report my views along with any recommendations.

He was only able to give me a few days for the job but anyway I came up with the report which he said was exactly what he wanted and gave me a strong hint that we would be working together again very soon. I was intrigued.

It was early in '93 that I got a call to the ACC's office and was asked if I was up for another challenge. He explained that Fred Page who by that time had taken over responsibility for the Career Development Branch had asked for me as his assistant as his current Inspector was moving on. Well, I knew I could get on with Fred, and the job, being just a two person department, appealed to my preferred work style. I accepted without a second thought, although given the pressure we were under on the home front with the house build going on, it might have been wiser to have thought twice. Time would prove that to be the case.

A year or two earlier a Home Office directive had required all police forces to establish a career planning or development department which it said was to have ACPO support and this was not just to be 'lip service' but real support. So, what was all this about?

I spoke earlier about the force rank structure with its broad base of many constables and sergeants rising to a sharp point of relatively few senior officers and the problems this created in maintaining morale and providing for career progression to the higher ranks. It was also an issue in relation to wastage of very capable officers seeking more interest and responsibility by transferring to other forces or leaving the service altogether for greater challenges and remuneration outside.

Fortunately not every constable aspires to be a superintendent or even a sergeant but most would like to think that over their careers they might get some variety or the chance to specialize. It seemed that this had also been recognized by Home Office which was the reason for the directive that a more proactive approach be taken to the problem by setting up structures to *"manage and develop where appropriate, the careers of each and every officer."* Fine words indeed.

Achieving this was inevitably going to mean moving people about a bit on occasion which was never going to go down well with divisional commanders especially if a replacement could not always be offered. It was for this reason that the directive indicated that a strong ACPO commitment was required and that an officer of senior rank should run the office, in our case a superintendent.

Every officer had annual appraisals which were supposed to be the time when career plans were reviewed and preference expressed for any future training or specialization. The problem tended to be that the paper work then disappeared into the blue and the hoped-for action often didn't materialize.

Once the Career Development branch was established all appraisals went over our desks and where possible we would try to arrange desired moves, training or specialization or at the very least acknowledge the wishes and offer some hope for the future.

Fortunately at that time both the job and technology were evolving very rapidly so there was often the opportunity to offer people some new experience or specialism to pique interest and raise morale even if only on a temporary basis. After all, who would have imagined when I first joined the job, that I would ever have to work with the press or the impact that computerization would have and the jobs it would create for me and other colleagues within the IT section.

My responsibility within the office was for all the constables and sergeants in the Surrey force which at well over a thousand individuals was actually laughable when you think about it. ACPO commitment? Who in their wildest dreams could have imagined that as a reasonable workload? Fred's role was to oversee me and take responsibility himself for the careers of all Inspectors and Chief Inspectors.

Very often, in addition to actively planning and engineering moves to help people's careers, I found myself counselling individuals who dipped out on job interviews or were passed over for promotion. It is a sad fact that many ambitious individuals believe themselves to be far better than they actually are; the difficult part is helping them to identify and own their shortcomings without puncturing some surprisingly fragile egos.

As part of this we were also responsible for organizing promotion interview boards and then giving feedback to the unsuccessful as to how they might better prepare themselves in the future. It came as a huge surprise to me to discover the degree of anxiety, not to say paranoia suffered by some around the promotion stakes even to the point of keeping tables of runners and ticking them off as jobs were allocated or promotions published. To be frank if some of them had put as much effort into their day to day work they'd have probably done a better job and been rewarded for it.

Fred Page and I did this difficult job with a fair amount of success although it was always going to be difficult to deal with the resistance of local commanders when faced with losing one of their personnel for a career or experience move especially if a replacement was not to be immediately forthcoming. It was in this area I had most difficulty and invariably had to call on Fred's rank to make things happen because a local superintendent would not uncommonly simply refuse to acknowledge my authority.

32 DREAMS DASHED

Living in the caravan we were able to watch the daily progress on the site as foundations were dug and concrete poured and were surprised at how small the footprint of our future home actually looked. However, once the foundation walls were in and the concrete block and beam surface of the ground floor was in place the whole thing took on a new perspective as we were able to walk around from 'room to room' and now it started to feel more like a mansion.

Our home arrived on three huge lorries on different days. The first carried the main frame consisting of massive nine-inch square timber posts and beams that would provide an internal load bearing structure to support the entire building but which would, in the traditional English timber frame style, be left exposed as interior features.

Raising the main frame timbers.

The erection of these was quite a feat not dissimilar to the illustrations of how ancient structures might have been hauled upright except of course, John Pollen and his guys had a bit more mechanical muscle to call on. The erected frame looked just like a period barn without its cladding.

A couple of days later all the interior and external factory-made wall panels arrived which once erected created a shell around the main frame and finally a lorry load of roof trusses turned up and in the space of less than a fortnight the main structure was complete. It only needed the roof to be felted and the structure was weatherproof and by some miracle pretty much the whole job got done in the dry.

If we thought that was 'job done' we couldn't have been more wrong. As anyone who has ever been involved in having a house or extension built, or indeed, building their own will know, this is where the real work begins.

There was just so much still to do with all the internal finishing, installation of services and so on. Also, there always seemed to be questions about where this or that fitting, electric socket, light switch etc. had to go and this despite the fact that we had pored for hours over the plans to indicate just such details. We eventually got to the point of leaving the plot via the rear access in order to avoid being caught by the electrician.

One aspect that particularly pleased me though was the fact that I had managed to find a use for Peter's original roof water system. I couldn't bear the thought of all his labour going to waste and to tick my own environmental considerations as well we managed to incorporate it. I had all the gutters routed to the underground reservoir and then fitted an automatic electric pump that would fill a roof tank from which the toilets could be flushed and the washing machine filled. Being rain-water it was wonderfully soft and needed very little detergent so was very eco-friendly.

The other thing I did which wasn't in the end quite so clever was to have the garage built. It made perfect sense to me that while John and his machinery were on site they should build the double garage and workshop I so desired. However; me and my big ideas! I hated the idea of wasted roof space so arranged for the garage block to have an upper floor fitted and a toilet installed, imagining the perfect workshop and 'den' for myself in future years. They made a fantastic job of it albeit at considerable extra cost.

So impressive was the garage block that visitors to the site would admire our new house and then say *"And who lives there?" "No one."* I said. *"It's the garage."*

The risen Westwood on the day we moved in.

We put so much of ourselves into the place with all my fancy technical gizmos and a beautiful brick inglenook we designed together. Marilyn designed some pretty stained glass doors for the kitchen cupboards and with our Jacuzzi bath and lovely sun terrace we really were in seventh heaven. We moved in the October and on the very same day the weather turned and the water supply to the caravan froze. We couldn't have timed it better.

We had decided to do all the painting ourselves in order to save a bit of money but certainly hadn't realized quite how many square metres of wall and ceilings there were or how new plasterboard soaks up emulsion paint. The job seemed never-ending and it also seemed to take forever to get rid of all the plasterer's white dust that got everywhere and which was not helped by our dog running it round from room to room. We had acknowledged that we wouldn't be able to carpet the place for some time so the dusty floors were not such an issue and anyway we had our cool centralised vacuum system with long snaky tube you just plugged into the wall and all the rubbish was whisked away by the motor in the garage.

I don't remember the day that it dawned on us the extent to which we had overstretched our budget. Maybe it was the first or second gas bill when we realized that after everything we were probably not going to be able to afford to live out the dream so long imagined. We were devastated.

We had borrowed a bit to finish the job and by today's standards it was pretty small beer as mortgages go but to us at the time it was too much and neither of us are people who feel comfortable with debt. I was almost fifty with only about three years to serve so the rent allowance would have paid most of the mortgage for that time but beyond that it could have been a problem.

The plan had been to use the pension as a cushion to support a comfortable semi-retirement; accepting that I would have to do some work but setting about a new career as such was not what I envisaged.

We could certainly have stayed for a while but that would not have been facing the facts. The truth was that we had a lovely house in a great location but too much of a mortgage for that stage of my service and the knowledge that even if we could afford to stay there, things like carpets and furniture were certainly not going to come easy.

There always was a premium to house prices in Horsley so we knew the house would be worth a bit and while it was breaking my heart to even consider selling I just kept remembering Emma's words *'It's the land that's worth the money."*

Not surprisingly there was no shortage of interest in a brand new house in that area and when we got an offer the agent told us was good we just grabbed it and decided to go into rented while we gathered our thoughts and got Christmas behind us.

I did of course have all the salvaged building materials to consider not to mention an old Ferguson tractor that I'd bought as a restoration project when I imagined myself pulling a grass cutter up and down my green acre. I had actually done quite a bit of the restoration work on site at Horsley over the previous three years but with the demolition of the old garage it had been relegated to repose under a tarpaulin for several months.

The French tiles I had hoped might be snapped up by a dealer turned out not to be so 'sought-after' and unless I had more than five thousand and they were all palleted for easy collection he was not interested.

Fortunately for us the buyers agreed that I could leave all the timber, tiles and tractor until we found our new place which was very helpful.

Painful though it was at the time; in retrospect, and even disregarding the financial considerations, it was almost certainly the right thing to do.

There were a few ghosts for me that would undoubtedly have haunted our future there even if quite gently. I never heard any gossip but once word of my inheritance spread further afield as it always does in a village situation there would surely have been some sour grapes and the odd wagging tongue casting doubt on my friendship with Emma.

There was also the apparently common knowledge about my shaky marriage with Denise and all that followed, and then there was the issue of how Marilyn felt about simply slotting into to all that background. On balance we both feel now (if not at the time) that we made the most of Emma's gift even if not as at first imagined.

33 MY DARK NIGHT

i

In December 1993 we left Westwood and moved to a rented house in Elstead where we thought we would just let the dust settle over Christmas while we decided on our next move.

Life at work had been getting more and more difficult given the workload on our small unit and the aforementioned resistance we met from various quarters. As a result I had been wondering, given our now unexpectedly large bank balance, whether I might not actually take an early retirement.

The arrangement with the police pensions was that we had a pension entitlement after twenty-five years' service that was equivalent to half final salary but it could only be taken after the age of fifty. So obviously for the majority having joined in their early twenties it made sense to do the extra five years and get the full pension which equated to two thirds salary. My thought was that with a substantial sum behind us and no kids in education we could afford for me to leave at fifty after twenty-seven years and accept the slight reduction in monthly pension.

Having reached that conclusion we started to think about where we might try to buy our next house and decided that a move a little further away from London and the Surrey commuter belt would enable us to get a bit more for our money and we settled on West Sussex. This was particularly comfortable for us both as from childhood we had been familiar with the various coastal resorts and the different towns so often passed through on family outings.

Marilyn was still running her mobile clothing business with a good measure of success and in between was busily researching potential new homes in Sussex. Apparently we went and viewed a couple together but I have absolutely no recollection of that so perhaps things were already starting to go wrong for me.

I have a theory that we all have a kind of virtual 'backpack' where we stuff all the ups and downs of life. All the dramas like divorces and bereavements, disappointments and crises are jammed in and lashed down while we do what Monty Python recommends and Always Look on the Bright Side of Life. Mostly this seems to work even if from time to time things threaten to spill out but usually with the aid of the stiff upper lip we get by. But of course, it takes a toll and there is always that last straw.

ii

I still can't believe that I didn't see it coming but the truth is I hadn't a clue. True, some of my colleagues had asked if I was OK, as they'd thought I'd seemed a bit pre-occupied – tetchy even, which was unusual for me.

True, I knew I was under a bit of pressure. There was that huge relief at the end of the week and then after an all too brief respite, by Sunday lunch time my head would in work mode again and I'd be winding back up for the list of stuff to be done on Monday morning. But that was all normal wasn't it?

To be honest, at that time the police service was not very good at acknowledging the existence of work place stress and I was no exception. The organisation was very macho and even in the nineties, it was not a million miles from the type of organisation depicted in some of the TV series about policing in the seventies where there is no place for wimps and the attitude was pretty much *"If you can't stand the heat – get out of the kitchen"*

As far as I was concerned stress wasn't even in my vocabulary. Sure, I'd had all the difficulties. The family deaths, the almost mandatory divorce and custody battle, the various house moves and associated highs and lows. For goodness sake my own wife had even had to give up her job due to post-traumatic stress after the death of her mother. Yet still the thought that it could happen to me never entered my head because I was the one that could hack it. I always had hadn't I? Until that day.

I think it was the middle of January when Fred page told me he was going. He had been given another project which would involve him being away for several months. Before leaving he made a lot of noise about the general workload we were carrying but particularly about the difficulties he could foresee me facing with divisional commanders without a senior colleague in the office. Needless to say he was not replaced and I just carried on.

Following the recent promotion boards I'd spent most of the previous two weeks seeing individuals who had been unsuccessful – basically providing a shoulder to cry or whinge on – and trying to work out individual development plans to help with their success in the future. More difficult though had been several serious confrontations with divisional Superintendents who were not going to accept at any price that I – a lowly Inspector- wanted to take members of their staff away for what they saw as no good reason. So it was small wonder that I left the office on the Friday with a huge sigh of relief.

I'd got up as usual on the Monday morning and I think I was getting dressed when my knees buckled and I slumped on the bed and burst into tears. It's very difficult to recall exactly what happened apart from the fact that I was completely distraught and simply couldn't face going to work.

This wasn't just 'a bit upset' but more or less total collapse and through it all the one aspect that I recall so clearly was the guilt, the feeling that I was letting everyone down, that I'd failed to hold the line.

It was clear that there was something fairly serious going on so Marilyn phoned in sick on my behalf and I went off to see the doctor where the whole thing happened again and I broke down in the consulting room.

The doctor was brilliant and signed me off immediately but the 'responsible' me insisted on going into the office to see the Chief Superintendent where I found myself apologising for letting the side down and once again breaking down in tears. He was very understanding and told me not to worry about anything apart from getting better and packed me off home which was a bit rich considering it had been his decision not to replace Fred Page. God knows what sort of state I must have been in to drive because I don't remember the journey at all; in fact I think it must have been around this point that the lights went out and I shut down completely because I have virtually no recollection of the next six months of my life.

I guess that once you are as it were, 'given permission' to be ill, the body goes into a sort of recovery mode and all of the adrenaline that has kept you up to the mark and coping drops back to the correct level. What happened in my case was that I sank like a stone into a deep depression, a terrible black place that even now I find it hard to talk or even think about.

The first certificate that signed me off for a month said 'anxiety'. The next time I saw the doctor he signed me off for further month with 'anxiety and depression'. This triggered a referral to the force medical officer who offered me counselling with the force psychologist.

I have only vague recollections of my visits to the counsellor who seemed most interested in how much I'd been thinking about suicide. To be honest, up until that point it had only crossed my mind on the odd occasion but she kept on about it so much that I began to wonder if it was obligatory. The main problem I had in my conversations with her was stopping myself from crying and apologising for letting everyone down. It was this aspect that disturbed me more than anything.

She eventually wrote to the force that I was suffering from 'severe depression' and it was her belief that I would need several more months to recover but that if I went back into any sort job that involved stress or responsibility I would probably break down again and possibly more seriously.

The next few months are pretty much a blank space as far as my memory is concerned. I apparently spent most of the time curled up on the settee while Marilyn found us a house and organised a removal none of which I remember. I guess I must have signed off the necessary paperwork but I don't remember doing so.

By the middle of the summer I was beginning to surface although I still felt terribly fragile, a particularly curious element of which was the complete inability to formulate any type of decision. Simple things like whether I wanted to go out or not or what to wear caused me real stress and perhaps most worrying was that decisions that should have been automatic caused me to dither terribly. For example, driving has always been a great love of mine but I found that when getting back behind the wheel I even had to deliberate over whether to brake or not which was seriously unsettling.

Little by little with Marilyn's love and immense understanding I began to creep back into the world and while the sun shone on our lovely new country home the old me began to re-appear but any mention of the police or the old job caused real anguish. Even driving near HQ stressed me up and that continued for several years.

It was in the September that the force medical officer asked me to go in and see him and he broke the news that the force was considering 'casting' me on an ill-health pension. Well to be honest I could have kissed him. It certainly was not the way I would have chosen to go and of course it raised anew the issues of guilt and failure but I knew in my heart that they were correct in that there was virtually no role in which I could have returned that would have been within my resources at that time.

And so it was that after 27 ½ years I ended my service with Surrey Police but that is not quite the end of this story.

All the time I'd been on sick leave I had been in receipt of sickness benefit and according to the doctors being compulsorily retired did not preclude me from that benefit and so I continued to claim it. However after another month or two as I began to feel even better the old conscience began to kick in and I wondered at the honesty of continuing to pick up the sickness benefit.

At a pre-retirement course the previous year we had been reminded that as police pensioners we were still of working age in the eyes of the state system. As such, until we found other employment we were entitled to claim unemployment benefit and so it occurred to me that perhaps I should give up the sickness benefit and proclaim myself ready to work but presently unemployed and so claim the benefit. To this end I went off to the Job Centre for my interview where I discovered that it was now called 'Jobseekers Allowance' and a condition of which was that one was actually seeking work and that in order to qualify I had to have the jobseekers interview.

The benefits officer sat me down and opened the interview which began by her asking me what I was qualified to do. Well clearly 'police inspector' was out of the question so the next stage was for me to complete a form stating my strengths, skills and so on. "*No problem*" I thought "*No different to making an internal job application in the force*" and I'd done loads of those over the years.

As I started to write out my management skills; leadership, ideas man, problem solving, planning, team building, budgetary control, time management, etc. I started to tremble. I felt as though someone had just literally kicked by feet from under me and I looked up through tear filled eyes at the benefits officer.

She smiled gently and said, "*You're not ready yet Brian. I just wish everyone were as honest as you. Give yourself a bit more time and don't be in too much of a hurry. Don't forget you've paid in for years so just relax and accept the sick pay. I think you still need it*"

I never did go back because it slowly dawned on me that I was no longer the same person, no longer the team leader and problem solver but a different person. The most difficult thing was learning to accept over time that the other person really had gone and that I am now someone else. Not unlike a bereavement when the recovery process lies in getting used to the idea that a person has gone and that you have to move on except that the person who has gone is the old you.

Just occasionally over the last twenty-three years there have been times as there are in anyone's life when I've been a bit down. When I've caught a glimpse as it were through a chink in the door of that place where the lights are out and the darkness terrifyingly intense and I never ever want to go again. It is then that I remind myself not so much who I was but who I am now and all I've learnt and the experiences and blessings that my life since has brought me over the last few years.

Somebody said to me recently "*Perhaps we all need to experience that dark night of the soul to really know ourselves.*" I certainly never want to go back there but I believe she was right.

THE FUTURE

It took a while to adjust, but life since I left the police has been interesting and exciting.

We settled into our Sussex village and gradually started to pick up local threads and as we then had a little money behind us and my police pension as a cushion we decided to just chill for a bit and see what happened. Without a mortgage or children in uni to support I decided I certainly didn't want to take up another career that required me to clock in regularly to a 'normal' job. We also had a bit of a 'wish-list' of travel destinations that we would now be able to start ticking off.

Without giving too much away, as I've already decided that there is to be a third volume to my story; it's sufficient to say that we have reinvented ourselves several times over the last twenty three years, followed up our Spanish dreams including a lot of travel and a couple of periods actually living there. New skills and abilities have been discovered and utilised very profitably.

Following the first period in Spain we returned to live in Surrey again where we ran a successful B&B alongside several other part-time activities. However just recently (September 2017) our itchy feet have brought us back to West Sussex again where we are busy getting to know our new area.

This has been the story of an ordinary guy that I suspect may chime with the experiences of many other ordinary guys and I have always found even ordinary lives interesting which is what I hope has made this readable.

If you have enjoyed my story thus far I would be delighted to hear from you on brianseye@outlook.com and will be happy to let you know when the next volume is written.

You may not know that there was a previous volume entitled Born in 44. This is no longer available as I revised it recently under the title Stepping Out from Ashtead 1944-1964 which relates my early years growing up in Surrey. It includes the usual silly but quite entertaining juvenile experiences and teenage angst around sexual experience and my attempts to get some followed by my first job in electro-chemical research. Then came my hugely enjoyable and often hilarious trip around the world as a steward with P&O and my introduction to the ship-board gay scene – definitely not as a participant. This was followed by my first very brief encounter with the police service when I spent just ten months as an officer in London; and all that before I was twenty years of age.

ABOUT THE AUTHOR

New to writing, Brian Simmons is at pains to say he is "Just an ordinary guy" and the offering of these memories is in no sense an effort to suggest otherwise.

This, Brian's second book, follows on from Stepping Out from Ashtead and is, like the first, an affirmation of a long held belief that everyone has a story to tell filled with laughter and tears, adventure and routine, success and failure and a myriad of other experiences. All of which can be at once informative, interesting and frequently amusing if told well.

Now bitten by the writing bug he intends to carry on with further memoirs covering subsequent years and adventures.

Brian's background is about as ordinary as they come. But it came with the benefit of having a secure home and loving and supportive parents who allowed him, often against their better judgement to find his own way and make a few mistakes too.

After stumbling 'interestingly' through his early years he eventually returned to a career with Surrey Police before retiring in 1994

In the twenty-three intervening years until now there have been several very different occupations and hitherto unknown skills discovered. These have led to some interesting and entrepreneurial ventures, quite a lot of travel and many more lessons learnt. Together with the police years, they too promise to make an interesting and entertaining read.

When not writing, Brian is a passionate photographer as can be seen by visiting his website at www.surreyhillsimages.co.uk

Printed in Great Britain
by Amazon